OUTCASTS ON THE MARGINS

OUTCASTS ON THE MARGINS

Exclusion and Discrimination of Scavenging Communities in Education

RATNESH KATULKAR

GenNext Publication

Published by

GenNext Publication
5, Ansari Road
Daryaganj, New Delhi-110002
Phone: 011-47034999, 9811692060
E-mail: gennextpublication@hotmail.com

Distribution Network
gyanbooks.com
India, USA, Canada, UK, Australia, France

ISBN: 978-93-5663-188-5 (PB)
First Published, 2023

Printed at: Gyan Press, Delhi.

OUTCASTS ON THE MARGINS
Author: RATNESH KATULKAR

Contents

Acknowledgments

I am pleased to present this book, which is an outcome of my institutional project "Discrimination and Exclusion in Education". The project started with the study of four northern states of Uttar Pradesh, Rajasthan, Himachal Pradesh, and Haryana, and in subsequent years expanded to the states of Bihar, Jharkhand, Madhya Pradesh, and Chhattisgarh. Later, the study was extended to four southern states of Andhra Pradesh, Tamil Nadu, Telangana, and Karnataka, under the guidance of Dr. Selvaraj Arulnathan.

The study of the first four states was sponsored by ICSSR. During that time I was working in the Department of Dalit Studies as a Researcher and my department was headed by Dr Denzil Fernandes. It is indeed my pleasure that at present Dr Denzil is heading the institute as an Executive Director and has written a Foreword for this book. I express my heartfelt thanks for his positive and motivational support and guidance during my tenure as a Researcher and Social Scientist at the Institute. It is indeed his proactive approach that made this work to be published in this form, which is otherwise lingering in the offices of mainstream publishers who for one reason or another were delaying its publication. Dr Denzil also read the manuscript sincerely and did final copyediting. Therefore, I am thankful to him for his support, guidance and labour that made this book possible. I am also extremely thankful to the Research Director Dr Tom Perumalil and senior faculty Dr Lancy Lobo for approving this manuscript.

When this research project was initiated, the Institute was under the leadership of Dr. Joseph Xavier, who played a pioneering role in connecting the team to ICSSR. At that time, Dr. Paul D'Souza headed the Research Department. Both of them are experts in the study of scavenging as they obtained their PhDs in the same field. They played a crucial role in preparing the proposal. Later, Dr. Paul took over the Department of Dalit Studies and became a key partner and ally for all these studies. He provided crucial support for both the projects and this book. Dr. Paul proposed that the book based on these studies should not merely replicate the research projects in a book format, but should be much different and lucid enough for both laypersons and professional researchers to understand. Accordingly, a blueprint of the book was prepared and approved by him. During the COVID-19 lockdown, I started writing this book and completed its draft while working from home. Writing this book became my official task, and I used to report each day's work to Dr. Paul. Some days were difficult, especially when I spent most of the day thinking or reading books without writing a single page. On such occasions, Dr. Paul's kind, sincere, and understanding nature helped me a lot. As a researcher, he understood that I did not waste my time on such days. Although it was difficult to prove my daily tasks, his insistence on submitting daily reports helped me adopt a disciplined lifestyle. His support and role have undoubtedly been valuable.

I also wanted to remember Researchers of the other departments firstly Dr Vincent Ekka for his help and support. My research team consisting of Renuka Ramanujam from Women Studies, Dr. Archana Sinha HoD of Rural and Urban Studies, and our Research Associates Kiran Dungdung and Nidha Khan played significant roles in the first edition of the project which had become a base for subsequent studies. Dr. Archana Sinha took responsibility for the field study of Uttar Pradesh, and Renuka Ramanujam did the field study of Haryana. The young researchers Kiran and Nidha took responsibility for the study in Rajasthan. Dr. Tina Anil enriched the research by writing a conceptual framework for this report. During the initial course, we received consistent guidance and support from leading academicians, Prof. Surinder Jodhka, Prof. N Sukumar and Prof. Vimal Thorat along with activist scholars Harsh Mandar and Bezwada Wilson, who played a significant role in guiding this study. I am highly indebted for their valuable suggestions and guidance.

I am again grateful to Bezwada Wilson for his active role in providing contacts of his local partners who helped us in our data collection. The senior activists of SKA Pavan Valmiki and Jyoti Valmiki of Madhya Pradesh, Rajkumar Bohat of Haryana, Sikandar and Ram Chaudhary of Korba, senior Gandhian social activists Karu Ji and Jagat Bhushan of Bodhgaya and Rameshwar Lashkare of Jabalpur not only helped in data collection but also shared their rich experiences which helped in enriching the research. I am also indeed thankful to all respondants who shared their views to me and my team. Their contribution is immense; however, in thos book names of all the respondents have been changed to conceal their identities.

During writing this book, scholar-activist Dhamma Darshan Nigam played an important role by reading the drafts of the manuscript and commenting on it. He also shared his observations and views on the problem. I also consulted with another senior scholar-activist Raj Valmiki. Both these scholar-activists are associated with SKA therefore their clear and critical comments proved to be practical and valuable. Arun Kumar Oraon an Activist Scholar provided valuable suggestions on tribal issues. I used his reference based on his knowledge of oral tradition. My friends Dr. Sunil Ramteke and Laxman Salve kept reminding me of the need for this book.

My friend and colleague Shabih Anwer played a commendable role in reading and proofreading its first draft. He always provided me with the motivation to finish the writing of this book on time. My friend Manikanta Pallikonda, who for a short period joined the Institute helped in data collection from Patna.

Kuffir Nalgundwar, Moderator of roundtableindia.co.in played an exemplary role in copyediting a large part of the manuscript. I also received active support in copyediting from Abha Jeurkar, working in the USA and Sundeep Pattem, who shared their precious time in copyediting some of the chapters. These three brilliant copyeditors who always run short of time due to their serious professional engagements did not delay in supporting me and finished their work on time. Their impressive copy-editing skills make this work to a great extent error-free and easy to read.

I cannot forget my friends and colleagues of Insight Foundation Anoop Kumar, Gurinder Azad and Manju Rao, especially for their role in documenting the evidence of discrimination and exclusion in premier educational institutes. This experience helped me understand the problem of exclusion of Dalit and Adivasi students more sharply.

The Librarian of my Institute, Rameshwar Dayal, played a commendable role in providing me with all the references as per my needs. He also taught me some professional skills for seeking references which proved to be helpful. I also extend my thanks to all the staff of the Indian Social Institute because of my close bond with them and their friendly gesture that eased my work.

I am immensely grateful to kindledirectpublishing (amazon.kdp.com) for offering me a platform to publish my work. Thanks to their service, my manuscript was not left to gather dust on a publisher's desk, but instead was able to reach its intended audience. I am confident that this opportunity will help me share my ideas with the world and pave the way for future success.

Last but not least I would like to mention my family whose contribution and support are immense and this book would not be possible without their support. I like to mention again that a large part of the manuscript was written during the first and second phase of the COVID-19 lockdown when we all were locked down at our homes. My three year old beloved daughter Roshi, who is now five years of age allowed me to work even though this was the only time when we got an opportunity to share time. This was the time when my spouse Sevanti Patel being engaged in Nagar Nigam was loaded with extra responsibilities because of the coronavirus pandemic but despite her busy and difficult schedule, I received full cooperation and support from her. Being a student of Rural Development I also received her ideas and suggestions and her role in data collection from Himachal Pradesh was also a big contribution. My elder brother Rajesh Katulkar and my parents always kept my motivation.

Ratnesh Katulkar

Introduction

Recently, a small-time television actress named Munmun Datta was found to have tweeted, while getting her makeup on for a show, 'I do not want to look like a *bhangi*.'[1] This casteist and prejudiced comment, which is punishable under the Prevention of Atrocities Act (PoA), created a stir among a section of Dalits. However, as usual in the mainstream, there is no regret against this. Strangely, this was not a lone incident when any celebrity uttered such a casteist comment. A few years back on January 2016, Bollywood star Salman Khan, during one of the promotion events of his film 'Tiger Zinda Hai', used the word *'bhangi'* referring to his own dancing style.[2] While on December 2017, Shilpa Shetty said 'am I looking like a *bhangi*.'[3]Recently, a cricket star Yuvaraj Singh also used the term *bhangi* in a similar derogatory tone. The usage of *bhangi* by these leading celebrities shows that this word has become a common derogatory vocabulary of many.

However, the National Human Rights Commission and the National Commission for Scheduled Castes failed to take *suo-moto* cognizance of this issue. Even in the mainstream media, a general sense of regret about such a comment seems to have been lacking entirely. In each of these cases, the culprit celebrities mildly apologized for their choice of words, claiming ignorance of the meaning of the word *bhangi*. Their alleged innocence in using the term *bhangi* in a derogatory manner, shows that in mainstream society this term becomes a synonym for ugly or bad, and points to the deep-rooted hatred towards sanitation workers and Dalits, overall.

---

1. Taarak Mehta's Munmun Dutta issues an apology for her 'bhangi' comment in a recent video - Times of India (indiatimes.com)
2. https://www.newsbytesapp.com/news/entertainment/salman-and-shilpa-in-trouble-again/story.
3. https://www.news18.com/news/movies/bhangi-comment-row-shilpa-shetty-apologises-for-hurting-sentiments-1613663.html

One of the reasons for this innocence (if it is indeed true) is because, in mainstream discussions, the life and issues of sanitation workers have remained under the carpet. Yet, we cannot ignore Dalit activists like Bezwada Wilson and others, whose efforts have foregrounded the problems of sanitation workers and have led to the passing of an Act prohibiting manual scavenging and formulation of policies for the rehabilitation and upliftment of the scavenging community. The problems of the scavenger community have, to an extent, appeared before the common public through the Aamir Khan led popular TV Show, Satyamev Jayate. A documentary film 'Jai Bhim Comrade' by Anand Patwardhan, also raised this issue along with socio-politics before a set of audiences.[1] Much earlier, Martin Macwan was a pioneer in introducing the problem of manual scavenging in the development sector narratives. In addition, Stalin's documentary, 'Lesser Human', was a revelation for many.

In the field of academics, Prof. Shyamlal's books, particularly 'The Bhangis in Transition' and 'The Bhangi: A Sweeper Caste, It's Socio-economic Portraits', discuss the status of the scavenging community in detail. Whereas, for creating awareness among the Dalits, the writings of Bhagwan Das are a landmark. '*Main Bhangi Hun'*, which is a history of Dalits, particularly the scavenging communities in a semi-fictional form and his booklet '*Dr. Ambedkar aur Bhangi Jatiyan'*, are prominent pieces of work. They elaborate upon the tactical strategies of Hinduizing this community that ultimately resulted in their socio-economic deprivation and turned them into foot soldiers of rightwing forces. A similar attempt but with rigorous academic research is brought forward by Vijay Prashad in his book 'Untouchable Freedom.' He provides meticulous details on the journey of the scavenging communities with historical and sociological perspectives. He describes the various stages of development of various scavenging castes known by a variety of names, such as Mehtar, Chuhra, Sweeper, Balmiki, and Harijan. One can talk about many other pieces of work, but they all share the limitation that they overlook the aspect of the status of education within the scavenging communities.

Scavengers in Contemporary Society

The occupation ofscavenging at one time was confined mainly to caste groups of Lalbegis, Mehtar, Bhangi, Chuhra, Halalkhors, Jamadar, Patharphor, Barvashias, Metariya, Rakhesar, etc in the North and Central India. But the most common name for them in North India is Mehtar,

1. The viewership of documentaries is always limited as compared to feature films and other popular medium.

which literally means prince or leader.[1] In other parts of the country, various castes such as Olgana, Barvashia, Metariya, Jamphoda[2] in Gujarat and Relli, Madiga, Arunthathiyar, Paraiyar, Kuravar, and Kattu Naicker[3] in South India are engaged in scavenging. Later on, many new castes such as Dom, Domar, Dumar, Musahar etc. joined this occupation. In northern and central India, many of the scavenging castes have begun to call themselves Valmikis. In a similar exercise, the Domar caste in Madhya Pradesh and Dumars in Chhattisgarh and elsewhere have begun to identify themselves with a Vedic sage named Sudarshan.[4] In some cities, for instance in Shimla, the Chamars have also gotten into this occupation.[5] There are also cases where individuals of the Dusadh castes in Bihar[6] and also Mahars in Maharashtra have joined this occupation.[7]This expansion was not restricted to Dalits but crossed overto Adivasis as well. The Hadis in Bengal and Jharkhand, a few of the Gonds in Madhya Pradesh and Chhattisgarh, the Oraons, Khadia, and a few other tribes too have opted for this occupation.[8] There is also a meagre presence of savarna caste individuals in this occupation. However, in most cases the savarna caste members are seen to have opted for this profession, when there is a permanent government position, where they further employ a proxy worker to actually perform the task of sanitation. This practice is also followed by many people from the scavenger community as well.

Traditionally as well as at present, this occupation is not confined to Hindus where there is a well-established philosophical defence to the caste system. The caste as a social institution may have its roots in Hinduism, but it later spread among all the other religions in India. The Muslims are divided into Ashraf, the upper castes, and Arjals, the lower castes, while the middle castes are known as Pasmanda. Among the Muslims, the scavenging castes are the Helas in the present times and the Lalbegis in the past. Interestingly, the Hela and the Lalbegi castes are found both among Muslims and Hindus.[9] At present in many parts of India, the Helas

1 Thaliath, Joseph. "Notes on the Scavenger Caste of Northern Madhya Pradesh, India." *Anthropos* 56, no. 5/6 (1961): 789–817.

2. These are the scavenging castes in Gujarat

3. The list of south India castes referred from our study on southern states of India, An article Out of Breath: The lives of manual scavengers in Tamil Nadu also referred to these castes as scavengers.

4. The Hinduization of scavenging castes is discussed in chapter 7 of this book

5. Field based observation.

6. Field based observation.

7. Field based observation.

8. Field based observation.

9. Field based observation.

are found to practise Islam. However, in Sagar, Madhya Pradesh, and adjoining areas, the Helas are Hindus. Lalbegis too at one point followed Islam, but later came into the fold of Hinduism under the Valmiki identity with the propaganda of the Arya Samajis. Among Sikhs, the scavengers are largely called Mazbi Sikhs. In Christianity, there are no traditional scavenging castes, but a sizable number of Hindu scavenging castes have later adopted Christianity.[1] A few people from the scavenging castes have also converted to Buddhism.

The scavenging community, within the Hindu fold and outside, is heterogeneous with the presence of several castes and sub-castes placed in the order of graded inequality. Some sections are considered to be more superior as compared to the others. We have also observed that the new individual entrants from other Dalit castes, owing to their numerical deficiency, often cannot dictate their caste superiority over traditional scavenging castes. Yet, in case of downward mobility of whole castes into this occupation, they can reinforce their caste privileges to a slight possible extent, for instance, in the case of the Musahars in Bihar. Yet, by and large, the numerical strength of the scavenging caste is the only deciding factor in determining the position of the particular scavenging community in the hierarchy of castes. There are ample cases to understand this feature. This issue is discussed well in Chapter 7 along with the socio-cultural practices of the community, their political allegiance, etc.

Prospects for the Younger Generation

Attaining education has been established to be critical for empowering children and youth of any community. However, educational opportunities for the children in the scavenging community are still inaccessible; enrollment as well as retention rate of these children in schools is very low across India.

There are multiple factors that have affected access to quality education for these children, including poverty, lack of awareness, and limited parental care due to occupational pressure. However, the most significant cause of educational disadvantage for these children is the increasing number of for-profit private schools in India. Mushrooming of for-profit schools in the country has widened the gulf between the rich and the poor. At one point, government schools used to cater to a wide range of students. Children of bureaucrats, uppermiddle class families as

1. Discrimination and Exclusion in Education: A Study of Children of the Families Associated with 'Unclean' Occupations of Uttar Pradesh, Rajasthan, Himachal Pradesh and Haryana a report submitted to ICSSR.

well as from poor households used to study together. Whereas at present, schools are segregated along class and caste lines. Families of the elite and middle class send their children to expensive private schools, and poor Dalit children get increasingly ghettoised in government schools that provide free education. This segregation has affected the quality of services provided in government schools.

In premier government schools that provide high quality education, such as the Navodaya schools and Sainik schools, one can notice a stark absence of students from the scavenging communities. Often, parents from these communities are unaware of the existence of these schools. In addition, due to lack of support, children from these communities are ill-prepared to pass the challenging entrance examinations conducted to screen students for entry into these schools. Public education systems in India have deteriorated drastically in recent years, due to anti-people policies and political forces. The enforcement of caste hierarchies, and heinous practices such as that of untouchability, are also enforced strictly. The practice of untouchability is one of the most notorious social traditions, wherein a section of the society is permanently labelled as 'unclean' and 'impure'. They enjoy no rights, but are burdened with duties and obligations. This was so strictly practised for centuries that people still find themselves in the trap of their traditional caste occupations.

Dalit activists have often applauded the role of British colonial administrators such as Macaulay in democratizing access to education to the deprived communities;[1] however, this book finds the impact of his policies to be questionable.

Locating the present book

This book is based on the insights gathered through an empirical study undertaken by the Indian Social Institute between 2014 to 2019 to gather evidence of discrimination in education and their causes and consequences on the attainment of education of the children from households engaged in a range of occupations considered 'unclean'. Over more than six years, we have been in direct contact with the scavenging and allied communities across the states of Haryana, Himachal Pradesh, Bihar, Jharkhand, Madhya Pradesh, and Chhattisgarh. I have also had indirect association with communities in Rajasthan and Uttar Pradesh through field investigators and research partners.

1. For instance, Chandrabhan Prasad in his series of articles published in the national newspaper claims this.

In each of these states, two cities were selected as a sample. Out of which the settlements of communities engaged in 'unclean' occupations were mapped and a sample of 8-12 settlements were selected. The researchers spent one month in each of the sample states to collect in-depth information from the communities. Apart from that, a team of field surveyors were employed to collect quantitative data. During the research, focused group discussions and in-depth interviews were conducted with community leaders, children and activists. The methodology also included school observations and interaction with teaching staff and other school authorities. A total of 8517 households, listing 19,821 children from 16 cities and towns (urban and semi-urban) of 8 states (Uttar Pradesh, Himachal Pradesh, Rajasthan, Haryana, Bihar, Jharkhand, Madhya Pradesh, Chhattisgarh) from northern and central India, were surveyed. Qualitative data was gathered from 260 schools and households by conducting 1080 interviews with parents, teachers, and other stakeholders; and 130 focus group discussions with students and community members.

Subsequent to the field data collection and analysis, research reports were produced in a technical format that includes the depiction of quantitative data by using tables, charts, graphs, etc. However, many important dimensions of this research work could not be included in these reports due to practical considerations. This book documents many of those facts, qualitative data, as well as useful bits of information from secondary sources that could not be included in the technical report. In this book, we have almost entirely excluded quantitative data and analysis, to keep it accessible to readers from non-academic backgrounds as well. Another aspect that makes this book different is that, unlike in research papers, this book does not study the scavenging community in isolation, but attempts to understand its problems as situated in the wider caste system.

This book is written by combining the methodology of sociology and history. As discussed above the primary information was collected through the sociological method of data collection. While in the secondary piece of information, historical writings along with contemporary literature on this subject are being used. In a brief but coherent form, the role of dominant religious and social ideologies in the systemic marginalisation and exclusion of Dalits in ancient India and a critique of the British education system that was initially inclined towards sustaining Brahmanic hegemony have also been discussed. This book attempts to understand the life of a poor Dalit in educational institutes and in the broader society and to expose the practices and socio-cultural pre-conditions of society that keep scavenging and allied communities in the trap of occupational immobility. The problem of contemporary scavenging communities and their poor educational attainment is not a present-day problem. This unclean practice is deep-rooted in our socio-political system that systematically denies rights and excludes entire communities. It compels ordinary people and celebrities to use casteist slurs against the Dalits. This book explores the processes that have created and fostered vulnerability and marginality for a section of society.

This book also discusses the issue of caste and sub-caste conflict at a larger level, its observance among Dalits and also within the scavenger community, and tries to understand the difference in the intensity of casteism in inter-caste and intra-caste conflicts. Chapter 6 focuses exclusively on the problems of women and girls, who face triple discrimination due to their caste, class as well as gender. The last chapter 'Responsibility of Responsible Government' critiques the existing policies and programs of the government and suggests an alternative approach. The focus of the book is on exclusion in education, yet education is not looked at in isolation but in conjunction with larger systemic factors that are beyond the control of students but nonetheless affect their educational prospects greatly.

Chapter - 1

Unclean India and Socio-Economic Challenges

> Under the rule of the Peshwas in the Maratha country, the untouchable was not allowed to use the public streets if a Hindu was coming along lest he should pollute the Hindu by his shadow. The untouchable was required to have a black thread either on his wrist or on his neck as a sign or a mark to prevent the Hindus from getting themselves polluted by his touch through mistake. In Poona, the capital of the Peshwa, the untouchable was required to carry, strung from his waist, a broom to sweep away from behind the dust he tread on lest a Hindu walking on the same should be polluted. In Poona, the untouchable was required to carry an earthen pot, hung in his neck wherever he went, for holding his spit lest his spit falling on earth should pollute a Hindu who might unknowingly happen to tread on it.
>
> **-Dr. Babasaheb Ambedkar**[1]

Indians are known for their strict observation of purity and pollution. The dominant Brahmanic philosophy lays so much emphasis on purity that not only people engaged in menial occupations had been treated as untouchables but even the people of other faiths and nationalities who came into contact with the Hindus were often seen as untouchables by them. In other words, whosoever is a foreigner would be untouchable to the Hindus. When Ancient Indians first encountered the Greeks, they called them *Mleccha*—lowly or untouchable. The Muslim and Christian rulers who came and settled in India in the medieval centuries were also treated as untouchables by the elite Hindus. At one time, there used to be two separate water taps for Hindus and Muslims in public places such

1. Annihilation of Caste, BAWS, Vol. 1, p. 39.

as railway stations.[1] Such a differential treatment against Christians and Muslims was however somewhat short-lived and less enforced, mainly because of the influential positions they had occupied in the society. The Muslims were a ruling class in medieval centuries, while the British-Christians ruled from the eighteenth century onwards. During both these reigns, the dominant Hindus were in subordinate positions; this restricted them from strictly practicing caste rules with the Muslim and Christian populations. Otherwise, the Hindus would not have spared any chance in observing the practice of untouchability against them. Caste hierarchies in Indian society were exacerbated mainly during and after the Gupta period (320-550 AD). The biggest victims of caste-based discrimination and exclusion have been the indigenous groups labelled as 'untouchables.' These people were stripped of all kinds of power: political, economic, social and spiritual.[2] These groups of people were considered to be outside the purview of the four-fold varna structure.

These pervasive notions around purity affect even those who belong to the caste Hindu fold, as some are temporarily branded with the label of being impure at times. Women, irrespective of their caste and class, become impure during menstruation. A mother in labour, a child at the time of birth, and the family where a death has taken place are considered partially impure. To regain purity after these short periods of untouchability, people are expected to perform rituals such as spending time in seclusion or spraying some water from the Ganges over the bodies of people and the places they inhabit. Among the purifying agents, even waste products of the cow, such as urine and cow dung hold special significance. These rituals still survive in both rural and urban Hindu households of our time. Apart from these mythical concepts of impurity, genuinely unclean items such as human excreta or sanitary clothes stained with menstrual blood were treated as filthy.

One must find it strange, however, to note that despite this obsession with the notion of purity, most Indian public spaces are filthy. Indians have a notoriously low sense of civic duty, and people commonly litter streets with waste, urinate and defecate by the roadside and spit tobacco.

1. This is also mentioned in Amrita Pritam's story 'Pinjar'. In 2003, Chandra Prakash Dwivedi made a film based on this story. In this film, there is a scene where two separate taps for Hindus and Muslims are shown on a railway platform.
2. The dominant Brahmanic philosophy treated them as outcasts. The untouchables were forced to believe that they are born low because of their evil deeds in their past lives. Such philosophy was forced upon the indigenous communities for a long time, until it was challenged by the likes of Kabir and Ravidas in medieval centuries.

Open defecation is a common scene beside railway tracks all over the country. The cities of Bihar and Uttar Pradesh, including their capitals, have a practice of open urination at public places such as at railway platforms, bus stations, and by the roadside, where the local people, particularly males, do not hesitate in urinating in public even in broad daylight. But this is not limited to small cities of backward states alone, metro cities including the capital Delhi witness open defecation not only at the outskirts but even in the posh areas of South Delhi. Even the sites of historical importance, such as the Siri Fort or the Qutub Minar, stink with the stench of human excreta, owing to the lack of toilet facilities for the local poor living in the neighbouring areas.[1]Open drains at some of the non-posh places of South Delhi[2] and other places on the outskirts of the city such as in JJ *(Jhuggi-Jhopadi)* settlements are very common.

The double standard of heeding to purity in ritualistic life while caring the least about public hygiene and sanitation seems to be an age-old tradition of Indians. Yet one cannot forget that the country once witnessed one of the oldest human civilizations, where utmost importance was given to public hygiene and public sanitation which perhaps no other contemporary civilization did.[3] This was known as Harappan or Indus Valley Civilization (2500-1800 BC).[4] In almost all Harappan cities every house, big or small, had its own courtyard and bathroom. The drainage system was very impressive. Water flowed from the house to the street through drains that were covered with bricks or stone slabs. The street drains were equipped with manholes.[5]Another remarkable feature of the public infrastructure was the grid system of arrangement of houses where roads cut across at right angles and divided the city into numerous regular blocks. This was true of almost all Indus settlements, regardless of their size. This civilization was a non-Brahmanic one that neither believed in the caste system nor untouchability.[6] The natives of the Indus Valley Civilization were far ahead of present day Indians in the quality of toilets

1. This is to some extent controlled after 2018, when MCD constructed public toilets at this place.
2. This is very common in Mehrauli. The Shahpur Jat area, also known as the Fashion Street, has a bad drainage system. Leakage from the drains is a common feature.
3. The archaeological evidence reveals this feature to be unique to the Harappan civilization. All the historians attest to this fact.
4. RS Sharma, Ancient India p. 53
5. RS Sharma, Ancient India p. 47
6. RS Sharma, DD Kosambi, Naval Kishore Viyogi, JL Nehru, Romila Thapar and almost all the historians, except the right wing ones, agree with the fact that Indus Valley Civilization was a pre-Brahmin indigenous civilization that flourished until the advent of Aryan invasion in India.

they constructed. Archaeological evidence suggests that people of the Indus Valley Civilization used western commode-like toilets which were well connected to covered drains.[1] Present-day India still lags behind this ancient civilization in these matters. Even in the later centuries, in the Buddhist period, one can find that public sanitation and hygiene were important concerns. Archaeological evidence suggests that during this time open defecation was not practised at all. In the text 'Vinaya Pitak', which prescribes a code of conduct for Buddhist monks and nuns, detailed paragraphs on personal and public hygiene, and methods of using and cleaning toilets can be found.[2] The toilets in this period, however, were less advanced than those in the Indus civilization.[3] The shape of the commodes during this time more closely resembled present-day Indian-style commodes.[4]

We cannot be sure exactly when the focus on constructing toilets began to dwindle in India. However, it may be the case that Brahmanic ideas around purity and hygiene influenced people's perceptions towards toilets. Judging by the opinions of caste Hindu elders in present-day India, one can see that Brahmanic ideas consider toilets at home to be unhygienic and favour open defecation. This may have greatly influenced Indians' practice of open defecation that continues till date in villages and outskirts of urban spaces. There are several disadvantages associated with the practice of open defecation. However, one benefit of the practice is the lack of need for any sweepers and scavengers for cleaning toilets, septic tanks or drains. Based on this argument, a few scholars have suggested that the practice of open defecation is unlikely to have created the need for a sweeper caste. They claim, thus, that the sweeper community first came into existence during the Muslim rule in India. It is said that the Purdah system amongst the Muslims forced them to build dry latrines in their homes. A well-researched book by Vijay Prashad—Untouchable Freedom—could not trace the existence of sanitation workers before the Mughal empire. It focused only on the British Empire to trace the creation of a scavenging community in Delhi. Therefore, it seems to attest to the above views. However, in Dalit thought, there have been serious attempts to trace the roots of scavenging and untouchability in Brahmanism.[5]

1. Bhagwan Das, "Main Bhangi Hun
2. Vinaya Pitaka, Trans. Rahul Sankrityayan
3. Bhagwan Das, "Main Bhangi Hun"
4. Remains of a toilet commode available at Patna Museum shows the change in its shape and design during this period. This is made of stone.
5. See for instance, Dr. Ambedkar's 'The Untouchables' BAWS Vol. 7

Unclean Brahmanism

Almost all historians agree that one does not find any evidence for the existence of caste, untouchability, or any form of slavery in the Indus Valley Civilization. Its egalitarian and progressive features and emphasis on public sanitation and cleanliness make it far ahead of present-day India. This compels DD Kosambi to call this period the golden period in Indian history.[1] Historians have traced a multitude of reasons for the eventual decline of the Indus valley civilization. However, a common thread of logic runs across many of these theories which connect the dawn of the successive Brahmanic Vedic Civilization to the decline of the Indus Valley Civilization. The Vedic period is believed to have lasted for one thousand years, divided into two sections: 1500-1000 BC as the pre-Vedic period and 1000-500 BC as the later-Vedic period. The Buddhist period is considered to have followed the Vedic period. This chronology has widespread acceptance among historians. Dr. Ambedkar, too, posits Buddha as a revolutionary figure who stood against the tyrannical and oppressive Vedic period.[2] Both Buddha and Mahavira are said to have developed their religions as a reaction against Brahmanism of the Vedic period.

However, recent developments in the study of ancient India propose an alternative to this well-accepted chronology. Johannes Bronkhorst—a Dutch Orientalist and Indologist—postulates that Brahmins had not entered India during the Buddha's time; and that they only arrived in later centuries.[3] This theory may be shocking to the students of history; however, one must note that this is not a new hypothesis. Dr Bhadant Anand Kausalyayan, too, has claimed that Sanskrit was developed later than Pali.[4] Therefore, quite naturally, all the Sanskrit texts including the Vedas, Upanishads and Puranas were composed much after the Buddha's time. HabirAngar studied this matter in further detail and came to the same conclusion in his book 'Pali is Mother of Sanskrit Language'. Prof PC Roy also proposes the same hypothesis based on linguistic arguments. Observing the pronunciations of Pali and Sanskrit words, one can notice that Pali words are much easier to pronounce than Sanskrit words, pointing to the likelihood that Sanskrit was developed much later than Pali. Recently, Rajendra Prasad Singh also picked up the same idea and propagated it among wider masses through his books, articles, and social media posts. These two arguments regarding the chronological sequence

1. The Culture and Civilization of Ancient India in Historical Outline
2. See for instance, Revolution and Counter Revolution in India, BAWS Vol. 3.
3. See, The Buddhism under Shadow of Brahminism
4. In the preface of his book , '*31 dino main aawashyakpali*'

of Brahmin immigration and Buddhist period, as well as the development of Pali and Sanskrit, call into question the widely accepted claims of a thousand-year-long Vedic period in Indian history.

The stark absence of any archaeological evidence of the Vedic period raises the same doubts. Ample archaeological evidence is available to corroborate the existence of the Indus Valley Civilization as well as post-Vedic civilizations. However, nothing by way of archaeological proof exists that can authenticate the claims of the Vedic age. If we believe this to be true, then we should answer the question of what were the religious and philosophical ideas that were prominent during this period between 1500 and 500 BC. Answers can be easily sourced from the textual records of this period. According to Buddhist sources, in the Sakyan republic, the Sankhya philosophy was dominant. In this republic and its surrounding regions, Ajivika and six other non-Brahmanic sects were popular. None of these sects believed in graded inequality and the caste system. At the political level, the Magadha Empire—the most prominent and powerful one at the time—was ruled by a lineage that could be classified under Shudras in Brahmanic terminology.

The Nagas, Nandas, Mauryans were called Shudras in Brahmanic texts while the Haryanks, who were contemporaries of the Buddha and Mahavira, were Khattiyas, not Kshatriyas as wrongly mentioned by later historians. Therefore, it is certain that the varna system was unknown at that time. According to DhammanandKosambi, the Khattiyas were agrarian landholder communities. He traced the origin of the word Khattiya to the Pali word '*khetta*' meaning farmland.[1]

However, the establishment of Brahmanic Vedic culture and the deterioration of the indigenous religious thought precipitated the decline of the egalitarian social milieu. For the first time, a religious explanation on the mythical origin of the four-fold varna system and its so-called rationale appeared in the Rigveda. This type of social hierarchy was so favourableto the Brahmins that they continued to propagate it through the later centuries. The Gita, the sacred text of the Hindus that is supposed to be the gospel of the great Lord Krishna himself, is likely to have been composed during the Gupta period. One can find justifications for the need for graded social inequality in the Gita, which says

> *valor, strength, fortitude, skill with the use of weapons, resolve to never retreat from battle, generosity and leadership abilities are the*

1. See, DhammanandKosambi, *Bhagwan Buddha Jeevan Aur Darshan*, LokbharatiPrakashan

duties and natural qualities of Kshatriyas. Agriculture, cattle rearing and trade are the duties of the Vaishyas, born of their own nature; and action consisting of service is the duty of Shudras born of their own nature. [1]

In addition to the Gita and Rigveda, justification for the caste system can be found in books of political nature – such as the Manu Smriti and Gautam Dharma Sutra. These books go a step further as they pronounce strict punishment for those who try to bypass or revolt against this established system. These texts impose harsher punishments for Shudras as compared to those who are higher up in the hierarchy. They also serve as legal documents that justify the caste system and the practice of untouchability. The most unfortunate part of Indian history is that these Brahmanical values, with graded inequality of the worst form reflected in the caste system, became the dominant culture for the largest period of time. As a consequence, a group of people in society were permanently labelled as untouchables. India in the twenty first century is still reeling from the effects of these practices.

The Emergence of Untouchable Castes

At present, discussions on untouchability are often linked with 'unclean' occupations such as leatherwork, scavenging and sanitation work. This was not always the case in the past; unclean occupations used to be performed by slaves in almost every civilization. There is a general consensus among historians that the practice of untouchability began during the Gupta period. A recent study based on gene analysis goes even further to establish that the practice of endogamy also found its roots in society during the same period. However, in the early days of Brahmanism, just like in any non-brahmin civilization, menial tasks were performed by slaves belonging to different castes, including Brahmins. According to Ambedkar, Aryans did not at all mind engaging themselves in filthy occupations. A Brahmin could have a Brahmin or Kshatriya or Vaishya or a Shudra as his slave. A Kshatriya could have a Kshatriya or a Vaishya or a Shudra as his slave. A Vaishya could have a Vaishya or a Shudra as his slave. A Shudra could have only a Shudra slave. With all this, the law of slavery remained and all Aryans whether they were Brahmins, Kshatriyas, Vaishyas or Shudras, if they became slaves, were subject to it.[2] His argument was based on the reference of Narada Smriti

1. Bhagavad Gita, Chapter 18, Verses 43 and 44, Commentary by Swami Mukudananda
2. BAWS, Vol. 7 p. 305.

which says[1]: 'Know that there are two sorts of occupations; pure work and impure work; *impure work is done by the slaves.* Pure work is done by labourers.

> *Sweeping the gateway, the privy, the road and the place for rubbish; shampooing the secret parts of the body; gathering and putting away the leaving of food, ordure and urine. And lastly, rubbing the master's limbs when desired; this should be regarded as impure work. All other work besides this is pure'.*

Therefore, according to the Narada Smriti, the 'unclean' occupations were not restricted to a particular set of castes but were performed by slaves, irrespective of their castes. However, Ambedkar raises an important point that slavery was followed in a graded form. A Vaishya could not have a Brahmin or Kshatriya as his slave but could have either a Vaishya or a Shudra as his slave; whereas a Brahmin can have slaves from any of the four castes, including his own. However, during the Gupta period, the caste system started being imposed strictly. Chandals, who were a separate tribe living on the outskirts of cities, became the first victims of the practice of untouchability. They were cut off from mainstream society in all possible ways. The Chinese traveler Faxian, who visited India in 400 AD, documents the status of these tribes as untouchables; he notes that their entry into the city was heavily restricted, and they had to beat a drum hanging on their neck to alert others to maintain a safe distance from them when they were allowed to enter the city on rare occasions. However, at that time this ban and restrictions were limited only to Chandals. According to Ambedkar, when Faxian came to India it was the reign of the Gupta kings, who were the patrons of Brahmanism. It was a period of the triumph and revival of Brahmanism. It is quite possible that what Faxian describes is not untouchability but an extremity to which the Brahmins were prepared to carry the ceremonial impurity which had become attached to some community, particularly to the Chandalas.[2] In later years, around 600 AD, many other castes were relegated to the status of untouchables. According to the description by the second Chinese traveler Xuanzang, who visited India in 629 AD and spent sixteen years, there seem to have been many more castes against whom untouchability was being practised. He writes:

Butchers, fishermen, public performers, executioners, and scavengers have their habitations marked by a distinguishing sign. They are forced

1. Ibid.
2. Quoted from BAWS Vol. 7, p. 378.

to live outside the city and they sneak along on the left when going about in the hamlets.[1]

Segregating habitations of castes engaged with unclean occupations, and marking those with distinguishable signs, can surely be called as the practice of untouchability. However, it is interesting to note that among the occupations mentioned in this list, only scavengers can be said to follow an unclean occupation. Most other castes in the list are related to those who engage in the job of killing animals or humans. At present, most of these castes such as fishermen do not fall within the ambit of Scheduled Castes, but are placed hierarchically higher up in the Other Backward Classes category. In any case, Xuanzang's description clearly describes ghettoization of untouchables—a practice that continues till date. Later on, many new castes such as Chamar, Mahar, Dusadhetc which are numerically larger than those mentioned by Xuanzang get included in this list of untouchables. About four hundred years later, around 1030 AD a renowned scholar named Alberuni visited India from Iran. He too was struck by the caste practices in India.

The people called Hadi, Doma (Domba), Chandala, and Badhatau are not reckoned amongst any caste or guild. They are occupied with dirty work, like the cleansing of the villages and other services. They are considered as one sole class and distinguished only by their occupations. They are considered like illegitimate children; for according to the general opinion they descend from a Sudra father and a Brahmani mother as the children of fornication; therefore they are degraded outcastes.[2]

Alberuni's explanation for these castes following 'unclean' occupations, as those composed of illegitimate children of Brahmani mothers indicates that this piece of information was possibly shared with him by those who were influenced by the Manu Smriti. This text, which is believed to have been composed between 170 BC and 150 BC, also gives the same explanation for the origin of Chandalas.[3]

'Unclean' Occupations in Present India

All the occupations that are broadly involved with cleaning work are considered to be 'unclean' occupations in India. Scavengers make up the largest portion of these 'unclean' workers; others include those involved in disposing of dead bodies of humans and animals, leather

1. Ibid pp. 378-79
2. Quoted from BAWS Vol. 5 p. 271
3. BAWS Vol. 3 p.271

work such as skinning, tanning, cobbling, as well as washing of stained clothes. In the northern, western and central parts of India, castes such as Bhangi, Chuhra, Mehtar, Valmiki are known to engage in scavenging work. In the north, the burning of the dead has become a caste occupation of the Dom. However, in the rest of India, this task is performed by the deceased person's family members. The Doms are restricted to certain centres such as Varanasi in Uttar Pradesh, where many Hindus go to perform last rites for their family members by the Ganges river, hoping to secure a place for the deceased in heaven. The increased volume of work that is needed to be performed in Varanasi necessitates the presence of experts such as those from the Dom community. However, in general, the funeral rites of Hindus are conducted out in the open in secular places in villages, towns and cities. The rituals are held without any hurry by family members and caste associates, and specialized funeral services from members of the Dom community are not usually sought. Since the Dom community's livelihood opportunities are largely restricted to holy sites, it has forced members of this growing community to take up other jobs like scavenging. Since the Doms have already been associated with the 'unclean' occupation of disposing of dead bodies, often they get offered similar 'unclean' occupations to which they also adapt to easily. The Dumar and Domar castes have also taken up scavenging jobs. At present in the Mahakaushal region of Madhya Pradesh, there are sizable numbers of Dumars engaged in scavenging. While in Chhattisgarh, there are a great many Domars from the Banda district of Uttar Pradesh who have migrated to seek scavenging jobs.

How and when these castes, which have not been traditionally involved in scavenging, came to do these jobs is not very clear. Scholars like Bhagwan Das, Vijay Prashad and others describe the professional and organized nature of the scavenging occupation during the Mughal rule, which underwent further systematization during the British rule. Urbanization and ensuing development of the sanitation system seems to have resulted in increasing the demand for the services of scavengers. As a result, poor or landless agrarian labourers from castes like the Chuhra, Bhangi or Mehtar, who were struggling to make ends meet in villages, migrated to the cities in search of employment. In later centuries, castes like Musahar also joined this sector.

Jobs like sweeping and cleaning of gutters, drainages, and septic tanks do not require one to have any special skill. 'Unclean' nature of these jobs confers them with a very low status, thus, resulting in very less competition for taking them up. The need for sanitation workers is very high in all sorts of public as well as private spaces. Municipal corporations, Indian railways, government offices, private companies, as well as households fitted with dry latrines—all need the services of scavengers. Therefore, these jobs are always available for those who are desperately seeking any means of livelihood. Thus, it seems to be that many poor Dalit communities did not hesitate to take up scavenging, which eventually became their caste occupation.

On the other hand, leather work involving the processes of skinning, tanning and cobbling requires a lot of skill and is dependent on market demand, which is often less than that for sanitation work. These jobs, therefore, have remained under the domain of the Chamar caste and its allied castes such as Raigar and Mochi. Due to the lack of demand for this work, many individuals from these castes look for alternative occupations as well. However, unlike Valmikis, Doms, Dumars, and Hadis were able to secure jobs in other sectors as well. They toiled hard as labourers in the construction industry and in other fields, and have managed to achieve some degree of occupational mobility. At present, only a few of them are engaged in their traditional caste occupation. Among the Dhobis, there are further subdivisions: those who wash regular clothes claim a higher status as compared to those who wash stained clothes. Therefore, it is no surprise that in some states like Uttar Pradesh, Bihar, and Kerala, Dhobis are included in the list of Scheduled Castes. Whereas, in other states like Madhya Pradesh (except in Bhopal) and Maharashtra, they are included in the Other Backward Classes list.

Sanitation work is not only pursued by traditionally scavenging castes but also by some members from other prominent Dalit castes such as the Dusadhs of Bihar, Chamars of Himachal Pradesh, some Mahars in Maharashtra, and Koris. Sanitation work has begun to seem lucrative to some tribal communities as well. Tribes like the Gonds of Madhya Pradesh and Chhattisgarh, and Oraons, Santhals, and Mundas of Jharkhand have also been opting for this occupation owing to their migration to cities due to rising populations and dwindling control over natural resources. It is an interesting but little-known fact that Musahars used to be called Bhuinyas, and they originally belonged to a branch of the Munda tribe; the other two branches being the Oraons and the Maltos.[1] The Oraons and Maltos have successfully retained their tribal identities, but Bhuinyas have lost their tribal identity since they encountered settled Hindu communities, started working first as agricultural labourers and later as sanitation workers

1. This based on oral tradition of Oraon, shared to me by an Adivasi scholar activist Arun Kumar Oraon.

when some moved to the cities. There are also stray cases of individuals from OBC and other castes falling into this occupation.

Those who are new entrants into the scavenging occupation, whether Dalits or tribals or anyone else, are seen to be more vulnerable as compared to those who are traditional scavengers. These new entrants have far less collective bargaining power, and earn lesser wages. Another reason for this marginality also lies in their hesitation in claiming their real caste identities. In most cases, these workers in a new city conceal their caste and make false claims of being Rajputs or Brahmins.[1]

This display of false caste pride detracts their attention from the real fight. While, among traditional castes of scavengers, there is no question of hiding their caste. As a result, both individually and in a group, local scavengers are ready to fight for the real issues of wages and also manage to succeed. For instance, in the Delhi Metro Rail Corporation (DMRC), it is observed that the local Valmikis who do not hesitate to reveal their caste receive higher wages, while the migrant workers falsely claiming to be Rajputs or Brahmins are employed at much lower wages.[2]

Vulnerability of the Communities Engaged in 'Unclean' Occupations

Economic vulnerability of scavengers is less in the government sector, since profit-making is of little concern to the socialist, democratic, republic form of government. Jobs provided by the public sector are not dependent on the rules of demand and supply, but are rather considered to be the state's duty to provide for its employees. Thus, sanitation workers are recruited by the government in much the same way as all other staff members are. They are paid a decent salary, along with provisions for casual and medical leaves, HRA, housing facilities, provident funds, increments, pensions and other social security measures. These factors have made sanitation work in the public sector lucrative for members of communities traditionally engaged in this work. However, the fall of the communist regime in the USSR led to a worldwide shift towards liberalization and privatization in the 90s. The government began to withdraw from its responsibility in the service sector and production. Municipal services also began to be privatized by inviting tenders from private entrepreneurs. As a result, permanent recruitment of sweepers in municipalities, railways and other government departments has dwindled. Manual occupations in all the sectors have begun to be given on daily-

1. Field based observation in Delhi while data collection for a project 'Delhi on Margin: A Study of Delhi Metro Contract Workers' study by Dr Denzil Fernandes.
2. Ibid.

wage or contractual basis. The new economic policy has been the biggest blow to the job security of the impoverished scavenger community.

Rapid increase in the population of people in the scavenging communities has also exacerbated the pressure on the job market. As a result of the abundant availability of labour, the cost of hiring has gone down drastically. Often contractors are seen to hire sanitation workers at wages far lower than the minimum wages fixed by the government. However, the contractors receive full wages from the government according to the Minimum Wages Act. This surplus is pocketed by the unscrupulous contractors right away, as they continue to make profits without putting in any effort by merely reducing the wages of the workers and by hiring fewer workers than what the task demands. As the contractors exploit the workers to reap the harvest of higher returns, sanitary workers end up becoming beasts of burden. In most of the municipalities, the contractors are given a free hand. Workers do not get their wages directly transferred to their bank accounts, nor do they get any payment slips. Payments rely upon the whims and fancies of the contractor. The basic law of demand and supply has the worst impact on these labourers, since there is a decline in the demand for their services but accompanied by an abundance of supply. Livelihoods of private service providers such as washermen, tanners, cobblers, scavengers, and those who associate themselves with dead bodies are heavily dependent on the market. Due to the increase in the population of the unemployed, semi-literate Dalits cannot all be employed because of the low availability of work. A sanitation worker Ravikant who works with the Municipal Corporation shared:

I am working with the Nagar Nigam as a cleaner and my dad also does the same work. For the past three years, I have done this work from 6 AM to 2 PM every day. My responsibility is to clean the roads and drains. The supervisor tells us that this large chamber is clogged, you have to go there and clean it, otherwise, you will be thrown out. Sometimes the employer does not pay money. We are very poor. I started this work from my town, but it paid me very little, so I moved to the city. After coming to this city (Patna) I started working with the Municipal Corporation. People talk about us and say that 'these people clean drains with their bare hands, we must not eat food with them as they are untouchables'. Sometimes when people of our village see us working, they recognize us. Our kids are tortured by their classmates in their schools for the work we do.[1]

In some cases, where the government is more vigilant towards the practices of contractors, such as in the Delhi Metro Rail Corporation

1. Discrimination and Exclusion in Education…Bihar and Jharkhand, p. 55.

(DMRC), workers' salaries get transferred directly into their bank accounts. This protocol ensures that labour rights are upheld, and minimum wages are being paid. But the contractors have devised crafty and cunning tactics to overcome these barriers. They distribute the salaries directly into the bank accounts, but they keep the passbooks and debit cards of the workers' accounts with them.[1] The salaries are then withdrawn by the contractor himself through his agents, and paid in cash to the workers thereafter. There is little doubt that the salaries that are handed to the workers in cash are far less than what is shown on record. There are several such ways that the contractors use to circumvent labour laws to make profits. The liberal turn of the economy has proved to be quite detrimental to the interests of the sanitation workers. As Lalla, a contract worker in Korba, Chhattisgarh, shared: "During the *Swachh Bharat Mission*, we work even at 2 in the morning; our contractor used to call us at any odd hours to complete some of the tedious work".[2]

Continuation of Manual Scavenging

The practice of manual scavenging continues in all its forms in India till date. According to the data released by the SafaiKarmachariAndolan (SKA), there are a total of 26 lakh community dry latrines and individual dry latrines in India. Manual scavengers are employed for cleaning these toilets daily.[3] Indian railways is the biggest employer of manual scavengers. Most trains have a hole in the toilet that opens up right onto the tracks. With 23 million people riding India Railways every day, that makes for a shitty situation.[4] Railways often directly and sometimes indirectly hire manual scavengers to clean the track. This inhuman and unhygienic system was challenged by a Dalit politician Ram Vilas Paswan during his tenure as the Railway Minister in 1996, but not much came to fruition since the fall of his government. Yet one of his biggest contributions to the railway sanitation workers was that he regularized all the contractual sanitation workers that were hired by the railways. The bio-latrine plans that were proposed by him did not make much progress at the time; the idea was later re-introduced on an experimental basis.

1. Field based information collected during Delhi Metro project.See, Delhi on Margins: A Study of Delhi Metro Contract Workers, A Study Report by Denzil Fernandes and Ratnesh Kumar, p. 92.
2. Discrimination and Exclusion in Education…Madhya Pradesh and Chhattisgarh, p. 100.
3. https://safaikarmachariandolan.org/
4. Cassie Carothers in her article https://www.globalcitizen.org/en/content/toilets-trains-india/?template=next

The first rake with bio-toilets was developed with the help of DRDO (Defence Research and Development Organisation) for Bundelkhand Express on 18th January 2011.[1] The Swachh Bharat Mission has sped up the process of refitting old train toilets with bio-latrines, yet some trains continue to use the old toilet model. Later chapters discuss many ill effects of the Swachh Bharat Mission on the lives of the scavengers, but the transformation of traditional train toilets to bio-toilets on a massive scale has proved to be a major milestone towards securing the rights of the scavengers. Yet, in some cases, clogging or structural damage to the toilets often leads to leakage on the track. In such a case, the services of a manual scavenger are needed. In many other government sector enterprises, manual scavenging continues. Public sector entities, such as the SECL (South Eastern Coalfields Limited) regularly invite tenders to clean their septic tanks. The cantonment boards also employ manual scavengers. The situation has persisted even after the passage of the Employment of Manual Scavengers and Construction of Dry Latrines (Prohibition) Act 1993 and even after the introduction of the Prohibition of Employment as Manual Scavengers and their Rehabilitation Act 2013.

Risk of injuries and even death are unfortunately a part and parcel of the scavenging work. Nearly 2,000 manual scavengers die every year in the sewers due to exposure to poisonous gases. The number of deaths in septic tanks is even higher.[2] Minor accidents are far too common in this occupation. Bodhdas Valmiki, a sweeper engaged in manual scavenging at Korba, Chhattisgarh, describes the risks in his occupation:

I used to clean the gutter by getting down inside it. I use spades to collect the dirt in a pan, and then I pass it on to another labourer who stands outside the gutter. This work involves direct contact with dirt and human excreta. We are not provided with any safety gear, gloves or even gumboots. The contractor does not even provide us with soap and water to wash up. We have to depend on the nearby houses for water to clean ourselves. Sometimes there are blades, glass pieces and other sharp objects which cut our hands.[3]

Such work often results in wounds, cuts and skin infections. These physical problems are not minor, but are openly visible. A manual scavenger is easily recognizable by his infected hands, body smell and

1. https://irimee.indianrailways.gov.in/instt/uploads/files/1435551621486-IR-DRDO%20Bio%20toilets.pdf
2. Crisis | SafaiKarmachariAndolan.
3. Discrimination and Exclusion in Education...Madhya Pradesh and Chhattisgarh, p. 100.

other outward appearances. They hardly get enough money to spend on their dress and other necessities, adding to their dishevelled looks. In an interview with the scavenging community, a youth said:

One can easily identify who is a manual scavenger. These persons usually suffer from visible skin infections and their dressing sense is quite different from others'. They also have a regular drinking habit, which is another identifying marker. When such parents interact with teachers, their children get branded negatively by the teachers.[1]

The scavenging community of Sagar cantonment in Madhya Pradesh says that the army administration issued a strict law to prevent the construction of new buildings or renovation of any old building. There are many big bungalows in the cantonment areas that were built during the British period. These big bungalows are now portioned into many small quarters and are serving as residential spaces for the lower grades of employees. Being old structures, there are no facilities or toilets in them. Moreover, the residents are not permitted to build any toilets or septic tanks. This results in the widespread practice of open defecation, and manual scavengers are hired to clean up the mess. Manoj, who is working as a sweeper in the Sagar cantonment area for the past five years says:

We are hearing in the media that manual scavenging is banned in India. There are a lot of campaigns going on under the banner of Swachh Bharat Mission. But here in Sagar, the army openly perpetuates conditions for manual scavenging. If we are not allowed to build toilets in our homes, what else do we do other than go out in the open ground. When the ground stinks because of human defecation, our people are recruited to clean up. Ironically, this is because of the Army's order. Does the Army stand above the Government of India?[2]

Indian history shows that ruling regimes have been responsible for the creation of a separate scavenging class, and their marginal position in society. Establishing a democratic government in India has done little to alleviate the conditions of the communities at the lowest rungs of the caste hierarchy. Poverty and social marginalization greatly impact children from these communities who are suffering as they attempt to gain access to education. In this modern age that valourises individual liberty, entire communities of people are continually trapped in this occupation generation after generation.

1. Field based information shared by a scavenger at Shimla.
2. Discrimination and Exclusion in Education...Madhya Pradesh and Chhattisgarh, pp. 33-34.

Chapter - 2

An Overview of Education in India

> In this country, education is in the lowest grade. Not only that is so but for some reason which all of us know, education has not been universally spread among all the communities in this country. There are communities, which are highly educated and there are communities where education is very, very low.
>
> **-Dr Babasaheb Ambedkar**[1]

Mass education is one of the critical responsibilities of a nation, particularly of a democratic or socialist nature. This is important because it is a known fact that education is the key to knowledge, success and development of both individuals and society. This is precisely the reason why all the reformist movements which were rooted in religion laid much emphasis on education, besides efforts to propagate their religious teachings. Among major institutional religions —Christianity, Buddhism, and Islam — the concept of mass education had been deep-rooted. TheConvent schools, Viharas and Madrasas, respectively, were the educational institutions for mass education. Interestingly, these religions had been followed by the ruling elites of India for many centuries. Therefore, it is not a surprise that mass education was also an essential feature of Indian society for a significant period until the establishment of brahmanic supremacy.

Education in Ancient India

The education and literacy of the masses in the third century BC can be traced to the Asokan inscriptions engraved at various remote places in

1. BAWS Vol. 15, p. 190.

India. This was, however, not the first evidence of writings in the country. Much before 2500–1900 BC[1] or even earlier, Indians were known to have developed an indigenous script in what is called the Indus Valley Civilization. The archaeological evidence suggests this civilization was egalitarian. Therefore, we can rightly assume that mass literacy was its essential feature. This script, however, was lost with the decline and diminishment of this civilization. We have no records of reading and writing in later centuries. During the Buddha's period (563 BC), there was a great development in philosophy, but the art of writing was not developed. Yet, the *viharas* began to develop as education centres for the common masses, where the monks and nuns imparted education to people. This system was later streamlined during the Asokan period (268-230 BC). This was also a period when a new indigenous script called Dhammalipi was fully developed and popularized.[2] The uniqueness of this era was that this script did not remain confined to the elites but became known to the masses. Asoka also recruited a new set of officials called Dhammamahamattas to reach the ordinary people through the *viharas* to spread education among the masses. Based on this fact, Prof. PL Narasu observes that 'the percentage of literacy among the Indians in Asoka's time was higher than it is now in many provinces of British India.' He opined:

> The care taken to publish the imperial edicts and commemorative records by incising them in imperishable characters most skilfully executed, on rocks and pillars situated in great cities, on main lines of communication, or at sacred spots frequented by pilgrims, implies that knowledge of reading and writing was widely diffused and that many people must have been able to read the documents. The same inference may be drawn from the fact that inscriptions are composed, not in any learned scholastic tongue, but vernacular dialects intelligible to the common people, and modified when necessary to suit local needs. It is probable that learning was fostered by the numerous monasteries and that the boys and girls in hundreds of villages learned their lessons from the monks and nuns, as they do now in Burma from the monks.[3]

Education through Buddhist *viharas* is a surviving feature even in

---

1. RS Sharma in his Ancient Past mentions 2500-1900 BC as the mature phase of Indus valley civilization.
2. In mainstream History this script is known as Brahmi Lipi. However, Asoka himself mentioned this script to be Dhamma Lipi in his inscriptions.
3. PL Narasu, A Study of Caste, p. 53.

the present century in the Buddhist dominated areas of Bangladesh.[1] Education in the Buddhist period in India was not restricted to schooling alone. Higher education in the form of universities had also become a feature of the education system. The universities, such as Taxila, Nalanda, Odantpuri, Nagarjunkonda, Kanchipuram, Manaketa, Ujjain, Pushpagiri, Ratnagiri, etc., were excellent examples of higher education in the pre and post-Mauryan period.[2] These universities were open to all castes and creeds and there were even a sizable number of students from foreign countries studying there.[3]

However, with the decline of the Mauryan Empire, and more pertinently with the decline of Buddhism, the concept of mass education went astray. The emergence of Brahmanic kingdoms was the most significant setback to the idea of mass education. Brahmanism believes that knowledge should be restricted only to the elites, and commoners should be deprived of it. The Gupta period (320-550 AD) which is claimed to be a golden period in Indian history,[4] particularly by right-wing historians, is no doubt a period of development of the classical language Sanskrit and its fine literary compositions, and of magnificent architecture.[5] But it was a golden period only for the upper classes, the masses were neglected. We cannot forget that Sanskrit was the language of the elites, and this period proved to be the worst for the depressed classes, including women of all castes and classes. The *sati* system emerged during this period. The first example of the immolation of a widow after the death of her husband appears in Gupta times in AD 510.[6] The formation and genesis of the institution of caste and its operation through endogamy also came into practice from this period onwards. This historical fact is also attested in a study by the National Institute of Biomedical Genomics (NIBMG) at Kalyani, West Bengal. In this study, the researchers analysed the DNA samples of 367 unrelated Indians belonging to 20 population groups. It is found that 1,575 years ago, during the Gupta Empire, caste endogamy,

1. This piece of information is shared to me by friend a Bangladeshi monk Ven. Suvinaya.
2. Sandesh Wagh available at https://mu.ac.in/wp-content/uploads/2014/05/2016-Ancient-Buddhist-University-in-India-compressed.pdf
3. See, DG Apte, Universities in Ancient India, Faculty of Education and Psychology. This point is raised prominently in Dalit-Bahujan discussion where it is often claim that ancient India, gained the title of Jagat Guru (universal teacher) not becauces of Shankaracharya but because of the Buddhist unversities which cater to the students of various nationalities.
4. For instance see, https://www.worldhistory.org/Gupta_Empire/
5. This is claimed with much intensity among the rightwing scholars.
6. RS Sharma, Ancient India 1990, p. 160.

the staunchest step towards the hereditary hierarchical system, came into strict practice and it continues even today.[1]

The ancient Sanskrit dramas composed during and after this regime suggest that the caste and patriarchal division in education had reached its height. Sanskrit became a distant dream even for the females of elite castes as it was restricted only to their male counterparts.[2] The dialogues of ancient Sanskrit dramas suggest that even while in communication with their husbands and male relatives, the women speak in Prakrit while the males respond to them in Sanskrit. This insistence on Sanskrit in royal courts but depriving its access to females, the Shudras and commoners further created a rift between elites and ordinary people. The total disregard for a *lingua franca* and mass education by the Brahmanic kings subsequently turned Indians into illiterate masses.

This happened continuously and systematically for centuries since the country had been under Brahmanic kingship for the longest period. The immediate successors of the Mauryans — the Sungas, Kanvas, and Satavahanas — belonged to the Brahmin caste. The Gupta kings who came later belonged to the Vaishya varna, followed by the Rajputs, who were originally casteless hordes from Middle Asia. Among these dynasties, the Sunga was known to be the worst and most violent attackers on Buddhists, while the Gupta period is infamous for the revival of Brahmanic literature. The Rajputs, being a foreign tribe, were sanctioned the status of Kshatriyas by the Brahmins. As a result, they too became staunch supporters of Brahmanism.[3]

It is a known fact that the brahmanic culture from its beginning had been opposed to the concept of mass education. Manu Smriti, composed in the Gupta era, imposed severe penalties on the Shudras who dared to seek admission in educational institutions. Apart from this, Shudras and women were subjected to many punishable restrictions. According to Ambedkar, Manu is the only divine lawgiver who has denied the commoner the right to knowledge. The education under this scheme was

1. https://timesofindia.indiatimes.com/india/70-generations-ago-caste-stopped-people-inter-mixing/articleshow/50859632.cms
2. Such inter-lingual diaglogue is common among all the sanskrit dramas. See, Vaidya, P. L. "ON THE USE OF PRAKRIT DIALECTS IN SANSKRIT DRAMAS." *Annals of the Bhandarkar Oriental Research Institute* 33, no. 1/4 (1952): 15–25.
3. The anti-Buddhist and castiest attitude of Rajput is well discussed by Dr K Jamanadas in his article 'Rajput Period Was Dark Age Of India', available at http://www.ambedkar.org/research/Rajput_Period_Was_Dark_Age_Of_India.html

restricted only to Brahmins and Kshatriyas—the two upper classes of the Indian society. According to the laws of Manu, it can be rightly said that writing had become the right of the high-class few and illiteracy had become the destiny of the low-class many.[1]

In the mythological legends of Mahabharat and Ramayan, which are also believed to have taken final shape during the Gupta period,[2] we have a classic example of exclusion and discrimination against the outcastes. Eklavya, a tribal youth, was denied admission in a *gurukul* by a Brahmin teacher Dronacharya. This discriminatory behaviour does not stop here. The outcastes of that time were also strictly restricted from learning and practising any skill using any other alternative means. Eklavya's thumb was chopped off by Dronacharya as a ritual fee called *Guru Dakshina*, despite the fact that the former had mastered the skill of archery all on his own. In a similar attempt, Ram beheaded a Shudra teacher Shambuka for the alleged crime of spreading education among the Shudras! This denial is persistently designed to exclude a certain group of people from achieving any progress, material or otherwise.

Education during the Islamic Period

The Brahmanic kings had ruled India for over three dozen centuries until the establishment of the Muslim kingdom. During this long stretch of time, there remained no hope for mass education. However, with the establishment of Islamic rule, there began a little change in the scenario. In 1203, following Muhammad bin Bakhtiar Khilji's conquest of Bengal and Bihar, Islamic education spread widely throughout this land. As a result, several Mosques, Madrasas, and Khankas were established. Initiatives undertaken by the recently arrived Muslims, alongside the increase in the Muslim population resulted in the growth and expansion of the Madrasa education system in major cities like Delhi, Lucknow, Rampur, Agra, Dhaka, and other major cities of the western region of India.[3] An Islamic scholar Abul HasnatNadabi compiled a list of Islamic centres of learning, from historical relics and artefacts, established during the long Muslim rule. He mentions the Madrasas in Multan, Ucha, Ajmer, Delhi, Punjab, Agra, Awadh, Bihar, the Deccan, Malab, Kashmir, Gujarat, Surat, and Bengal. The Bengal section reports that ancient Madrasas were

1. BAWS Vol. 3, p.43
2. RS Sharma, Ancient India 1990, p. 164
3. Hilal Wani, Madrasah Education in India: A Need for Reformation available at https://www.researchgate.net/publication/312146408_Madrasah_Education_in_India_A_Need_for_Reformation

found in Rangpur, Dhaka, Murshidabad, Laxmanabati, Gour, Asthipur, Ghorasheed Mahalla, Shilapur, and other towns.[1] This list shows the intensity and extent of Madrasas on Indian soil. Their presence and utility can also be traced in the vocabulary of the older generations who used to call schools in British India and independent India, Madrasas. However, despite this effort at mass education by the Muslim rulers, a large section of the masses remained deprived of education. There are three primary reasons behind this; first, compared to modern education efforts in a democratic setup, the Madrasas were less in number. Secondly, the Shudras and the untouchables who at this time were broadly clubbed in Hindu categories—the shackles of Brahmanism prevented them from studying. Thirdly, and equally important, is the close relationship of the Muslim aristocracy with the dominant Hindu castes.

The socio-political situation of that time resulted in the acceptance of the Brahmanic custom of hierarchy to the extent of acquiescing to the four-fold Vedic system of varna division of society. It is evident that despite the castelessness in Islam, the Muslim rulers accepted the supremacy of Brahmins in Indian society. This is quite natural because there was no absolute Muslim rule across India. It was sometimes in support and sometimes in coalition and sometimes in partnership with the Hindu elites and dominant castes, such as Rajputs, Brahmins, Jats, Marathas, etc. It is, therefore, no surprise that except for Firoz Shah Tughlaq (1351 to 1388) and Aurangzeb (1658 to 1707), the Muslim rulers, in general, whenever they levied a poll tax, *Jizya*, it was imposed on all non-Muslims except the Brahmins. Jizya was a discriminatory tax, but the Rajputs, the Brahmins and all those in the Mughal service were exempted. In terms of collection, the jizya was graded: the richest man was to pay Rs.12 per annum, while the less prosperous were supposed to pay Rs.8 per annum. According to Jadunath Sarkar, it was Rs.3 ¼, Rs.6 2/3 and Rs.3 1/3 per annum for the three classes. The harshest aspect of the jizya was that it was a tax on the poor, who had to pay an average of one month's salary as tax.[2]The Brahmins were exempted on the flimsy ground of them being philosophers.This was a strange argument to exempt the Brahmin caste without bothering to identify their mental level. Even a foolish Brahmin was exempted from the tax on the ground of exemption (of tax) to philosophers. But there is hardly any evidence of exemption to any Dalit intellectual in *Jizya*. In other words, during

1. Ibid.
2. Sayed Ali Nadeem Rizvi, 'Revisiting Aurangzeb' ref: https://frontline.thehindu.com/the-nation/article24441441.ece

Muslim rule, there was not a radical shift in society and the Manu Smriti continued to be accepted in practice. In such a political scenario, mass education is bound to be affected. However, the upper class of Hindus, the Brahmins and Kayasthas, mastered the court language Persian and became part and parcel of the administration. The Islamic rule of over 700 years in India, or more specifically in north India, between 1206-1857 CE may not have brought a radical change in the field of education, but the introduction of Madrasas at least provided an opportunity to a commoner, irrespective of one's religious faith and to some extent caste, to study and get educated. Despite the shortcomings and limitations of the Muslim rulers and Madrasas, this was certainly a noticeable change in society.

Education in British India

In the eighteenth century, the European forces began to make inroads in the country. The East India Company, 1747 onwards, had taken substantial control over India. This was the first example of European governance witnessed in modern India, centuries after Greek conquests happened in ancient India. Liberal Western thinking, the impact of the Renaissance and the industrial revolution were imprinted on the British rulers' minds. The Governor-General of Bengal Warren Hastings (1750), took steps to expand education. However, in the initial days, the oriental school of thought was dominant among the British. This was said to be essential for them in understanding society's local culture and customs to rule over them. Society at that time was dominated by two religious philosophies—the Islamic and the Brahmanic. The British, when they encountered Mughal officials, learnt and mastered Persian. Sir Thomas Roe, who visited the court of Jahangir, was fluent in Persian. Moreover, Islam, as practised in a large part of the eastern world, was well known to the British. Later, in 1781, Warren Hastings set up the Calcutta Madrasa for people to study and teach Muslim law and related subjects.[1] Hinduism on the other hand was still surreptitious to them. Similar to present-day right-wing thinkers' attempts, the Brahmins of that time cleverly claimed to possess' magical crafts and secrets in their Vedas and claimed the divinity of Sanskrit. This was made possible because their dominance was visible in all walks of life, including their ritually highest position in the Hindu social order. They claimed the identity of *Bhudevas* (Gods on earth) and achieved the highest status in society. Their presence is equally noticeable in the Muslim courts and administration as they have the upper hand among the Hindu population. The formidable status of

1. Bipin Chandra, Modern India p. 119.

Brahmins in Indian society motivated the Britishers to learn and master the Sanskrit language. When Bengal and Bihar came under the rule of the East India Company in 1765 the lawbook of Manu, which was presented as the most authoritative legal text of the Hindus, was translated into English as the *Code of Gentoo Laws*. The pandits were associated with British judges to aid them in administering the civil law of the Hindus; the Maulvis played a similar role in interpreting Muslim civil law. The initial efforts to understand ancient laws and customs, which continued largely until the eighteenth century, culminated in establishing the Asiatic Society of Bengal in 1784 in Calcutta. It was set up by a civil servant of the East India Company, Sir William Jones (1764-1794), who translated the drama known as *Abhijnanashakuntalam* into English in 1789; the *Bhagwat Gita*, the most popular religious text of the Hindus, had been rendered into English by Wilkins in 1785. The Bombay Asiatic Society was set up in 1804 and the Asiatic Society was set up in London in 1823.[1] A German-born scholar F. Max Mueller (1823-1902) translated the Vedas into English. Under his editorship, the *Sacred Books of the East*, altogether fifty volumes, came into existence. This also includes a few Pali, Chinese and Iranian texts but the most substantial part of it contains the Brahmanic texts.

In the process of learning Sanskrit, the British scholars were dependent on the traditional ritualistic Brahmins. This exercise resulted in increasing the influence of the Brahmins on British learners. A modern scholar Mudrarakshas rightly commented that while mastering Sanskrit, the learners became as Brahmanized as the Indian Brahmins were. They too sang the glory of Brahmanic culture and literature in a similar tone as the Brahmins do.[2] As a result, the institutions in British India were greatly Brahmanized. This is evidenced by the fact that the court of Calcutta used to refer to Manu Smriti as the law book of Hindus in the case of disputes between the Hindus. The Brahmin continued to influence the British even in later days. Bal Gangadhar Tilak, despite his violent struggle and hatred against the English, had tried to build a racial link with the British by devising an Aryan invasion theory. He created the myth that the Brahmin-Aryans were the original inhabitants of the Arctic region who had migrated to India.[3] There is not the slightest doubt that in

1. RS Sharma, Ancient India, 1990 p. 4.
2. Mudrarakshas discussed in detail in his book *'Dharmgrantho ka Punarpath'*
3. Interestingly the Aryan invasion theory is believed by the English intellectuals possibly to justify the colonization of India. Among Indians JL Nehru and other mainstream historians do propagate this theory. Among the Dalit-Bahujan circle

this whole exercise, the Dalits and wider Hindu masses became outcasts.

The British also started the promotion of Sanskrit under a modern university system. In 1791, Jonathan Duncan started the Sanskrit College at Varanasi.[1] In Calcutta, the Sanskrit College was established in 1824 during the administration of William Pitt Amherst. The dominance of Brahminic influence on the British can be traced to the fact that only the Brahmins were allowed to take admission in this college. The other castes were debarred from taking admissions. This is a strange rule echoing the ancient Gurukul system but surprisingly, this happened in modern India with Britishers like HT Princep, Thomas Babington Macaulay, and Hayman Wilson as members of the committee of this college! The exclusion of non-Brahmins continued for many years until January 1851 when Ishwar Chandra Vidyasagar took over as the Principal. Being a progressive Brahmin he widened the door of the college for the Kayasthas.[2],which is one of the Shudra castes, traditionally involved in clerical occupations and had produced intellectual leaders like Vivekananda. The leniency towards the Kayasthas resulted in their upward mobility to an extent that at present none of the Kayasthas is ready to accept the Shudra tag. However, for other castes, particularly for the Dalits, the doors of education were still closed. Mass education was beyond imagination.

There was of course a debate on education but it was centred around two issues; first, whether education should focus on oriental studies or western education. The second issue was the medium of education, whether English or vernaculars. While one section of opinion wanted it to be exclusively for the promotion of modern western studies, others desired that, while western sciences and literature should be taught to prepare students to take up jobs, emphasis should be placed on expanding traditional Indian learning. Even among those who wanted to spread Western learning, differences arose on the medium of instruction to be adopted in modern schools and colleges. Some recommended using Indian languages for the purpose, while others advocated the use of English.[3] This debate was put to an end with the emergence of Macaulay's famous Minute. He seemed to have modern and secular leanings. He was against oriental studies for the reason that they lacked scientific and rational perspectives. He also opposed teaching in vernaculars because there is no

---

this theory is much popularised by the Jotiba Phule in his text '*Ghulamgiri*' and it is later picked by Mangoo Ram in Punjab and Periyar in Tamil Nadu.

1. Bipin Chandra, Modern India, p. 90.
2. Referred from en.banglapedia.org written by Rachana Chakraborty.
3. Bipin Chandra, Modern India p. 90.

single or major uniform language spoken across the nation. Each region has its dialects. Macaulay also rejected the need for Sanskrit and Arabic on the ground of their non-existent legal utility. He said that a new legal code would be formed for a new India.

Parliament commands us to ascertain and digest the laws of India. The assistance of a Law Commission has been given to us for that purpose. As soon as the Code is promulgated the Shasters and the Hedaya will be useless to a moonsiff or a Sudder Ameen. I hope and trust that, before the boys who are now entering the Madrassa and the Sanscrit College have completed their studies, this great work will be finished. It would be manifestly absurd to educate the rising generation with a view to a state of things which we mean to alter before they reach manhood.[1]

He was also against state funding of Sanskrit Colleges and Madrasas. Therefore did not hesitate in expressing his views against these languages. He said:

I would at once stop the printing of Arabic and Sanscrit books. I would abolish the Madrassa and the Sanscrit College at Calcutta. Benares is the great seat of Brahminical learning; Delhi of Arabic learning. If we retain the Sanscrit College at Bonares and the Mahometan College at Delhi we do enough and much more than enough in my opinion, for the Eastern languages. If the Benares and Delhi Colleges should be retained, I would at least recommend that no stipends shall be given to any students who may hereafter repair thither, but that the people shall be left to make their own choice between the rival systems of education without being bribed by us to learn what they have no desire to know. The funds which would thus be placed at our disposal would enable us to give larger encouragement to the Hindoo College at Calcutta, and establish in the principal cities throughout the Presidencies of Fort William and Agra schools in which the English language might be well and thoroughly taught.[2]

The rationalistic arguments of Macaulay and his opposition to Brahmanic languages and institutions raised his modern image among many including, the present day Dalit thinkers. For instance, Chandrabhan Prasad, in his series of articles published in the national daily Rashtriya Sahara, and Vijay Trisharan, in his write-ups including his book *Manu Banaam Macaulay* (Manu versus Macaulay), showered praises on

1. Minute by the Hon'ble T. B. Macaulay, dated the 2nd February 1835 retrieved from Retrieved from Macaulay-Minutes.pdf (iitk.ac.in)
2. Ibid

Macaulay for what they called removing the clutches of Brahmanism in education and opening a door of education for Dalits. However, this argument is a little flimsy both in theory as well as in practice. Macaulay's Minute was silent on mass education and uttered nothing on the inclusion of Dalits in the education system. The ideas and opinion of Macaulay reflect only the arguments of his contemporary progressive Brahmins, such as Raja Ram Mohan Roy, Ishwar Chandra Vidyasagar and others. There was no insistence on mass education or inclusive policy in this document. The critique of Macaulay frequently mentioned in mainstream history on the other hand says that it was based on 'downward filtration theory' which believes in educating a few persons from the upper and middle classes.[1] In other words, the beneficiaries of this policy were the Brahmins and their subsidiary castes. It was expected that education and modern ideas were thus supposed to filter or radiate downwards from the upper classes.[2] This was a strange assumption and similar to one modern interpretation of Manu Smriti which says that if education is imparted to a Brahmin, what is the need of imparting education to Shudras because a learned Brahmin will take care of the intellectual needs of illiterate Shudras.[3]

Moreover, the prevailing socio-economic character of Indian society gave access to schooling also to a great extent unreachable to villagers irrespective of their castes. The masses in general thus remained illiterate. Yet, with all its limitations, there isn't the slightest doubt that the school system in British India was a revolutionary move in the history of education in modern India. Bengal became a great centre of learning and as a result, it produced revolutionary thinkers like Raja Ram Mohan Roy, Ishwarchand Vidyasagar, Devendranath Tagore, and Satyendranath Tagore. This legacy was carried forward by WC Bonnerjee, Rabindranath Tagore, and many elite Brahmins, who critically relooked at Indian culture and successfully brought revolutionary changes in caste Hindu society. Yet in this serious attempt, the Dalit question and the problems of caste, class and untouchability remained untouched. Ambedkar in his famous 'Annihilation of Caste', was critical of the blindness on the Dalit question by the leading socio-political leaders of the time. They believed that their concerns should be focused only on bringing reform in their

1. Bipin Chandra, Modern India p. 91.
2. Ibid.
3. The defenders of Manu Smriti in modern times frequently defend it as liberal and rationalistic document. Dr Ambedkar in *Annihilation of Caste* critiqued such arguments.

community and the Dalit question was beyond their purview.[1]

The British Indian government was, however, to some extent aware of this limitation therefore it tried to bring a policy change. Much before the birth of the Indian National Congress, William Adam was the first British Officer to suggest introducing compulsory primary education in 1838. Captain Wingate (1852) even suggested that 5% of the land revenue be utilized to provide compulsory primary education to agriculturists.[2] However, none of the recommendations came into practice. In 1854, Sir Charles Wood, the President of the Board of Control in the Government of India, submitted his official report, popularly known as Wood's Dispatch. The Dispatch asked the Government of India to assume responsibility for the education of the masses. It thus repudiated the 'downward filtration' theory, at least on paper. In practice, the government did little to spread education and spent very little on it. As a result of the directions given by the Dispatch, Departments of Education were instituted in all provinces and affiliating universities were set up in 1857 at Calcutta, Bombay and Madras. The Report of the Royal Commission upon Decentralization in India in 1908 said that the Local Boards represent the rich, educated and land-owning classes; they are not really in favour of increased primary education, because it makes labour more difficult to handle; they are not in favour of a reduction of lower secondary education because they like to have the lower secondary schools to which men of their type send their children.[3] As a result, mass literacy in India was hardly better in 1921 than in 1821. As many as 94 per cent of Indians were illiterate in 1911 and 92 per cent in 1921. The emphasis on English as a medium of instruction in Indian languages also prevented the spread of education to the masses. It further tended to create a wide gulf between educated persons and the masses. Moreover, because the students had to pay fees in schools and colleges, education was quite costly and became a virtual monopoly of the richer classes and the city dwellers'.[4]

The concerns of the masses were pushed under the carpet until they were brought to notice by Mahatma Phule in Maharashtra who was one

1. See for instance the speech of WC Bonnerjee quoted by Dr Ambedkar in his Annihilation of Caste. This speech was centered around the reform in elite Hindus and their concern for the elite caste women. But in this there is no mention of caste problem and Dalit question. p. 53, Vol. 1.
2. Deb, Prasenjit, British Education Policy in India, Indian Journal of Applied Research, Volume : 4 | Issue : 10 | October 2014 | ISSN - 2249-555X
3. Referred from Chaudhary, Latika, Caste, Colonialism and Schooling: Education in British India (May 2012). Available at SSRN: https://ssrn.com/abstract=2087140
4. Bipin Chandra, Modern India, p. 92.

of the indirect beneficiaries of English education. He was able to raise the issues of Dalits and other backward castes—whom he called *Shudra-Atishudra*—before the British regime.[1] He made a consistent effort to raise the issues of marginalization of Dalits, Shudras and women in education. As a result, the British government made substantial changes in education policy. The Education Commission of 1882 especially recommended policies that would popularize education among the 'lower' castes. This gave certain sections of the marginal castes access to education. He also raised the issue of mass education before the Education Commission in 1881 (also known as the Hunter Commission) and as a result, he achieved some success in opening up schools for the Dalits, Shudras and women. For Dalits, this was the first experience of entering educational institutions in modern India after centuries. The government was never ready to spend more than a scanty sum on education. As late as 1886, it devoted only about one crore of rupees to education out of its total net revenue of nearly 47 crores.[2]

A section of Dalits with martial race backgrounds such as the Mahars, the Chamars, the Parriyas and the Dusadhs also got an entry into schooling if their parents were in the army. This was made possible as it was a rule in the British army that the children of the soldiers should be compulsorily admitted in school.[3] Dr. Ambedkar, whose family had served in the army for two generations, was one of the benefactors of this rule. Interestingly, he was one of the first beneficiaries of the new education policy among Dalits—later, he played a successful role in spreading education among the common masses, particularly the Dalits.

Christian Missionaries' Role in Imparting Education

The British rule in India was largely secular. The British officials paid little heed to spreading Christianity among the natives. In practice, they kept their personal religious beliefs separate from governance. This approach could be understood with Macaulay's comment in his famous Minute, where he said 'We abstain, and I trust shall always abstain, from giving any public encouragement to those who are engaged in the work of converting the natives to Christianity'.[4]

1. Accessed from https://roundtableindia.co.in/index.php?option=com_content &view=article&id=5296:memorial-addressed-to-the-education-commission&catid=115&Itemid=127
2. Bipin Chandra, Modern India, p. 93
3. Dr Ambedkar mentioned this in his autobiographical notes Waiting for Visa
4. Macaulay Minute http://www.columbia.edu/itc/mealac/pritchett/00generallinks/macaulay/txt_minute_education_1835.html

Moreover, the British officials were also looking at the Portuguese, Dutch and Scottish missionaries with a bit of suspicion. Many of these missions came to India before settling of East India Company during the struggles between the French, Portuguese, Dutch and English conquests for settling their colonies in India. This happened in the sixteenth-eighteenth century. However, the active Protestant engagement in India dates back to the early eighteenth century when German and Danish evangelicals established missions in South India and set up schools for men and women for all social classes.[1]

A change in policy in 1813 further opened a door for the missionaries under the Charter Act of 1813. This act granted permission to Christian missionaries to spread the use of English and propagate their religion. Later the Charter Act of 1833 laid down regulations about the permanent presence of missionaries, from Britain and other countries, also to carry out their educational work in India and increased the educational grant from 10,000 pounds per annum to 100,000 pounds per annum.[2] The contribution of the Christian missions in pioneering modern education in India has been both qualitative and quantitative. The Christian educational institutions were among the best organized and managed in the country. Christian missionaries take special care of the country's youth, irrespective of sex, creed, colour, and caste and have built for them numerous elementary, secondary and higher educational institutions. It was St. Francis Xavier who led the way in elementary education by exhorting his companions to build a school in every village. St. Francis Xavier was the first Jesuit to come to India and started the Indian mission in 1542. These schools were the pioneers of the modern system of primary education. Several schools and colleges were established by the missionaries. Many Christian colleges existed in Goa, Angamalle, Cochin, Vaipin, Cranganore and Bassein from as early as the 16th century. Jesuits founded several educational institutions in India and engaged in scholarly pursuits following the legacy of St. Francis Xavier during the 16th, 17th and 18th centuries. Gradually many colleges were established in different parts of the country. The idea of teacher training schools was first established by Christian missionaries as early as the 16th century. The system of boarding schools was also first initiated by Jesuits in India.

1. Frykenberg, 'Christians in India'. quoted from Lankina, Tomila V. and Getachew, Lull it (2013) Competitive religious entrepreneurs: Christian missionaries and female education in colonial and post-colonial India. British journal of political science, 43 (1). pp. 103-131.
2. Choudhary and Koh, The Contribution of Christian Missionaries to Educational Development: A Study of Tribals in Jharkhand, 2019 p. 187

The missionaries were also pioneers in promoting vocational education. Not only that, they also worked enormously for the education of Indian women. The Christian missionaries were the first to realise that no sound community could be created under conditions in which women were incompetent to teach the young and heal the sick. Thus, it is not surprising that the three major needs of Indian women — for teachers, doctors and nurses—were met almost entirely by Christian women first. The Catholic missionaries began to build schools in the villages from 1885 onwards. Formal education was hardly known here before the arrival of the Lutheran missionaries. Within one year the Jesuit missionaries had opened 30 schools. By 1887, the number of schools had risen to 70 with 2400 boys and 70 girls.[1]

The arrival of Christian missionaries had brought in a new culture of schooling that was open to all irrespective of caste, class and gender. Yet, in many places, particularly in Kerala, there wasa sizable number of converts, Syrian Christians, of Brahmanic caste backgrounds. With such developments, the missionaries compromised on their egalitarian mission. In many such places, the untouchable converts were denied admission because their presence would pollute the elite caste Christians. The Church practised existing caste taboos and hierarchies, until the end of the nineteenth century and did not actively promote mass education until the 1880s.[2] Elsewhere in India, the process of conversion proceeded from accepting a handful of socially marginal individuals initially to voluntary petitions of entire villages to convert later.[3] The remote tribal areas also came under the ambit of missionary educational activities. The known tribal leaders such as Birsa Munda, Jaipal Singh (who is now popularly called Jaipal Singh Munda in an effort to reclaim his tribal leadership) received English education through the missionaries.[4] Jaipal

1. Ibid p. 194.
2. E. T. Mathew, 'Growth of Literacy in Kerala: State Intervention, Missionary Initiatives and Social Movements', Economic and Political Weekly, 34 (1999), 2811-20. Quoted from Lankina, Tomila V. and Getachew, Lullit (2013) Competitive religious entrepreneurs: Christian missionaries and female education in colonial and post-colonial India.British journal of political science, 43 (1). pp. 103-131.
3. Juergensmeyer, Religion as Social Vision; Frykenberg, 'Introduction' quoted from Lankina, Tomila V. and Getachew, Lull it (2013) Competitive religious entrepreneurs: Christian missionaries and female education in colonial and post-colonial India. British journal of political science, 43 (1). pp. 103-131.
4. Despite the first generation beneficiaries of Christian Missionaries, none of them supported missionaries' activities. Birsa turned deadly against Church while Jaipal initially took a personal career as prime act and later organized the tribals

Singh even went to Oxford to earn his degree and became an ICS (Indian Civil Servant). He later became a member of the Constituent Assembly. The missionary activities in the tribal region had brought about sizeable mobility, predominantly in Jharkhand, Chhattisgarh and north-eastern states and among a few tribals in other regions.

However, it is a little strange that among Dalits other than Advocate Bhagwan Das—a known Ambedkarite, none of the names appear to be the direct beneficiaries of Christian missionary education. In terms of masses, there seemed to be little impact on Dalits. According to Bhagwan Das, there could be more beneficiaries among Dalits, especially among those who were engaged in 'unclean' occupations in the early twentieth century. However, with the appearance of the Shuddhi movement and Arya Samaj movement, the Bhangi, Lalbegi and other Dalit castes engaged in 'unclean' occupations were tactically linked to Valmiki lineage.[1] As a result, they got dissociated from missionaries and became foot soldiers of Hindutva politics.[2] Another reason for finding a negligible number of Dalit beneficiaries of educational activities by Christian missionaries was pointed out by Eleanor Zelliot. A large number of Dalits benefitted from converting to Christianity in the early stages because there was no caste hierarchy among Indian Christians back then, so they achieved a casteless Christian status. This mainly happened in Maharashtra where a sizable number of Mahars and Mangs were absorbed as Christians without any caste burden to shoulder.[3] On the other hand, we can also not deny that since the missionaries earned a certain elite status because of the image of imparting quality education, this resulted in attracting the upper class and upper-middle class families to admit their children in their schools. In this process, the Dalit-Christians and other Dalits were neglected and therefore, the impact of missionary activities on Dalit Christians was less. As observed by Ambedkar:

The services rendered by the Missions in the fields of education and medical relief are beyond the ken of the Indian Christians. They go mostly to benefit the high caste Hindus. The Indian Christians are either too poor or too devoid of ambition to undertake the pursuit of higher

of Jharkhand under the banner of AdibasiMahasabha and become a politician and later joined Congress.

1. Bhagwan Das described the tactics of Hindu rightwing forces in Valmikaization of scavenging castes in his *'Mai Bhangi Hoon'* and *'Dr Ambedkar and Bhangi Jatiyan.'*
2. Bhanwar Meghwanshi in "Why I could not be a Hindu" also discussed the continuity of Hindu rightwing tactics even in the post-independent era.
3. Eleanor Zelliot, in her booklet "Ambedkar's Conversion" raised this issue briefly.

education. High schools, colleges and hostels maintained by the Missions are, therefore, so much misplaced and misapplied expenditure from the point of view of the uplift of Indian Christians. In the same way, much of the medical aid provided by the Missions go to the Caste-Hindus. This is especially the case with regard to hospitals.[1]

At present convent schools are running professionally in urban centres serving only the upper class-caste students. There is hardly any presence of poor students or the Dalits, especially of those with 'unclean' occupational backgrounds, in convent schools and Christian colleges.[2] However, on the positive side, the missionary educational activities continue to be active in rural and backward areas with limited resources. The high quality, and costlier, convent schooling is limited to urban centres. The missionaries, particularly Jesuits, are known for imparting quality education to the masses. Their role in spreading education among the masses is commendable, yet in some cases, elite institutions such as Xavier Labour Relations Institute (XLRI) cater exclusively to the students of the upper-class, largely comprising caste-Hindus. The strict meritocracy and tough standards in these institutions deter promising Dalit and poor students from getting admission in these institutions.

Schooling and Education in Independent India

When British rule ended in India, with the transfer of power in the year 1947, the literacy rate was just 12%.[3] Among the meagre number of literates, the Bhadralok of Bengal comprising Brahmins, Kayasthas and Baidyas, and Brahmins and a few upper castes from other regions, like the Nairs of Kerala had the highest literacy rates. The leading national leaders of the time like the Tagores, Nehrus,[4] Bose came from families which had enjoyed the privilege of English education for 2 or 3 generations. The

1. BAWS, Vol. 5, p. 52.
2. Prakash Ambedkar and also Chandrabhan Prasad, in their talks and articles are raising this issue. Ram Punyanai is also discussing this issue and said that most of the Hindutva leaders of present days are the students of Christian Convent schools.
3. https://www.census2011.co.in/literacy.php#:~:text=In%20a%20country%20like%20India%2C%20literacy%20is%20the,years%2C%20India%20has%20changed%20socially%2C%20economically%2C%20and%20globally.
4. Jawahar Lal Nehru was son of Motilal whose grandfather Lakshmi Narayan was the first vakil of the East India Company at the Mughal Court of Delhi. In 1857, his father Gangadhar served as a police officer. PanditMotilal Nehru spent his childhood in Khetri, where his elder brother was the Diwan; Motilal got trained in Arabic, Persian, and English ref: https://therealgems.com/father-of-political-science-in-india-motilal-nehru/

credit of educating the upper caste elite mainly goes to the missionaries. But hardly any one among them had given any thought to the religion which brought these institutions into existence.[1] There were only a limited number of Dalits who had acquired school education and hardly a few could go into higher education. There was no question of schooling among the castes directly associated with the 'unclean' occupations. There was hardly any school facility in villages, particularly the remote ones, while the urban elite had easy access to schools.

A minimal number of Dalits in education is mainly because of social and economic reasons. Further, their location in rural areas adds to their troubles. The matriculation exams were conducted at the city level; therefore even if rural children get admitted into schools, they have to go to cities to appear for their matriculation exams.[2] This requires money for stay and food in the cities. These pre-conditions scuttled the prospects of many promising students attempting to pass the matriculation exams. The open practice of caste and untouchability in school premises and all the public places harmed them more. The Dalit students were not allowed to sit along with other students and they could not draw water from the common source.[3] In such a situation, a vast mass of toiling masses, the castes lower in the hierarchy remained outside education.

To correct this imbalance and counter this challenge, the Constitution of India—which was enacted in 1950—had taken several initiatives to correct the historical injustices against a section of the people. It makes a provision under Article 45 of the Directive Principles of State Policy stating, 'the state shall endeavour to provide within ten years from the commencement of this Constitution, for free and compulsory education for all children until they complete the age of fourteen years.' Articles 15, 17 and 46 safeguard the educational interests of the weaker sections of the Indian community, that is socially and educationally backward classes of citizens, and scheduled castes and scheduled tribes. Article 15 states, 'Nothing in this article or clause (2) of Article 29 shall prevent the state from making any special provision for the advancement of any socially and educationally backward classes of citizens or the scheduled castes and the scheduled tribes.' Under Article 46 of the Constitution, which is part of the Directive Principles of State Policy, the federal

1. BAWS, Vol.5, p.439
2. This piece of information is shared with me by a senior Ambedkarite.
3. This was a common practice across India, Dr Ambedkar also faced such caste-based exclusion and discrimination in his school days. He narrated such incidents in his autobiographical note 'waiting for visa'.

government is responsible for the economic and educational development of the Scheduled Castes and Scheduled Tribes. It states,'the state shall promote with special care the educational and economic interests of the weaker sections of the people and in particular, of the Scheduled castes and Scheduled Tribes and shall protect them from social injustice and all forms of exploitation.' Further, to counter untouchability and caste-class-gender-religion-language based exclusion, Article 29(1) states 'no citizen shall be denied admission into any educational institution maintained by the State or receiving aid out of State funds, on grounds only of religion, race, caste, language or any of them.'

The Constitution of India is the most radical and revolutionary document the country has produced over the past centuries. It is a frontal attack on Manu Smriti and against all the prevailing biases of Indian society. However, in a nation full of prejudices against sections of its own countrymen, it was extremely challenging for successive democratic governments to implement the spirit of the Constitution. The Government of India tried to some extent to bring change in the society. As mentioned above, on the eve of Independence, the literacy rate was just 12% in 1947, which had gone up to 73 per cent in 2011. Currently, India's higher education system is the largest in the world, with a total enrolment of 38.5 million students in 2019-20.[1] Educational reconstruction was reviewed by several committees and commissions, including the University Education Commission (1948-49) and the Secondary Education Commission (1952-53). The Education Commission (1964-66) was appointed to advise the Government of India (GoI) on the general principles and policies for developing education at all stages and in all aspects.

New schools had been opened at both village and city levels. The increase in the education budget and efforts of the government had brought in a substantial change in the status of education. Initially—both British India and in the initial period afterIndependence—the quality of education in government schools was up to a mark. The teachers used to be very strict and disciplined. Schooling used to be so tough, and corporal punishment was so hard that it resulted in many discontinuations and dropouts.[2] However, on the positive side, those who were able to complete schooling gained proficiency in the skills of writing and arithmetic. Many

1. Vinay Umarji, Business Standard, https://www.business-standard.com/article/education/india-s-gross-enrolment-in-higher-education-rose-marginally-in-2019-20-121061001249_1.html
2. This information is shared the persons of older generation who witnessed this.

of today's eminent scholars, for instance, like Ashis Nandy,[1] and Virginius Xaxa[2] were students of government schools. It is still a common proverb in the Hindi heartland that a 'fifth class pass of the '40s is better than today's post-graduate'.

The status of government schools at present, however, has fallen to a great extent. The standard of the government schools has come down to such an extent, nationwide, that even students in the 8th standard are unable to read and write properly and lack basic arithmetic skills. This observation is also attested in ASER 2017, which reveals that about 25% of the 14-18 age group still cannot read basic text fluently in their own language. More than half struggle with division (3 digit by 1 digit) problems. Only 43% are able to do such problems correctly. The ability to do division - a task that is usually done in ASER - can be thought of as a proxy for the ability to do basic arithmetic operations.53% of all 14 year-olds in the sample can read English sentences. For 18 year-old youth, this figure is closer to 60%. Of those who can read English sentences, 79% can say the meaning of the sentence. Even among youth in this age group who have completed eight years of schooling, a significant proportion still lack foundational skills like reading and arithmetic.[3]

One of the major reasons behind this debilitating condition of government schools is because it seems like ghettoes of poor Dalit students while the middle and upper classes are opting for convent schools, Public Schools and International Schools.[4]This separation, worst affected the prospects of government schools, however, it was not there from the beginning as we have seen that some of the leading intellectuals of our time were students of government schools. This division has mainly resulted from liberalization, globalization, and privatization that were initiated in the 90s. But still, among the government-owned schools, the Kendriya Vidyalaya (KV) is the most popular. The central government also runs Navodaya Vidyalayas, Sainik Schools, Air Force schools, and Naval schools. These central government schools have

1. Ashis Nandy shared his school education background in his talk delivered in Indian Social Institute, New Delhi.
2. Prof. Xaxa shared this fact in his address on Indigenous day celebration at New Delhi
3. http://img.asercentre.org/docs/Publications/ASER%20Reports/ASER%202017/aser2017nationalfindings.pdf
4. This is fact is established in our field survey of the states of Haryana, Madhya Pradesh, Chhattisgarh, Jharkhand, Bihar, Himachal Pradesh, Rajasthan, Uttar Pradesh for the project ' Discrimination and Exclusion in Education: A Study of the Children of the Households Associated with 'Unclean' Occupations.' .

better infrastructure and quality than the state government and local body governed schools.

However, until the 90s, for the masses across caste-class categories, government schools remained popular, even among a wide range of lower bureaucrats and government officials. However, this does not mean that they continued to have the same reputation and quality as during the British period and the early years after independence. The quality, both infrastructural and otherwise, was declining in the government schools. The graduates of these schools have to struggle hard in their careers. The medium of education—Hindi or any vernacular —was adding more shackles to their prospects. Many of the government services like civil services, staff selection commission (SSC), banking, railways, etc. require substantial knowledge of English. For a state government school student, such competitive exams are increasingly becoming a challenge and therefore, their schooling has become irrelevant. It is commonly observed in many cities and towns that the second generation of state-level bureaucrats studying in government schools go astray.This is my observation in Bhopal and many cities and towns of Madhya Pradesh where I found a sizeable number of children of the bureaucrats in government schools till late 90s. However, at present most of them are struggling for a decent livelihood. Interestingly, the grandchildren of these bureaucrats are found studying in elite private schools due to the grace of their grandparents. This situation gave rise to resentment and frustration among the middle class. However, at that time they had no alternative.

The convent schools at that time were very few in number, and therefore, they catered only to the English-speaking elite. The middle class did not have any alternative. The origin of convent schools was, however, said to be rooted in Christian missionaries' serious attempts to spread education. But over time, the fee structure and prominence of the English-speaking environment among the elite turned these schools into distinct entities which worked as status symbols for their students and teachers. This was the beginning of the first rift between the masses and the elite in schooling. We have discussed earlier how these schools were catering to the elite Hindus during the British regime. Later, many new private players came up in the field of education and this resulted in the flourishing of private schools promoting themselves as *public* schools in almost all parts of the country. According to the Unified District Information System for Education (U-DISE), 43.18% of students from grades 1-12 attended private schools. India has nearly 400,000 unaided private schools, with more than 7.9 crore students enrolled.[1] The term *public* school is a strange nomenclature as these schools were not for the public at large but only for the upper-class students. The popularity of private schools after the 90s spread to even the rural areas. According to ASER 2018, between 2006 and 2014, private school enrolment increased steadily from 18.7% to 30.8%. Since then, it has remained at about the same level, i.e. 30.6% in 2016 and 30.9% in 2018.[2]Many private players, with the sole motive of earning profits, have entered the field of education. As a result, Public Schools and International schools came onto the scene in high numbers. These schools are business ventures of corporates and as a consequence, the fees and other expenses are much higher than in other schools. Unlike convent schools, these schools have a clear agenda of profit-making.[3] Therefore, to attract a wide range of middle-class students, mainly of Hindi-speaking background, the school managements make sure that the Hindi medium parents feel comfortable in visiting these schools for admitting their children. This openness, comfortable and spacious infrastructure and English medium of education quite naturally attracted the middle class. Thus, the push factors of poor quality of education, Hindi medium, improper infrastructure in government schools and the pull factors of English medium, quality education, good infrastructure and status symbol evoking image of Public Schools motivated the middle-class population towards private schools. This resulted in a massive shift from government to private schools. Later, even bigger investors came into the scene. As a result, International schools with many more added facilities, like swimming pools, horse riding arenas, fully air-conditioned classrooms, etc., are becoming common.

This change suddenly created a sharp division among Indians between the Hindi and vernacular medium students on one side and the English medium students on the other. The Hindi and vernacular medium majority are lower in terms of wealth and largely lower in the caste hierarchy. Their poverty and inability to access education at a higher cost persuaded them to remain in government schools. The exclusive presence of poor Dalits in these schools automatically made them vulnerable. Interestingly,

1. https://www.centralsquarefoundation.org/privateschools/#:~:text=India%20has%20nearly%20400%2C000%20unaided,than%207.9%20crore%20students%20enrolled.
2. Wilima Wadhwa, Equity in Learning, ASER 2018 ref: https://img.asercentre.org/docs/ASER%202018/Release%20Material/aserreport2018.pdf
3. Throughout the sample states, we have observed that the convent schools are catering mainly upper class and middle-class Indians, yet compared to International schools their fee is less.

the teachers recruited in these schools are mostly from middle class and upper-middle-class backgrounds, whose kids are studying in elite private schools. The class-caste difference between the teachers and students creates a further rift between the two.[1] The local slangs and vocabulary used by the students in government schools are so different from the language used by teachers that it becomes difficult to understand each other. This creates a communication gap between the two. As a result, students are bound to feel a sense of non-belonging. Further, the casteist approach of teachers restricts them from performing their duties well. This is one of the prominent reasons for the declining quality of government schools. Apart from these two above discussed factors, there are many more reasons for the exclusion and discrimination faced by both the schools and their students. Chapter 5 of this book discusses this in detail.

Besides the issues of quality and the medium of education, there are also other reasons behind the middle class' shift to private schools. This can be traced to the deep-rooted customs of exclusion already prevalent in society at large. The admissions in government schools according to mandate should be open for all, irrespective of caste-class barriers. It thus provides an opportunity for the children of the poorest and most humble backgrounds to be part of the student community along with kids from other backgrounds, from the other extreme of the social spectrum. The government schools had been a platform where children from lower class-caste backgrounds could mix with the upper class-caste children. The forward caste parents accepted the mixing of these two separate groups until there was no other option available. However, with the emergence of private schools in large numbers, middle-class parents found a good alternative to separate their children from the poor Dalit students. Hence it resulted in a dynamic shift of the middle class from government schools to private schools. This pattern is similar in all the states, from north to south and east to west. However, we have observed exceptions in two states, Haryana and Bihar. In Haryana, we have observed that the ghettoization of government schools is a fact only in the boys' schools. The girls' schools are still serving students across caste-class communities and thus retaining their cosmopolitan nature. However, the reason for acceptance by girls' parents of government schools is not an outcome of their protest against privatization but due to the prevailing patriarchal mindset in Haryanvi society which considers its daughters as *parayadhan* (other's wealth). This mindset prevents them from spending and investing money

1. See, Ratnesh Katulkar's Exploring Lack of Interest as a Cause of Dropout, Social Action

in the education of their daughters. The lower fee structure of government schools thus becomes a pull factor for the middle-class parents to admit their daughters in government schools to save money for their dowry. The pain in the eyes of middle-class girls was seen when they were responding to the fact that their brothers are studying in private schools.[1] The differential treatment of girls in the family is a regular practice in this state.

In Bihar, some schools cater to students of middle-class backgrounds. But this is just only on paper. The students of middle-class families do take admission in government schools for the sake of accessing various government benefits. But in reality, these children hardly go to the schools. Instead, they are regular in coaching centres or private schools. These students take admissions in both government schools and private schools simultaneously.[2] Admission in government schools is just a formality to seek benefits. Thus such admission has little effect on the profile of the student community which remains ghettoized by poor Dalits.

The other side of the picture is the mushrooming of private schools in both urban and rural areas. It has become a fashion even among the poorer communities to admit their children in private schools. At many places, admission in government schools is in a steep decline to the extent that many government schools have been locked down and in some cases, two or three schools in the same area were merged. The ASER 2013 (Annual Status of Educational Report) shares that private schools are also increasingly becoming popular among the poor. It said that amongst children aged 5-10 years (primary–upper primary) living below the poverty line, 14.8 per cent attended private schools (8 per cent in rural and 36 per cent in urban India). The corresponding figures for ages 11-14 (upper middle school age) and 15-17 (secondary school age) were 13.8 per cent and 7.0 per cent, respectively. Most of these schools have poor infrastructure and below-average human resources, much lower than the government schools. The quality of teachers, administration and infrastructure in most cases is poorer than in government schools. The staff salaries are meagre, and most of them think of their jobs as stop-gap positions before they move on to other jobs or view them as avenues for passing their time. However, the poor parents had developed a feeling that private schools are qualitatively better than government schools. The parents being ignorant, however, is no yardstick to measure the quality of these private schools. This tendency is cashed in by the petty business-

1. Field based observation while data collection from the state of Haryana.
2. Field based information from Patna and Gaya.

minded people who entered the business of running private schools. The English medium school, in most cases, is just nominally one. In practice, both the English medium and quality education are just lures for advertisement. Being ignorant of this practice, the parents, on the other hand, place high hopes in these schools. This is because of their low education levels and perhaps their inability to understand the politics of these petty entrepreneurs. According to Geetha Nambissan, these schools are Private Budget Schools (PBS), an emerging alternative to the non-performing government schools described asdysfunctional government schools.[1] These schools cater to children from low-income groups and charge lower fees compared to big private schools. Amongst the poor, the popularity of private schools is very high. The net result of admissions in these schools is depriving poor students of quality education despite their investment in it.

Among the private schools, the network of Saraswati Shishu Mandirs is one of the prominent ones run by right-wing Hindu groups which cater to most of the communities engaged in 'unclean' occupations.[2] These are Hindi edium schools. One of the reasons for scavenging communities› leaning towards right-wing Hindu politics could be traced to their admission in Sarswati Shishu Mandir schools. Our data[3] indicate that despite a shift towards private schools, a higher percentage of children are attending schools with Hindi as the medium of instruction while a small percentage are attending schools with English as the medium, for instance in Madhya Pradesh 78%, and in Chhattisgarh 87% students are found enrolled in Hindi medium schools.[4] In government schools or private ones, the children have access to only Hindi as a medium of instruction in all the selected northern and central states. Language as an instrumental factor has turned out to be a barrier to quality, and inclusive education for children of households associated with 'unclean' occupations, particularly within the education system and outside the education system, by limiting their occupational opportunities. The marginalized sections' *preference* for private schools indicates that parents do desire quality education

1. Geetha B Nambissan, Business as Usual? Private Schools for the Poor, EPW, Vol. 47, Issue No. 41, 13 Oct, 2012.
2. The Saraswati Mandir Schools are found more visible in Madhya Pradesh and Chhattisgarh catering to the poor students comprising of scavenging community.
3. Referred to the data collected during the survey of the project, Discrimination and Exclusion in Education: A Study of the Children of the Households Associated with 'unclean' Occupations, conducted by the Indian Social Institute, New Delhi.
4. Discrimination and Exclusion in Education...Madhya Pradesh and Chhattisgarh, p. 52.

for their children despite their tight economic conditions. These budget schools seem to pander to the aspirations of the marginalized sections. The false promise of providing good quality English medium education is a clear case of discrimination. A government teacher, working in a private school after retirement, shared the opinion that the poor performance of government schools has given leeway to private unaided schools, which are nothing, more than '*Baniye ki Dukan*' (a grocer's shop).[1]

The elite private schools on the other hand have the best infrastructure and the quality of education they offer is above the mark but they are beyond the reach of the poor. The children from the scavenging communities cannot even dream of these schools. A parent from Faridabad said, 'the big and good English medium schools are beyond our reach. In our locality, there are Ryan Public School, Gold Field, but I don't think anybody from our community goes to these schools. It is not that we cannot afford them, but we get eliminated during admission due to our occupation and illiteracy. We cannot fill out the admission form.'[2]

In Panipat, the parents opined that the exclusive private schools discriminate based on parents' education, income and occupation. The school authorities on the other hand justify this norm. A principal of an elite private school responded,

How can illiterate parents attend an interview? Therefore they cannot apply to my school. We apply a suitable mechanism to deny the entry of children from the slum.[3]

Well educated and well-settled parents are bound to admit their child in a quality school at a proper age,whereas the poor and illiterate parents with their minimal understanding of the schooling system and education are bound to follow their peers. There is none to guide the parents about the age of admission and suggest the names of possible schools where one could admit their children in the backward settlements. The net result is it is purely a matter of a child's fate whether she gets admitted at the proper age and in a good school. Our data also show that they are struggling hard to even complete school education. The dropout rate in Rajasthan is 25.10%, Haryana 21%, Uttar Pradesh 21% and Himachal Pradesh 11%. The consistent decline in the completion rate of Dalit students at each stage of schooling is another severe problem.

1. Renuka, Ramanujam, Discrimination in Education...Haryana. p. 59
2. Ibid p. 58.
3. Ibid p. 59.

One of the most significant lacunae of our education policy before the enactment of NEP 2020 was that pre-schooling—nursery, KG1, KG2—remained outside of the scope of government schooling. Pre-schooling has always been left to the purview of private entities. This means that it remained inaccessible to needy students. The communities engaged in 'unclean' occupations being the lowest social strata also in terms of their incomes, are thus not able to avail pre-schooling facilities for their children. When admitted into the first standard of the primary section in school, these children are unable to compete with other students from better economic backgrounds who had started their education with pre-schooling. Thus, right from their first day in school, these students develop a negative feeling towards their teachers and their peers. The initial schooling thus does not start at the same point for these two kinds of children. The children of mainstream society have their starting point far ahead of the children from the scavenging community. With time, during completion of schooling, the difference does not remain the same but becomes more steep. Students with a strong foundation can learn much more than the average student. Further, the availability of sources of information, motivation, and support systems keep the mainstream students far ahead of the unprivileged students. The habit of reading reference books and competitive magazines along with text books, tuitions and coaching makes their career prospects much brighter and promising. Therefore, toppers of 10+2, IITs, JEE, NEET and other national and regional level entrance exams emerge from this section. On the other hand, a flood of dropouts and backbenchers emerges from the scavenging and poor Dalit community students, who later turn out to be jobless or work in sanitation or other blue colour jobs.

Chapter - 3

Systemic Factors of Marginality

> The Hindu Social Order is based upon a division of labour, which reserves for the Hindus clean and respectable jobs and assigns to the Untouchables dirty and mean jobs and thereby clothes the Hindus with dignity and heaps ignominy upon the Untouchables.
>
> **Dr Babasaheb Ambedkar**[1]

It is discussed in the previous chapter how the political and social system consistently denied basic human rights to a certain group of communities and in the longer run relegated them to a permanent status of 'untouchables'. On the contrary, we have also discussed that with the establishment of a democratic setup in India, the humanitarian measures and the positive discrimination policies enacted by the State resulted in the mobility of many ex-untouchables, who reached a commendable position. Yet, this community at large is suffering discrimination and exclusion. Among these groups, the castes engaged in 'unclean' occupations are one of the prominent groups. These people are still to a large extent struggling with an untouchable identity despite the fact that the Constitution of India banned untouchability in any form.[2]

The prevailing social custom resulted in maintaining a 'safe' distance from those engaged in 'unclean' occupations. The sanitation workers whether in private spaces or working in public places often face discrimination and untouchability in their day-to-day lives. Their work requires them to be in direct sight of the people. The work of sanitation in

1. Essays on Untouchables and Untouchability, BAWS Vol. 5, p. 258.
2. Article 17 of the Constitution of India declares that Untouchabilityis abolished and its practice in any form is forbidden. The enforcement of any disability arising out of Untouchability shall be an offence punishable in accordance with law. See. https://samistilegal.in/article-17-of-the-constitution/

open and public spaces such as sweeping, garbage collection cleaning of drains, etc. results in their separate identification. Common people, who look at these workers daily, may not be aware of their names but they sure identify and label these workers with their occupation. Consequently, their work becomes their identity. Moreover, apart from their engagement in sanitation work, another factor that separates them from the mainstream is their separate and distinct habitation that accentuates their exclusion.

Spatial Segregation and Exclusion

The caste-based settlements or separate settlements of people engaged in 'unclean' occupations is an age-old system of Indian society. The sociologists, Kathleen Gough[1], MN Srinivas[2] and SC Dubey[3], have discussed the settlements based on castes as a natural social process and system. In Brahmanic literature, there is a mention of a distinct settlement of Brahmins called agrahar and a separate settlement for the untouchables. However, Ambedkar looked at the caste-based settlement from below in a revolutionary tone. He writes:

> Every village has two parts, the quarters of the touchables and the quarters of the untouchables. Geographically the two are separate. There is always an appreciable distance between the two. At any rate, there is no contiguity or proximity between them. The untouchables' quarters have a distinct name such as Maharwada, Mangwada, Chamrotti, Khatkana, etc. De jure for the purposes of Revenue Administration or Postal Communication, the quarters of the untouchables are included in the village. But de facto it is separate from the village. When the Hindu resident of a village speaks of the village, he means to include in it only the caste Hindu residents and the locality occupied by them. Similarly, when the untouchable speaks of the village, he means to exclude from it the untouchables and the quarters they occupy. Thus, in every village, the touchables and untouchables form two separate groups.[4]

The caste-based settlement is still a surviving practice in present India. In rural areas of Maharashtra as said by Ambedkar there isMaharwada, Mangwada, Chamarwada, while in the north,Domkhana or Dompada, etc. still have their distinct presence. However, interestingly, this is not the reality of the village alone. In fact, it is continued well in urban

1. https://www.epw.in/system/files/pdf/1952_4/21/the_social_structure_of_a_tanjore_village.pdf
2. See, The Remembered Village
3. See, Indian Village
4. BAWS, Vol. 6, p. 229.

setups until the present day. The cities follow the same pattern sometimes openly and many times under a shade of class. The upper class, consisting exclusively of castes placed above in graded inequality, resides in posh colonies. The middle class comprising of all the castes across the hierarchy and mainly of middle rank have their different settlements while the Dalit bastis at the outskirts have their separate and exclusionary settlement. The caste-based settlements in urban centres in most of the cases are not a new development but they are a continuation of the old pattern of settlement. In fact, most cities have evolved and developed from rural settings. This fact is well attested in the pattern of habitation in the city of Delhi, which is composed of a number of villages under its periphery. These villages like any other Indian villages are exclusively based on caste. Therefore, the existence of dominant castes with their peculiarities is surviving feature of Delhi. The settlements such as Shahpur Jat, Adhchini, and Mehrauli are the dominant settlements of Jats.[1] In fact, there are 207 villages where the Jats have a higher presence.[2] Most of these settlements at present are located in posh locations thereby providing an opportunity for the local Jats to continue their dominance as landlords over the rich urban businessmen and middle class service people who came to this city for their earnings. The second in this line is Gujjars who are dominant in 70 villages of Delhi city concentrated in South and East Delhi.[3] This pattern is ubiquitous in the city where Sainis, Chamar, Brahmin, Balimikis and many other castes have their own settlements. The known settlements of Balmikis in Delhi are Ambedkar Nagar in Dakshinpuri, Sultanpuri, Mangolpuri, 100 quarters of Karolbagh, Kalyanpuri, Ranapratap Bagh, Madangir, Tigari, Sangam Vihar, Baljit Nagar, Valmiki settlement in Panchkuiyya, etc. Some of the Dalit settlements of Delhi are close to posh localities, which in pre '90s were almost equally underdeveloped but later developed into posh hubs. The striking difference is visible between the two. An Ambedkarite activist-scholar Dhamma Darshan opines,

> The sheer casteism is visible in the developmental agenda. Karol Bagh is a posh business hub but it's close by Raigarpura,a settlement of Dalits, is still backward. Dilshad Garden is another case which is a posh locality but in its neighbouring places of Nandnagari and Sahirpur, the Dalit settlements remained backward. Similar is the case of Mayur Vihar and Trilokpuri. At one point of time, there was not a big difference

1. This information is based on primary data.
2. Source: https://www.jatland.com/home/Delhi accessed on 13.10.2021.
3. Source: https://gurjarindelhi.blogspot.com/2012/09/history-origin-statue-of-samraat-bhoj.html accessed on 13.10.2021

between these two sets of settlements but it increased tremendously with time. This shows the castiest nature of Delhi.[1]

However, one unique feature in separate settlements of scavenging castes in most of the cities, is that their settlements are not age-old but comparatively a new development. This is mainly the result of urbanization in the early eighteenth century. Scholars popularly believe that scavenging as an occupation is a creation during Islamic rule and expanded and was better regulated and managed from British rule onwards[2]. How a section of Dalits fall into this occupation is not difficult to understand. There are many reasons for opting for this occupation by the marginal castes. The pull factors for this are firstly, because of its unskilled nature, which makes it suitable to opt for any newcomer. Secondly, there was no competition in opting for this occupation because of its lower grade and impure feature. It thus provides an opportunity for the poor castes placed lowest in graded inequality to join the workforce of sanitation workers. These two factors stimulate the poor castes of rural areas, who were struggling to meet both ends, to migrate in large numbers to cities. As discussed in Chapter 1, the castes such as Musahars, which is originally a tribe and later in an agrarian set up became skilled agrarian workers, converted to scavengers. At that time, plenty of free lands were available in the outskirts where the new migrant scavenger group could settle. Therefore, the scavengers ghettoized them in slums at the periphery of cities. Many such settlements continued to show its presence in contemporary times. However, often with the passage of time, the expansion of cities resulted in their inclusion in the central and posh locations. Yet, the geographical inclusion of these settlements does not result in their social inclusion in the urban culture. These poor settlements even after reaching close to central urban locations continued with their poor and excluded identity. In different cities, these settlements are called by different names. In Patna and Gaya, the live remnants of the separate settlements of erstwhile untouchables are called by the names of Domkhana or Dompada. In the city of Jabalpur, one such settlement is called Chandalbhata—which is at present located at the center of the city—showing its identity with the Dom castes which is also called Chandals. These settlements are located in central locations. As mentioned above, at one point of time, these settlements were also beyond the periphery of the respective cities but due to the gradual expansion of these cities at present, they automatically

1. Dhammadarshan Nigam in https://www.academia.edu/104779592/Our_Society_My_Observation he also shared this in a personal interview
2. For instance, see Vijay Prashad's Untouchable Freedom

get into the prominent locations. In a similar case, it is observed that in Ranchi, a Valmiki Basti gets into a prime location of the city.

The Dalit localities in urban spaces often have separate identifiable names, such as, Bhim Nagar, Ambedkar Nagar, Valmiki Basti, Harijan Colony, Sudarshan Nagar, etc. These names show the allegiances of its residents with a particular cult or ideology of a Dalit movement. Sometimes the Dalit bastis are also found to be named after political leaders such as Indira Basti, Rajiv Basti, etc. In the city of Bhopal, there is Rahul Nagar extensively resided by the Buddhists of ex-untouchable caste and other Dalit communities. This settlement is not however named after Rahul, the son of Gautam, the Buddha, as it is understood by outsiders owing to the presence of a large number of Buddhists in this basti. Neither, as a few local people believe, it is named after Rahul Gandhi, but this basti is named after the son of the then Chief Minister of Madhya Pradesh, Arjun Singh[1], whose name was Ajay Singh but was popularly called Rahul Bhaiyya. This example suggests that on many occasions, for the encroachment of free land, the poor inhabitants have to lure and tempt the leaders of the ruling party.

In the cities of Shimla and Solan, there are exclusive settlements of sanitation workers comprising of Balmiki and Chamar castes called Krishna Nagar and Kargil Nagar respectively. In the case of Solan, this settlement was made possible at the behest of local BJP leaders. It settled in the year 1999 after the Kargil war between Pakistan and India. The respondents informed that to occupy the land in a city was no less than a battle. Referring to the story of the occupying of the land, a local Valmiki leader shared:

> People say that we are Indians and we do believe in it. However, actually speaking we had nothing in this country (that belonged to us). Leave about home, land, and other materialistic comforts. We are not even treated as humans. In my hometown (Uttar Pradesh) untouchability still persists. There was no employment for us over there so we migrated to Himachal. Here people are quite good... far better than the people of Uttar Pradesh. Here we do not feel discriminated against. However, it was equally true that here also we were landless. To get a place for our living was like a war for us. Our enemies were not foreigners but the citizens of this city! The locals at any cost were not allowing us to settle down. They might be thinking that poor people disturb the scenic beauty of the open

1. Rahul Singh is the name of a son of veteran Congress leader Arjun Singh.

> space. Therefore, they are not allowing us to settle. Nevertheless, we do not have any option and we need a place to settle down in this city so we struggled hard. Fortunately, we got political support from BJP. One local BJP leader gave us confidence and supported us in capturing the land. At that time local people used to guard the place so that we could not build our houses here, but one night, we all climbed down the hill and erected our structures on this place. The environment was tense, but as we had political support, the police took our side. Finally, we got patta in our names. This BJP leader also got our names registered in the voters list. It was our victory. Now we are full-fledged citizens of Himachal... It was really a fight for setting up our desh (nation). It is no way different from Kargil war. It was not my words alone but each of us felt so. Therefore, to keep the memory of our struggle alive, we named this place Kargil.[1]

On many such instances, the support of local political leaders becomes a blessing for the migrant Dalits. This relation is two-way. The settlers in return become loyal and trusted vote banks of the concerned political leaders. There is a trend in getting land for settlements by poor Dalits. In the pre-‘90s, it was mainly the Congress party, who came forward to support them but in the later decade with its decline in most of the states and the emergence of right-wing politics in the form of the appearance of BJP, there is a shift in political tutelage. This also results in increasing Dalit votaries in right-wing political parties. The parent organization RSS is running its activities in these areas. It is observed especially in Madhya Pradesh, where it is running its Saraswati Shishu Mandir schools in the vicinity of the poor settlements. As a result, almost all the children of poor Dalit backgroundswere admitted to this school. The continuous influence of the right-wing both in the school curriculum and through its shakhas results in making them the foot soldiers of Hindutva politics. However, opposite is the case with Christian missionaries who are mandated to serve the poor but in practice their presence in scavenger bastis is hardly visible.

Back to the pattern of settlement, it is observed that there are four different patterns of settlement in the urban space. First, is the settlement based on revolutionary spirit and struggle by claiming their identity based on their socio-political ideology such as in the case of Bhim Nagar, Ambedkar Nagar, etc. The second pattern is the settlements based on humble submission to existing social and religious orders such as in the case of Valmiki Basti or Sudarshan Basti. The third pattern is based on

1. Discrimination and Exclusion in Education...Himachal Pradesh p. 231.

negotiations with local political leaders by luring and tempting them by adopting their political imageries and leaders such as what has happened in the case of Indira Basti, Rajiv Gandhi Basti, Rahul Nagar and Kargil Nagar. While the fourth is, the age-old continuation of traditional settlements in the urban places due to the expansion of the periphery of the city such as Chandalbhata, Dompada, and others. Anyway, the settlements do face similar exclusion and discrimination. The localities of Dalits, irrespective of any of the above-mentioned four patterns, are branded negatively not only because of the castiest mentality of the society but also because of many physical features. The surroundings are full of filth and slush flowing from open drains that make the living conditions, most unhygienic and create several health hazards for all.The settlement anyway has no service for garbage collection and sweeping. The administration thinks it is useless to recruit any sweeper in these areas on the ground that since it is the traditional occupation of this community, there is no use of appointing any sweeper! 'You people clean the whole city; can't you clean your settlements?' is a common answer from the Municipal Corporation whenever the locals demanded the need of implementing sweeping services in their settlements.

Problems in Settlements

The lack of water supply, electric connection and supply make their life terrible. The slum dwellers throw hooks to electric poles in the evening to get electric supply. The water connection in most of the settlements is not available. In some slums, especially in Bihar and Uttar Pradesh, hand pumps locally called *champakals* are an available option. However, with decreasing groundwater levels, the residents began facing the problem of water scarcity. In some settlements, the water connection is provided by the municipalities but it is in a pathetic condition. It is observed in Chandalbhata, Jabalpur, the tap water connection was two feet down the ground. The people used to put their buckets below this connection to collect the water. With the limited supply of water in summer, people face a lot of problems. However, the rainy season proves to be even worse. The muddy rainwater enters into the pit of the water connection and it reaches above the pipeline. As a result, while collecting water from the tap, the dirty rainwater gets into the buckets. The people have no option but to drink the muddy water during the rainy season. The tasks to fulfill their daily basic necessities like water, sanitation and electricity arethe responsibility of both parents and children which reduces the possibility of kids learning in their homes.

The congested space and the lack of availability of free space make their lives difficult. There is no place for pastime activities or celebrations. The homes are small, dilapidated with no repair and without proper ventilation.The size of houses is very small in a range of 8 x 10 square feet of one or two-room sets which serve all the purposes of kitchen, bedroom, drawing room and all the necessities. There is no private space for parents and children. The limited space also results in poor ventilation and the non-availability of sunlight in the daytime. The unventilated, small houses and no free common space affect the children much. One of the negative impacts of this is that it affects their mental and physical growth. Due to lack of open space, the children do not find space to play. This further impacts their physical and mental development and it of course directly affects their prospects of learning.

The absence of toilets in the home or community latrine is common. In some settlements, there are community toilets. The community toilets do not have water supply and a mechanism of cleaning and maintenance. As a result, these toilets are choked and unusable. In such condition, open defecation is the only available option for them. In Madhya Pradesh and Chhattisgarh, the sides of the railway tracks are being used for this purpose. In most places, there is a division of open space as female area and a male area. The people themselves are socialized to follow this separation. However, when settlements are located at the fringes, such as Dom tola in Gaya, the people prefer open defecation as the mountains are available close to it. In this tola, there is one community latrine but due to lack of water supply, it remains unusable. The expansion of cities and towns and the growing population and developmental activities make land dear to such an extent that the slum dwellers are unable to carry out their day-to-day activities. The problem becomes acute with the spread of colonies near the slums which ends the availability of free land and ends the possibility of open defecation. It is often believed that a woman faces more problems than a man. This comment is, however, impractical and patriarchal in nature because the position of the male in these settlements is equally pathetic. In some cities, where the government is strict against open defecation, the dwellers face a lot of problems. In these localities, they are forced to maintain community latrines but with much difficulty. The Municipal Corporation seldom provides its services in these slums. The users have no other option than to clean and maintain it themselves.

Apart from the absence of toilets, the absence of bathrooms in homes or in the community is a big problem. For grown-up girls, its absence creates a big problem as they find difficulty in having a daily bath. This results in a lack of hygiene. During the time of menstruation, they encounter extra difficulty due to the lack of a private space. The one in-charge of Jeevan Sangham Kendra, a social centre at Bodhgaya, who is extensively working with the Musahar community, in a personal interview shared the pathetic situation of girls:

> There is no bathroom in the Musahar slums. The people used to take bath in the open. The males, age-old women and kids do not find much difficulty in bathing in the open. But the girls face many problems. When they takea bath in the open, the males of the slums and outsiders stare at them and even try to molest them. For this fear, the girls do not dare to bathe for months… Bathing which is a daily act of a normal person is a big achievement for these girls.

The absence of bathroom is the result of limited availability of land which apart from causing many problems in daily affairs also worst affects their livelihood and income opportunities. The traditional caste occupation of pig rearing by the poor Dalits is affected to a great extent. This occupation was once believed to be the easiest and a casual occupation of this community. For the reason that apart from being treated as an unclean occupation, this occupation appeals to the poor for the fact that it doesn't require any special diet, medical expenses and care. The pigs used to feed on human waste and rotten food and they do not require any farm but are also free to roam and eat whatever waste is available to them. The only requirement of piggery is free space for their movement and grazing. But with decreasing land this becomes challenging. The pigs often bring trouble to the community whenever they encroached on the area of other people. This situation many times becomes troublesome and have led to violent conflict. On many such occasions, the pigs have been shot dead by the dominant castes using their *katta* (local pistols).

Absence of Meaningful Leisure

The most common scene especially in broad daylight is a group of males sitting in a circle and playing cards. This is not in one or two groups but many such groups are seen in the common space together. This is a simple time-pass activity, which also involves gambling. This becomes an addiction, therefore, the people involved in it often suffer a great monetary loss. The after-effects of it are visible in their both mental as well as physical health. Moreover, the parent's engagement in such games diverts them from their family responsibilities. As a result, the prospects of children are affected. Another peculiarity of the slums is frequent quarrels between the people. Sometimes this turns into fight and violence to such an extent that it needs police interventions. Anyway, a person, whether a child or an old inhabitant of these slums, is believed to be 'different' by mainstream city-dwellers.

The common people are involved in various time-pass activities such as playing cards, marbles (*kanchas*), and other such things. Both the males and females of the community are busy in such conversation that is simply to pass the time and do not engage in any meaningful discussion. For the dropout seniors of the scavenging communities, life is idle; they spend much time keeping themselves abreast with the latest fashion. Such attractive fashionable youth becomes a natural role model of the younger generation, who start thinking of school-going as a burden and hampering activities in the way of a fashionable and idle lifestyle. The attraction of such a lifestyle also results in a lack of interest in studies (*padhai me man nahilagana*).[1] The lack of education in adult members also affects the education of the younger generation as these pupils, in case of any difficulty in their studies, do not get any support from them. A scavenging community student of Shimla who is pursuing a law degree from a university describes the situation of his locality in the following words:

> Children playing after their school hours and on a holiday is a common thing but what is different in our community is that there is no one in the family to restrict the time of play. The children play as long as they want. This culture is fundamentally different from the general caste colony where parents prepare a timetable for their children, which includes a specific time for games and sports and the rest of the time for study and other meaningful activities. In my case, whenever I faced any problem in understanding any topic while reading at home, I do not find a single one with whom I can discuss my problem. In our basti students lack in getting guidance and direction. They are helpless in case of any problem or query in their mind.[2]

Poverty in Community

The communities engaged in 'unclean' occupations are living in acute poverty and marginality. Many of the sanitation workers are forced to work under oppressive terms and conditions put up by the contractors

1. Ratnesh Katulkar, Exploring Lack of Interest as a Cause of Dropout of the Children of Scavenging Communities, Social Action, October-December Issue: No. 04, Volume: 68 p. 422 New Delhi, 2018.
2. Discrimination and Exclusion in Education...Himachal Pradesh p. 254.

and supervisors, and this affects their children in both subtle and direct forms. This influences them in two ways; first on their health, including their mental and physical growth, as this is mainly due to the lack of affordability of a balanced diet and second on the minuscule expenditure on their education. It is observed that all the slum children are physically weak. Their pale face, big tummy, lean and thin hands and legs show a clear sign of malnutrition. The limited free space and absence of playgrounds as discussed earlier also add wounds in their growth and development. This restricts them to play in their free time and as a result, they remain stunted and underdeveloped.

The Musahar in Bihar and Jharkhand, whose caste occupation also include pig rearing, is also found struggling with deficiency diseases. This community does intake pork at frequent intervals of time but the lack of other nutrients and the absence of a balanced diet resulted in their malnutrition. While on the opposite side, a section of the upper class despite being vegetarian gets full nutrition, as their diet is rich in all the essential nutrients, which the non-vegetarian scavengers are lacking. This fact breaks the much-popularized myth that meat-eaters are healthier than vegetarians. However, there is also another side of the story, which is shared by an activist of Bihar that in many instances, it is not the Musahars but the forward caste Hindus such as Brahmins, Rajputs, Banias who are the actual owners of piggeries and purchase the piggeries without getting directly involved in it. These caste-Hindus are the investors who give the task of domestication of piggeries to the poor Musahars. In such a case, the Musahars are just caretakers of these animals while the right over its meat in the form of cash or a kind belongs to the masters of forward castes. This business is run in secret and hidden for the fear of concealing ritualistic 'cleanliness' and superiority of these 'upper' castes. Anyhow, in such a case also the actual servers of piggeries have no right over the pork. Therefore, they remain deficient in a protein-rich diet.

In some cases, the scavenging community children are following a strict vegetarian diet. It is mainly because of the influence of new religious sects such as Radhaswamy or the Aad-Dharmi movement. These vegetarian poor sanitation workers, however, are unable to purchase milk and other protein-rich diet for themselves and as a result, they lack a balanced diet that the vegetarians of other castes could bear easily. While in some cases, pork intake is restricted because of practical issues such as in the cities of Shimla, Solan and Sagar because the municipal corporations have strictly banned pig rearing in these cities. Since other meat, such as mutton, is costlier than pork,therefore, the poor are bound to take cheap vegetarian diet that is much more economical than chicken and mutton.

Anyhow whether being a pork eater or vegetarian, in both cases the scavenging communities lack essential nutrients because of a lack of a balanced diet. A poor diet results not only in a weak physical body but also in improper mental development. Their cognitive skill remains undeveloped due to a lack of nutrition.[1] This deficiency is not a post-birth problem but it starts before pregnancy. A pregnant woman due to lack of proper care and improper intake of nutrients gives birth to a child with physical and mental ailments. Such children when admitted to school remain inattentive and are bound to be weak in studies. This stigma remains attached to them as long as they study in the school. The nutritional deficiency among the poor Dalit children impacts the lifelong journey of these individuals and as a result, the mainstream society does often strongly and firmly believe that Dalits are naturally stupid. Such comments become popular, especially during anti-reservation agitations. It is not surprising that the then Chief Minister of Gujarat Narendra Modi who has now ascended to the position of Prime Minister of India once drew parallels between Dalit children and the 'mentally retarded'.[2] The mental ability of a Dalit whether middle class or poor is always under a question mark. Nevertheless, the background of the performance of these poor Dalits lies on the ground of inadequate nutrients and lack of a balanced diet. However, it is hardly an issue of discussion in academic as well as political debates dealing with meritocracy. Poverty, in combination with lower caste status and lack of cultural capital, makes parents vulnerable to getting their entitlements. In such a case, there is no support system available to the parents to assert their rights. Moreover, as they are aloof from the education system and have no culture of education among them, they easily accept the dictates of school authorities and do not attempt to fight for their rights.[3]

Evacuation and Forced Resettlement

The poor and shabby looks of the slums affect the beauty of the city

1. For details of ill impact of lack of balance diet on the brain see, AnettNyaradi, Jianghong Li, Siobhan Hickling, Jonathan Foster and Wendy H. Oddy's article 'The role of nutrition in children's neurocognitive development, from pregnancy through childhood.'
2. https://economictimes.indiatimes.com/news/politics-and-nation/congress-slams-modi-over-anti-dalit-remark/articleshow/5879649.cms?utm_source=contentofinterest&utm_medium=text&utm_campaign=cppst
3. Described in details in chapter 4 of this book.

and are seen as aneyesore. In any expansion and beautification drive, there is always a risk of forcible evacuation and resettlements. They are bulldozed and the settlers are forced to evacuate the place. The city of Delhi has witnessed the intensity of such drives twice. First, in 1982 at the time of the Asian Games and second in 2010 during the Commonwealth Games. The slums of the city were bulldozed and the habitants were forcibly taken to the outskirts of the cities in what is called *Jhuggi-Jhopadi* (JJ) clusters.

The city of Ranchi has also witnessed such a forcible settlement at ChirondiBrambeAawas. This place is located 30 km away from the city. There is no public transport facility to connect this settlement with the city. Two-room flats are constructed but the material is of extremely poor quality. The worst thing is that these apartments are built without any foundation. As a result, the ground floor in almost all the cases and in some instances even the first floor buried under the ground. Even a casual walk on its stairs and upper floors causes trembling of the whole structure. There is no sanitation facility. Open and uncovered channels for wastewater and open sewer for a toilet are a part of the settlement design. The risky and pathetic situation is further accentuated by the distance from the city, which results in the abandonment of these quarters by a large number of settlers, who left this place within a few days of this forced settlement. At present, hardly a few families reside there. The forced resettlement without any basic facility resulted in the loss of occupation and proved the biggest setback to their income generation activities. This also led to widespread discontinuation of the study of the children and youth who became dropouts. Some years later, the government started a school close to this settlement but this proved to be meaningless for the dropouts, consequently, they remain semi-literate. However, this attempt of the opening of the school in the vicinity proved to be beneficial to the younger children, who got admission in this. Yet, this again proved to be a short-lived success as they too were bound to drop out with the permanent closure of this school. This happened because of the brutal murder of a teacher's relative on the school campus. This resettlement is a sample, enough to show the discomfort and pain of the people who are forcefully evacuated. As said above, one of the biggest problems with such a forceful settlement is that the people lose their source of livelihood. Thanks to UPA's Food Security Act, the provision of supply of free rations to the people at least saved their lives. Otherwise, the situation would be pathetic.

Even in some instances, when the slums resettled within the limit of the cities,the size of the house always remains small and lacks necessities.

Such settlements whether in cities or on the outskirts are not properly connected with roads and they do not have proper concrete streets or sub-roads in the settlements. A famous film Director of Tamil film industry, Pa Ranjith in his blockbuster film Kaala picturised the pathetic situation of this scheme with a background emotional narration, which says that these buildings are like matchstick boxes put over one another. The forceful settlements are however comparatively better than the forceful destruction of the settlements without paying any compensation.

Forced Duties in Religious Mass Functions

The Hindu festivals and gatherings such as Kumbh Melas are events of joy, pleasure and festivities among Hindus. Being a staunch follower of Hinduism, the scavenging communities, in general, do participate in such events. In May 2016, at Ujjain Kumbh, Home Minister Amit Shah took a holy dip with a Dalit Saint.[1] The leaders of the scavenging community shared that this Dalit Sadhu belongs to a scavenging community.[2] This event was named 'samrastasnan'. Three years later in the year 2019, Prime Minister *Narendra Modi moved a step ahead of his political partner while visiting the Kumbh Mela at Allahabad. He washed the feet of five manual scavengers, which included two women workers. He thanked them for what he called their karma yog and their role in keeping the Kumbh clean.*[3]The other side of this political gimmick is that despite the enactment of the Employment of Manual Scavengers andConstruction of Dry Latrines (Prohibition) Act, about 28,000 dry latrines have been built in the Kumbh area which openly defy this Act. Moreover, the Kumbh Mela authorities have also recruited 5,000 people to keep these toilets clean, apart from cleaning health clinics and the maze of roads in the Kumbh Mela area.[4] The media reported that scavengers from Uttar Pradesh had been recruited for this event. However, the community leaders of Madhya Pradesh informed us that a large force of manual scavengers for Kumbh Melas had always been from Madhya Pradesh. They assume that probably Madhya Pradesh is selected for this recruitment, as there was a lot of outcryin the media on employing the sanitation workers of Uttar Pradesh at a lower wage rate. Therefore, to avoid media attention, the temporary workers were recruited from Madhya Pradesh, which is always away

1. Amit Shah to take holy dip with Dalit sadhus at KumbhMela today | Latest News India - Hindustan Times
2. A senior SKA activist of MP, shared this piece of information to me.
3. Mr Prime Minister, Manual Scavenging Work is Neither Spiritual Nor Glorious | NewsClick
4. Scavenging still a reality - Reporter At-Large (reporteratlarge.org)

from media hype. Anyway, this was not a spiritual exercise as claimed by the Prime Minister but it was an open and blunt form of exploitation of sanitation workers against labour laws and the Prohibition of Manual Scavenging Act. *Bezwada Wilson of the Safai Karamchar iAndolan has called this an insult to the manual scavengers. In his tweet, Wilson said, 'What a pity! As a CM, he spiritualized shit cleaning, now as PM he is glorifying injustice. This act is against Babasaheb Ambedkar's mission.*[1]

However, the Kumbh Melas and Hindu festivals are not the only occasions of victimization of the scavenging community. It is noticed, that Jainism also plays an equal role. A strong evidence of this linkis found in the city of Sagar, which has a sizeable population of Jains and is dear to a famous Jain Monk Tarun Sagar.[2] He often visits this city along with his monk disciples. There are retreats organized on these occasions. Being a business community Jains keep a high hold in civil administration. The municipal commission and bureaucrats are always ready to serve their needs and demands. The problem to scavengers appears because the Jain saints forbid using the toilet for the reason that it results in the killing of microorganisms. They, therefore, relieve their excreta on the ground. In the olden days when open defecation was common in India, it was not a big issue as there were plenty of lands available for such purposes. However, at present when the retreat centre is surrounded by a large number of devotees, open defecation is difficult for the monks while it is equally a fact that their religious norm does not allow them to use toilets. Therefore, the Jains devised a way out. They used to build a temporary structure covered from three sides with white cloth and put a curtain on the front side. Inside it, they put two bricks adjacent to each other, which act as footrests while they release their faeces. This arrangement seems to be all right to follow the dictum of religious sanction. However, the problem arises while discarding this waste. For this purpose, a manual scavenger is appointed. The scavengers on such occasions are bound to have their presence for twenty-four hours. Moreover, in the case of retreats where there is a large number of participation of Jain Monks, there is greater demand for manual scavengers. The site of the retreat centre is often on the outskirts of the city. Therefore, the sanitation workers of the city were forced to move to this site during the whole period of the retreat, which often runs for fifteen days or sometimes a month-long. Yet, these sanitation workers were neither compensated with any leaves nor provided any

1. https://www.downtoearth.org.in/news/waste/dalit-activists-leaders-decry-prime-minister-s-christ-like-act-63353
2. Traun Sagar is no more he took his last breath on September 2018, ref. https://www.indiatoday.in/india/story/jain-monk-tarun-sagar-dead-1329172-2018-09-01

overtime. Even travel expenses are not provided to them. The municipal officials and bureaucrats are very harsh and strict in enforcing this dictate to the sanitation workers. The poor workers however have no choice but to follow the dictates of administration and leave their family and their responsibilities aside. Santosh, one youth of Sagar, was forced twice by the local administration in this work. He angrily said:

> Religion is fine; strict practice is also good. However, if it is a Jain tradition why not let Jains clean the shits of their revered sages? If they are so strict with their custom and cultures, they must come forward to earn their religious merits by lifting the shit on their heads. If they want they can even worship it… it is none of my business. My question is why the administration is forcing us to clean this holy shit! Is it not against the law? On one side, Amitabh Bachchan and Modi are ridiculing those who do have all sorts of comfort in their home but still go out for the toilet in the open. But why there is no voice against this custom? At one time Hindus used to burn their widows in the name of religion, and at many places, parents used to sacrifice their children in the names of *bali*… many such atrocious customs were being practised in the name of religion but they were all banned and declared unlawful. What is wrong if our government declares this Jain practice of holy shitting as unlawful and strictly bans it? Or else let these religious people come forward and do these tasks for their merit and at least relieve us…[1]

Duality of Swachh Bharat Mission

This mission is celebrated with the advertisements of film stars such as Amitabh Bachchan, Shilpa Shetty, Kamal Hassan and prominent sports personalities, with a broom in their hand. It is said in the popular discussion that this move will break the stigma of broom. Despite much claim and propaganda, in reality, it becomes just a show-off and publicity drive. The claim of breaking the myth of negativity associated with brooms is futile, as general staff and bureaucrats take brooms in their hands to clean their premises as an event in this mission. They do it only for a show and even in this short exercise the brooms used by them was not the one that is used by the sanitation workers of their offices but a new set of brooms being purchased for this one day show. A sanitation worker Shanta of Korba shared, 'these officers are just actors, and they cannot use our brooms for this event. This shows their casteist mentality.

1. Discrimination and Exclusion in Education…Madhya Pradesh and Chhattisgarh, pp. 34-35.

It is nothing but untouchability.' In fact, the Swachh Bharat Mission has not brought any sensitivity in the mind of a common citizen to take care of the cleanliness of the city as a personal obligation. The common people are as careless as they were before. Even those cities like Indore and Bhopal which are in the front rank of cleanliness, the common public seems equally insensitive towards the cleanliness of public places. They are seen littering the waste in public places and throwing chewed tobacco. However, with the continuation of these filthy habits, it is indeed true that these cities along with many others do become clean with the enactment of this drive. How they become clean should be a matter of question? If one believes this to be an impact of the popular advertisement campaign of Swachh Bharat, the answer is negative.

The cities became clean with the proactive role of municipalities in these cities. We have little information on how many people have been fined by the administration for spreading garbage or throwing dirt in public places, but we are sure that to maintain cleanliness, the sweepers have been forced to work beyond the official hours. In the name of cleanliness, there was open defiance of labour laws. The sweepers were asked to clean the places in two shifts. Their work was being strictly monitored and in case of any discrepancies, they were levied with the punishment of salary cuts. As a strict measure, the sanitation workers had to visit twice in the municipal office to punch in to ensure their presence in the duty no matter how far the actual site of their duty is from the office. The sweepers have to first come to the office to mark their attendance, and then have to leave for the actual site. This drive also promoted the contract system. The wages of the workers and their duration of work timings are at the mercy of the contractors. There is no fixed minimum wage, though there is a norm and fixed amount in the record but practically it all depends on the whims and fancies of contractors to pay the salaries. During the Swachh Bharat campaign, the work started as early as 4 o clock and lasted until 9 pm. There are no hours fixed for an individual worker, the work may last up to ten-twelve hours or even more. This mainly happened during the ranking preparation of the city for this Mission. The municipal bodies under this plan are pressurised to make their cities clean in a competition to earn a good ranking in the nation. This is no doubt a good exercise to make and keep the country clean.

However, the only victims of this operation are sanitation workers who were imposed with much more responsibilities and work without bothering to provide any overtime and other provision of the labour laws. There is no provision for sick leave, casual leave, medical leave, or other leaves. Even Sundays are not considered a rest day. The workers are given a choice whether they wanted a break on a Sunday or not. Those who opt for a break on a Sunday tend to lose their one day salary each month. The absence in case of an emergency or any genuine reason is bound to be treated as absent and resulted in a loss of pay. The worst thing is that even in case of an accident or an injury during work hours, the sanitation workers are neither provided with any medical relief nor do anyone get leave for recovery or rest. The municipal administration forces the sweepers to work extra hours. In the early days, this happened during special occasions or festivals but it becomes their daily trouble with the implementation of the Swachh Bharat Mission.

Stigma and Negatively Branded Identity

A sanitation worker has to carry this stigma throughout his life. However, the result of this is not merely psychological but this often resulted in encountering many practical problems. They are treated lesser humans in all stages of their lives. There are three immediate and direct causal factors for the exclusion and marginalization of scavengers. The first is their engagement in what is called 'unclean' occupation, the second is the low wages which leads to economic vulnerability and the third is their lowest position in the social hierarchy in the caste system.

The immediate outcome of low income is poverty which affects the overall well-being of scavengers and their families. The succeeding factors of poverty are poor habitation, unhygienic living, lack of nutritious food, and lack of involvement in recreational activities. These factors not only make a negative impact on the life of a scavenger but it creates a challenge for the children who, because of the negation of their basic needs and lack of any support system, are bound to perform poorly in school that ultimately results in their dropout. The exclusion and untouchability become a part of the life of every scavenger. Their position becomes severe both in workplaces and in public places. The Municipal Corporation or whosoever their employer seldom cares to provide basic facilities to them even in their workstations. It is observed that while collecting garbage or sweeping there is neither any facility available for the workers to have water for their drinking or to wash. Often for this basic need, the workers have to seek the mercy of common people. Being branded 'unclean', the religious and social customs of common people restrict them to help the needy. In case of mercy, the common people do provide water to the workers but with much 'care' and restrictions. Ramesh who is employed as a sweeper in Nagar Nigam said,

We used to clean the dirtiest drains. However, we do not get the wages every month. When I go to the chair's office, we are not allowed to sit on the chair. If we feel thirsty, we cannot drink water from the glass in the office. If we talk about raising the salary to the chairperson, he discontinues our services for 2-3 months and does not even pay money for our previous work. When we clean the drain, at that time if we are hungry they allowed us to go to the hotel. However, the hotel gives us snacks only on plastic plates and tells us to sit outside... After cleaning the drain even if we take a bath, still people hate us. No one drinks the water touched by our hand... We remember the tragedy of a time when I was wearing good clothes in the office a new officer recruit of Rajput caste asked me for a *khaini.* Therefore, I gave my khaini to him. After putting it in his mouth, he asked: what do you do? I told the truth that I am an employee of the Dom caste. Listening to this the officer becomes angry with me and said, 'being a Dom! How dare you share your Khaini with me? Can't you tell me earlier that you are a Dom... I will throw you out?' There is a big problem with the caste in a village than in a city. People do not give us good work after knowing our caste. How clean I am, but after knowing my caste and my work people start hating me. The village is more hateful than the city. To worship in the village, the temple is set according to the caste and one cannot go to someone else's temple if it is worshipped by the high caste - like Brahmin, Rajput, Bhumihar.[1]

Similar is the story of a sanitation worker Vinod. He shared:

Once I felt thirsty while cleaning a gutter. When my work got over, I asked for a glass of water from the family where I was working. A child of a family was about to bring water for me but he was suddenly scolded by his mother. She said to him, 'How can you serve water to him! Can't you see this man just cleared our gutter with his hand?' We are not allowed even to collect our money after our work gets over. The house will be polluted only after a bath I can come and collect the money. When I go to the master to ask for money, he gives us money by putting money outside the door. At that moment what could I do I say to myself that this thing is written in our life... we have to serve others? I know that this is a noble work we are saving others from all kinds of diseases by cleaning our country and the state. However, even today in our society, other community

1. Discrimination and Exclusion in Education...Bihar and Jharkhand, p.54

> members do not come here. People see the people of the Mestar[1] community with their notion of casteism. Therefore, the people of the Mestar caste are seated on the street outside the house in humiliation. Strangely, they serve the people but still, they are not considered as part of this society.[2]

Dharma Devi narrated how she faces discrimination in society, she says, 'because of my work as a sweeper, I am not even allowed to sit near the door of the people of other castes. If we take water from the tap attached to their door, they start abusing us.' She also narrated the vulgar behaviour of people towards her:

> Once there was a Rajput's son's wedding. At that wedding, I was supposed to throw the leftover food from people's plates but by mistake, I touched the bucket kept aside for serving food to guests. Unfortunately, a woman saw this, she immediately shouted to throw the entire food of that bucket and the entire food was thrown away.... At any wedding, we are given food only after everybody finishes their food that too by throwing it on our own utensil from above. We are asked to sit separately on the floor and eat....
>
> When I go to clean drains or for rag picking, dogs begin to chase me and the children from big houses make more dogs chase us. Society's perception of doing unclean work is very bad. Sometimes while walking or passing by, people look down upon me and use vulgar slang.[3]

There was even a brutal case that appeared in Uttar Pradesh reported in mainstream media where a nine-month pregnant Dalit woman Savitri Devi near a village in Meerut was beaten to death by a savarna Thakur woman and her son, when Savitri Devi touched the garbage bin of the savarna woman by mistake.[4]

The untouchability faced by sanitation workers is primarily occupation linked. Therefore, when a non-scavenging caste individual enters into this occupation, he faces similar experiences, as is the case of Pappu Paswan a Dusadh, who is working as a Sweeper in Patna Municipal Corporation. He shared:

---

1. Mehtar is called as Mestar in Bihar.
2. Ibid p. 55.
3. Ibid p. 56.
4. https://timesofindia.indiatimes.com/city/meerut/beaten-up-for-polluting-garbage-bin-dalit-dies/articleshow/61191230.cms

> From the beginning, my father used to work in the municipal corporation to clean the gutter and plant. I also got involved in this work. I have not studied before and have wasted my time roaming here and there with my friends. Then on the advice of my father, I was engaged in this work. I started the work with only 1000 rupees of monthly salary, as I was not working for the whole schedule in a day. However, when I got married it increased my responsibility. I took this work perfectly and I started working with full responsibility. I work for 6 to 8 hours. I am not literate so that is why I liked this work. This work is considered filthy and unclean but in my case the problem is even more than that of Musahars and Doms. They are lucky that they are traditionally been associated with impure work. But being a Paswan is more difficult for me. My caste was not anyway associated with impure work but in this settlement, I along with three more Dusadhs fall into the trap of this occupation. We all lost our relations with our caste men… but it is ok we have close fraternity with the communities in this occupation.…It is considered to be an unhygienic work and because of this the relationship with other castes and us is also worse. They do not talk to us. They did not have our *khaini*[1] made by us.[2]

A female respondent Radha, a sanitation worker of Chamar caste also shared her sorrow:

> People hated us, even after coming to the city, and there is a distinction because of caste. When people identify us as Chamars then they do not take us to work in their homes. I go to do the work of cleaning in Rajput, Bhumihar, Brahmin, Yadav, Kurmi, and Lala homes and if I touch the curtains of their doors, they wash them after I leave. The Kurmis, Rajputs and other caste people working in our office do not even eat the tobacco offered by us. Even if someone eats the tobacco offered by us and knows our caste thereafter then they get angry. Even if other caste people do the work of cleaning, after taking a bath they sit and eat with everyone and do not suffer discrimination like us. It is only because of our caste that we are discriminated against.[3]

The 'unclean' occupation-based exclusion and discrimination doesn't apply to the Dalit castes alone. But this is to a large extent also linked with the occupation.If at all people of other backward castes get into

1. A local variety of tobacco.
2. Discrimination and Exclusion in Education…Bihar and Jharkhand, pp. 54-55.
3. Ibid pp. 53-54.

this occupation, they too suffer the same. Sanjay, a Sweeper of Kumhar (OBC) caste, narrates his story,

> I initially used to weave and work as a tailor as my father used to do this work. Previously I was not connected to work that was called unclean. I started the work 11 years ago.I cleaned the drain in the municipal corporation and took up the garbage. I do this work for a total of 8 hours and with full responsibility. I am completely satisfied with my present work because my financial condition has become good and I can educate my children. After all, I got my job changed due to financial constraints. There was no obstruction of any caste in my work. I saw that in doing unhygienic things, with your work your relationships also matter. In the beginning, when I first started this work, my own family turned away from me. They broke us off by questioning whether there was no other work that Iare doing this work. But I did not care and now slowly they started coming to me. However, in the eyes of the public, I am a Mestar (Mehtar).[1]

The indifferent treatment and exclusionary practices against scavengers are common across India. The common people firmly believe in untouchability and its practice against the scavengers. It is not strange when these common people take up the responsibilities of teachers, school staff, and fellow students. They do practice the same against the scavengers of the schools and extend this behavior to the students of the scavenging community. Therefore, social distancing and exclusion are a natural outcome. The children of these slums have to bear the trauma and branding of their settlements in their schools. For a school with mixed categories of students, there is a marked distinction between middle-class and scavenging community students. Apart from this secondary impact of locality, in many instances, there is also a primary impact of these settlements on the children. There have been incidences where school authorities deny admission to children on the ground of being a habitant of a particular settlement. During my fieldwork in Bihar, I have come across such a case in Gaya, where the school authorities straightforwardly denied admission to children of a particular slum. As a result, none of the children of this settlement is school-going and they all are remaining illiterate.[2]

Hierarchies Based on Castes within Dalits

The Dalit is a heterogeneous group consisting of diverse castes, which were once considered untouchable by mainstream society. At

1. Ibid p. 56.
2. This matter is elaborately discussed in the chapter 4 of this book.

present, it has got a new constitutional name, the Scheduled Castes. On the one hand, it contains the castes such as Mahar, Dusadh, Kori, Jatav, Pasi, etc., who have almost no association with 'unclean' occupations—*at least for the past few generations.* While on the other, the castes such as Valmiki, Lalbegi, Bhangi, Chuhra, Mehtar, Musahar, Dom, Dhobi, etc., who are still much active in 'unclean' occupations like scavenging, washing stained clothes, disposal of dead bodies, etc. Apart from the distinction of 'clean' and 'unclean' work, the graded inequality, which is a quintessential feature of the caste system is equally present in the Dalit community. The alleged concept of purity and pollution keeps some of the Dalit castes in a higher position and assigns a lower position to others. Of course, being separate and diverse castes, none of the Dalit castes intermarries with each other. In a traditional setup, even intercaste-dining or commensality is also restricted. The castes involved in this occupation and other 'unclean' occupations are the most marginalized and vulnerable among the Dalits. The castes engaged in the lowest ladder of the hierarchy are thus bound to be the victim of caste-based discrimination even by the castes, which are a little higher in the caste scale. The castes such as Chamar, Dusadh, and Mahar treat the castes such as Valmiki, Bhangi, and Mehtar lower to them, and there are instances of untouchability practiced against them. The lowest treatment of the castes engaged in scavenging rightly resulted in the coining of a new phrase 'Dalits within Dalits' for them, for instance, used by Joseph Xavier in his study 'Excluded and Victimised City makers: Economic, Social and Cultural Rights of Dalits among Dalits.' In this study, he tried to measure the unequal treatment of scavenging castes by other Dalits and observed that the benefits of reservation meant for SCs are largelyconfined to the Pallars and Parayars and found that the Arunthathiyars, a scavenging caste is treated lowest even by other Dalits. They are being exploited by the moneylenders and good many of them are from the Scheduled Castes, other than Adi Andhras.[1] In each region and state there is a similar conflict among Dalits mainly between those who consider them ritually higher than scavenging communities[2] and those castes who are traditionally or otherwise employed in it. Yet, despite these hard and soft cases of discrimination against each other, one striking feature of the conflict is that there is not a single case of mass clashes appearing in the scene.

1. Joseph Xavier in his study 'Excluded and Victimised City makers: Economic, Social and Cultural Rights of Dalits among Dalits' traced the inequal treatment of scavenging castes by other Dalits and observed that the benefits of reservation meant for SCs is largely confined to the Pallars and Parayars. p. 192.
2. This issue is also discussed in chapter 7 of this book.

While on the other hand, the scavenging community despite their allegiance to Hindutva culture and religion consistently face brutal repression from the dominant Hindus. The infamous atrocities in Gohana, Pabnava and recently in Hathras of Uttar Pradesh where a Valmiki girl was brutally raped and murdered by the Hindu-Rajputs clearly show the intensity of the difference between the intra-Dalit conflict and inter-Dalit conflict. The conflict between various scavenging communities within and with other Dalits is merely a false replication of the Hindu caste system and sometimes more practically emerged out of competition in sharing of limited resources. On the contrary, the violent acts against the Dalits whether engaged in 'unclean' occupation or otherwise by the dominant caste Hindus show that all the Dalits are outcasts in Hindu society. One bigger unnoticed truth, however, is that the individuals belonging to Chamar, Dusadh, Mahar castes, who are found to be engaged in scavenging are found much more vulnerable than Valmiki, Bhangi, and Mehtar. The reason for their vulnerability within the scavenging community is not their social stature but it is more practical. Being fewer in number, they are unable to assert their ritual superiority over the traditional scavenging castes. Their poor numerical strength compels them to be submissive to the mainstream scavenging community. Therefore, they become marginal among the scavenging community. However, this fact is yet not covered in any sociological studies. During my fieldwork, I encountered many such cases, for instance in the Krishna colony of Shimla, which is predominantly a settlement of Valmikis but has sizeable Chamar scavengers. Their number is however much less than the Valmikis and are poorest settlers of this basti. They are located at the lowest fringe of the settlement. All these Chamars are engaged in daily wage scavenging or engaged in door-to-door garbage collection, which is the lowest form of scavenging. A few of these people of the previous generation got employment as sweepers in the municipal corporation. However, among the present generation, none of them got this opportunity. They are the most humble and poorest scavengers in Shimla. Their marginal status in the wider scavenger community prevents them to show their ritual superiority over Valmikis. However, they have maintained their separate identity by showing their allegiance to Saint Ravidas, and have built his small temple in their area. They shared that their relationship with Valmikis is cordial. In some cases, however, the new entrant castes in the scavenging occupation do face reverse caste discrimination.[1]

1. The term, reverse caste discrimination referred as a reaction of castes in lower hierarchy against the castes, which are socially upward.

The practice of graded inequality between various Dalit castes, and between diverse scavenging castes and between their different sub-castes is playing a major role in dividing this vulnerable community and keeping them at the bottom of the margins. The mutual enmity and their inability to come onto a common platform is the biggest hurdle before them to access their entitlements. As a result, the community is under the vicious trap of marginality. Moreover, with the introduction of liberal economic policies, the government job is increasingly been contractualised. The privatization of Public Sector Units (PSUs) and government sectors is nullifying the reservation of SCs, STs, OBCs, Persons with Disabilities (PWD) and women in these sectors. It is true that in the pre-liberalization era, many Dalits on the one side achieved occupational mobility but the communities within them who are associated with scavenging and other 'unclean' occupations have remained under the trap. The only change witnessed over these years is that many new Dalit castes which were in no way associated with scavenging and the tribes which are out of Hindu social order also joined the chores of scavenging. This downward occupation mobility increased the periphery of scavenging. Looking at the government's economic policy of liberalization and contractualization, it is no surprise that in the coming days more Dalits and marginal castes permanently fall into this trap.

Chapter - 4

The Unclean Practices in Campus

> In nearly 95 per cent of schools, the *Antyaja* (untouchable) children are made to sit outside in the cold, heat or rain, and they are made to fetch cow dung, fuel, droppings, dust, etc.
>
> **-Dr Babasaheb Ambedkar**[1]

We have discussed that the Dalits in general and those involved in scavenging and allied occupations continue to face discrimination and exclusion in their daily lives. Reflection of this marginalization is bound to confront their children in educational institutes. The practice of untouchability hounds this community, sometimes visibly and often in invisible forms. The life of Dalit students in school is full of trouble and oppression. The famous Dalit author, Omprakash Valmiki, in his autobiography narrated one such incident:

> A teacher scolded a Dalit student, '*Abey*, *Kala* Daroga, stand up straight or else I will make you crooked with my stick.' There was a loud burst of collective laughter… He then picked up a Dalit boy Surjan Singh. He began to kick and slap him mercilessly. It did not seem like a teacher punishing his student. Rather, it seemed like a ruffian was roughing up an innocent victim. Surjan Singh fell on the ground, and the teacher kept of kicking and beating him non-stop and commented '*Abey* brother –in-law, progeny of a Chuhra, let me know, when you die. You think you are a hero. Today I am going to gong to draw oil from your tresses…' All the students were standing dazed. The teachers were watching the spectacle quietly. The Principal stood

1. Ambedkar in 'The Times of India', 2 March 1928, quoted from BAWS Vol. 2, pp. 447-48.

quietly as well. No one protested or retaliated... After beating, Surjan Singh had lost interest in his studies.[1]

Apart from dropping out and discontinuation, the atrocious behaviour in educational institutes sometimes even results in loss of their lives.

The suicide of Rohit Vemula of Hyderabad Central University (HCU) was one of the most discussed cases, where due to institutional harassment a promising student was pushed into taking an extreme step. Parallel to this was the case of Delta Meghwal, a seventeen year old student of BSTC (a course after 10+2, to qualify as a school teacher) from Jain Adarsh teacher training institute for girls in Nokha, Bikaner (Rajasthan), who was raped and murdered on her hostel campus. She was a brilliant student and an amazing painter, having topped in an Art competition for the whole of Rajasthan while she was in class XI. One of her artworks was featured in an art magazine published by the Rajasthan secretariat in 2006 when she was just 7 years old.[2]Ajay Pandole, a fifth-semester student of BA LLB, was sodomised by his Brahmin senior Ashutosh Dwivedi, a final year student of Bachelor of Computer Applications.[3] As a result, Ajay committed suicide.[4] Recently Payal Tadvi, an Adivasi MBBS student committed suicide by hanging herself in her hostel room.[5] There are many such incidents of harassment against Dalit students on campuses. Some years ago, a Dalit organization named 'Insight Foundation' prepared a list of a few such cases and recorded some of them in its documentary series 'The Death of Merit'.[6] In the premier medical institute AIIMS, there have been rampant cases of discrimination and exclusion of Dalit students, which were kept under wraps earlier but started to intensify after the government decided to implement reservations for OBCs in the premier educational institutes. The Prof. Thorat Committee report on discrimination in AIIMS proves the practice of exclusion and discrimination against Dalits on this campus. This report says that Dalit students are socially segregated from the mainstream students. The two top floors of a common hostel were

1. Omprakash Valmiki, Joothan pp. 47-48.
2. https://www.sabrangindia.in/article/real-story-behind-rape-and-killing-dalit-girl-student-delta-meghwal
3. https://indianexpress.com/article/news-archive/latest-news/in-death-as-in-life-mystifying-all-who-knew-him/
4. This came up in the news in a different format accusing the victim to responsible for his death and painted it as a suicide. For instance, see http://archive.indianexpress.com/news/mystery-tragedy-in-mp-student-suicide/972415/1
5. https://www.ndtv.com/india-news/mumbai-doctor-bhakti-mehre-who-allegedly-targeted-her-junior-dr-payal-tadvi-with-casteist-remarks-le-2044288
6. https://thedeathofmeritinindia.wordpress.com/

ghettoized for the Dalit and tribal students. They were not allowed to participate in games and cultural events, and faced discrimination in the mess and ragging on caste lines.[1] Many of these practices continue till date, even after the release of this report, and have affected the life and liberty of the Dalit students. In March 2012, Anil Meena, a tribal student from Rajasthan committed suicide by hanging himself from a fan in his hostel room in this institute.[2] Another medical college of repute, Vardhman Medical College of New Delhi, was engaging in one of the most unethical practices of deliberately failing Dalit students in exams.[3]These are not exceptional incidents; it is almost a routine exercise. Many Dalit students prefer to discontinue their education in such cases and those who want to struggle on usually meet with a similar fate. Only a handful of Dalits could survive and earn their degrees in higher education.

The cases referred to above are related to higher education. The situation in schools is no different. The latest among the incidents is the killing of Indra Meghawal of Rajasthan. According to the police report shared by the NCSC, Meghwal was thirsty and tried to drink water from the pot meant for the head of the institution. Seeing that, the teacher started beating the boy due to which he fell and started bleeding from his ears.[4]According to news published in The Times of India, two Dalit girls appearing for their first board examinations in Narsinghpur district of Madhya Pradesh were stripped by female invigilators while 40 male students watched. During the Class X mathematics examination, the female examiners, Preeti Sharma and Reshma Simaiya, suspecting that some students were using paper strips to cheat, picked the two minor girls (both 15 years old) and asked them to strip. One of the girls told the sub-divisional magistrate that when she refused to obey the examiner's orders, one of them shouted 'strip or I will cut the cord of your salwar.' When the girls refused, the examiners stripped them while male classmates sniggered and cracked jokes. Nothing was found to suggest they had cheated and the girls were allowed to leave after the three-hour test.[5]

1. Thorat Committee Report, p.6 ref: http://ncsc.nic.in/files/mgz0001.pdf
2. Suicide exposes ills of system in AIIMS - The Hindu
3. https://www.thehindu.com/news/cities/Delhi/suspension-of-former-present-principals-of-mahavir-medical-college-demanded/article4015857.ece
4. https://economictimes.indiatimes.com/news/india/dalit-boy-death-father-took-child-to-6-hospitals-over-23-days-but-failed-to-save-him/articleshow/93620841.cms?from=mdr
5. https://timesofindia.indiatimes.com/india/two-dalit-girls-in-madhya-pradesh-stripped-in-examination-hall/articleshowprint/12386251.cms

In Pratapgarh district, Uttar Pradesh, a primary school accommodates students from nearby villages. Among them is Mansi, a student of Class 2, who made a startling revelation: the principal forced her to dispose of the carcass of a puppy. When she refused, she was brutally caned. That is not all; she is also regularly made to sweep the school premises. Investigation revealed that many children like Mansi are forced to perform menial tasks like this in school. The reason? They belong to the Dalit community.[1]

A personal experience from my school days is worth sharing. My school, the Kendriya Vidyalaya in Amla, Madhya Pradesh, like most of the KVs of defence cantonment, was open to all. It catered to a variety of students - on one hand, it had children of Air Force officers and on the other, children of extremely poor rickshaw pullers and labourers. This heterogeneous mix was because of being located in asmall town, where the children of air force officers had no other viable options available, since their transferable service restricted them from opting for private schools. In our school, amongst the many notorious teachers, the sports teacher was most ruthless and cruel towards Dalit students. He used to punch and biff them, and often used wooden sticks and sometimes even metallic pipes. There was hardly any Dalit boy including me who escaped from his merciless beating. Once a senior Valmiki boy of Class 11, who had a robust, tall physique matching that of a Bollywood star, was picked on by this teacher. He was targeted mainly because of jealousy of the sports teacher regarding his physique and even more because of his excellent sports skill in volleyball, for which he was selected for national level games. The sports teacher slapped him in the morning assembly. This was shocking to all the students because for the first time this teacher targeted a boy who was taller and more robustly built than him. There was usual pin drop silence among all, and the other teachers and principal as usual remained spectators. The matter however, did not end with this moment. A few days later, the same teacher accompanied this boy for a national volleyball competition to some far off city. After the practice match, this teacher again slapped him but this time he did not stop with this but began to beat him in his usual ruthless style. The boy was stronger and taller than the teacher, but he remained silent. However, a week later, when both of them returned to their hometown, the Valmiki boy retaliated. One fine evening when the sports teacher was on his walk, this boy confronted him with a stick and wire grip which is traditionally used to capture pigs. The culprit teacher understood the consequences and

1. https://www.videovolunteers.org/caste-discrimination-keeps-dalit-children-from-schools/

tried to run away. However, the Valmiki boy used the wire grip to hold the teacher by his neck and ruthlessly punished him in the same manner as he used to do with other Dalit students. However, the matter did not end with this; the next day, the teacher filed a complaint in the local police station. The police arrested the Valmiki boy. His career was ruined and he discontinued his study and later became a known history-sheeter. Out of fear, the teacher took a transfer to a far-off city.

During the field survey, we found almost all these practices of discrimination and exclusion in schools. However, it is also noticed that with the appearance of such cases in mainstream media as well as with the provision of the Scheduled Castes and Scheduled Tribes (Prevention of Atrocities) Act, 1989, fear is instilled in the minds of the school authorities to refrain from such acts in open and blatant form. During our survey across India, it is commonly observed that during the first interaction with forward-caste teachers, they strongly deny the existence of any discriminatory practices on the campus. However, after winning their confidence by appearing to belong to mainstream society, they feel comfortable and begin to share their internal feelings towards Dalit students. In such discussions, their biases and negative comments against the State's proactive policies for Dalits, mainly on reservation in government sectors, provision of scholarship, PoA and even RTE, are expressed with sharp criticism and opposition. Similarly, on the question of existence of discriminatory practices in school from the scavenging community students, their immediate response in most of the cases is of denial. However, after developing a close bonding with them and ensuring that the field investigator also belongs to the same caste community there began a revelation of the facts. In both opposite categories of respondents, the teachers and students winning their confidence is possible only after ensuring that the field investigator belongs to their caste-community. This was the strategy followed to gather true and correct primary data both from the school authorities and from the community. Using this strategy, many facts appeared in the scene. However, it is observed that the practice of exclusion differs from state to state, for instance, in most of the cases in Bihar, Rajasthan and Uttar Pradesh the practices of discrimination and exclusion is found open and blatant, but it is little milder in the states of Madhya Pradesh, Chhattisgarh and Jharkhand while in the cities of Solan and Shimla of Himachal Pradesh it is less. The reason for this is of course the prevailing socio-cultural practices of these states; yet, there is one more variable of admission pattern in the school that is playing a bigger and distinctive role. In schools which are catering to students of mixed communities including both forward castes and poor Dalits, there appears to be more discrimination while in those schools which cater only to poor Dalit students, there is almost a negligible appearance of caste discrimination. The reason is obvious because of the universal fact that friction occurs only with the opposites, therefore the schools with a diverse variety of students there appears to be more discriminations between them. The poor Dalits do face discrimination in almost every event, occasion and place including seating patterns in classrooms, drinking water from a common tap, mid-day meals, etc. and also there appears to be discrimination by teachers by giving preferential treatment to forward caste students and less attention to the poor Dalits. This, however, does not mean that schools exclusively ghettoized by poor Dalits are free from discrimination. It is true that in this case there appears to be no case of discrimination between students and occurrence of preferential treatment by the teachers. Yet, in such schools, the practice of 'tactical discrimination' in the form of careless attitude of teachers in performing their duties is common. However, in mixed schools, there emerges a blatant open form of discrimination through many illegal and inhuman practices.

Spatial Discrimination and Denial of Admission

Poverty, caste and culture make students and parents vulnerable to being denied their entitlements. There are ample cases where the school authorities directly or indirectly deny admission to these children. In such a case, there is no support system available to the parents to assert their rights. Moreover, as they are aloof from the education system and have no culture of education among them, in general, they easily accept the dictates of school authorities and make little attempt to fight for their rights. However, in some cases, when an individual or community tries to assert their rights, often they do not succeed. A girl in Patna was denied admission even though her parents attempted to enroll her many times. Nandini was not enrolled in schools even after four attempts. Her mother took her to the school but the teacher asked them to come afterwards. They went again and was asked to return the next day. The next day they were asked to come afterwards. When they went there after two days, the teacher was not present. The school was closed the next time they were there. On the last and fourth time they were there, the teacher told them to get enrolled the next year because the time for enrolment had passed. This is not an individual instance of discrimination but as referred in the previous chapter one Dom settlement of scavenging community in

Gaya is branded to such an extent that none of its children is welcomed in the government school. The school authorities are said to reject their admission outright with a casteist slur. The children narrated their pains and sufferings at the hand of their teachers:

> They beat us mercilessly and asked us to discontinue our schooling. They used to say, 'The school is not for you. You Dom-Manjhi!! Go and clean gutters.' They are so harsh to us that they beat us with pipes and sticks. They made our life hell. We have no option other than to discontinue schools.[1]

A mother of one of the victim girls shared how her six year old daughter's hand was wounded by a teacher, who beat her with a metallic pipe. She said,

> I know the importance of education. Despite being uneducated, I did my best to admit my daughter to school. I used to take special care of her despite my busy schedule in the morning. All was well for a few days but later my daughter has shown disinterest in going to school. I was not able to understand the reason. I accepted it as a normal part of child life. I know that children anyway are not much interested in school-going. But one day when she went to school. It was disastrous. Her hand was badly injured, it was bleeding and her skin was almost pulled off. It was so deeply injured that you can still see the mark. I asked what happened to which my daughter replied that she was beaten up by a Madam. She was in much pain. When I asked the reason for it she said my Madam doesn't want to see me in school. I understood that since we are poor and outcastes our presence on the campus disturbs others. This was not a stray incident but it was a regular exercise of the teachers. They used to beat our children and forced them to discontinue their studies. As a result, none of the children of our slum is going to school. The teachers used to make a slur by saying 'You Dom-Manjhi! Education is not for you. Why don't you get involved in scavenging and piggery? This is your caste profession. You can't become a doctor, engineer nor even a peon. Why are you wasting your time in school and making us polluted?[2]

This settlement of Gaya is traditionally known as Dom Tola but its modern name is Gayawal Bigaha. Both parents and children, together and

1. Field based information. Many such incidences are reported in the report Discrimination and Exclusion in Education...Bihar and Jharkhand p. 76
2. Discrimination and Exclusion in Education...Bihar and Jharkhand, p. 157

in separate meetings, shared about the discrimination and exclusion of the students in schools and the casteist prejudices of the school authorities. They informed us that the teachers blatantly and harshly discriminate against students, which forces them to discontinue their studies. They also informed that school authorities strictly ordered that they would not admit any child from this settlement in the future! This clear instruction leads young parents not to admit their children to school. Poverty and lack of any social security do not allow them to opt for private schools. The community members say:

> We all are semi-literate or illiterate, yet we know the importance of education. You see we have limited resources still we want our children to get educated. All of us admitted our children to a nearby government school. Nevertheless, this proved to be a bad experience. Within a few days, the school authorities forced our children to discontinue their school by directly taking strong actions against our children. The teacher beat our children so badly that some of our children took months to recover.[1]

However, as an exception, one parent managed to admit his son to a private school. The rest of the children are totally out of school. Could this one child from the settlement continue school? Without any support, motivation, and culture of school going in his neighbourhood, he is bound to discontinue in near future. This settlement is the worst example of spatial discrimination. When I inquired about the matter by cross-checking with school authorities. Their response was tactical. They said,

> You see we have limited seats in our schools, naturally, we have to give priority to the children of neighbourhoods first. This Gayawal slum is a little far away from our school, hence we cannot admit them.

On the question of forcible dropouts of the Dom community students from the school, the teacher responded,

> It was not the case of discrimination as you perceive. The Dom students are notorious; they do all sorts of mischievous activities on the campus which are not liked by anyone in this school. There is a frequent fight between them and other students as a result they prefer to discontinue the school. Anyway, learning is not the culture of the Doms. They are good in their hereditary occupations. This is the problem of modern democracy, which is forcing everybody

1. Ibid.

> to get educated from school. In our ancient *Gurukul* system, only the deserving child was admitted. What to say now? Macaulay and Ambedkar destroyed our social system.[1]

The comment above shows the cunning way to justify the non-admission of Dom students. The praise for the *Gurukul* system and negative comments on Dr. Ambedkar also shows the brahmanical mindset of teachers. In Patna, Neeraj Kumar, a Dom youth of eighteen years shared:

> The environment around us is of a discriminatory kind even though it is a city. We have suffered poverty and helplessness in our homes even after staying so close to the Nagar Nigam office. My parents took me for school admission but the teachers after knowing my caste and parents' occupation refused to give me admission even after us going to them repeatedly. After this, I told my parents that I would not go to take admission anywhere. No elder in my family has ever been to school except my mother and father. My three brothers and one sister, younger than me, all go to school. Many relatives told me to study but after that incident, I never even talked about studying.

In the absence of any support system, the parents are bound to accept the dictates of school authorities. This is such a common act across India, that many children are denied school entrance. Khushboo, a girl, tells that her mother had taken her to the school for admission. The teacher had sent them away saying that admissions have stopped. When they went, again the school was closed. The third time we went to school it was closed for summer vacations. When we went after the school reopened they said that I have grown old, what I will do after studying. Saying these things the teacher discouraged us. Khushboo says that the teacher said "what I will do after studying (what I will do by studying more). Because we belong to Dom caste, he said mean things and discouraged us. I felt very bad. When I told my parents then they also said the same things as that teacher."[2]

Another aspect of parents' poverty is that they are unable to spend on their children's educational needs. In all the state-government schools, textbooks are distributed to all the students free of cost. However, in this humanitarian exercise, the problem is that the schools are not receiving books on time. Sometimes the supply is delayed to such an extent that it reaches the school after the passage of half of the academic year.

1. Ibid p. 170
2. Discrimination and Exclusion in Education…Bihar and Jharkhand, pp. 61-62.

Thus, it hardly proves beneficial to students. Another problem related to the parents is that because of their poverty they are unable to purchase stationery and other supporting educational materials for their children. The community children thus are not able to get notebooks, pencils, erasers, sharpeners, which are essential for all the students during studies. The problem continues even in the later stage. Anyhow, if these students reach higher classes, they continue to face this problem. Moreover, for students of higher classes, graph books, atlas, geometry boxes, maps, guides and reference books became essential to them, however, due to the poor income of their parents these students are unable to buy these items. Consequently, they are bound to be below average in their performance.

Open Forms of Discrimination on Campus

The school campus is often lauded with many religious praises but technically is a secular space. In popular belief, the schools are believed to be the temple of knowledge (Vidya Mandir). The praiseworthy religious phrases attached to secular institutions condition people to strictly observe the religious norms of do's and don'ts in these places. It is, therefore, no surprise to see the reflections of the social customs of untouchability on the campus. The social practice of exclusion based on supposed purity and pollution at times does appear in some of the schools catering to a mixed variety of students. The states with feudal and casteistlegacy are upfront in this practice. There are ample cases where the Dalit students are separated and segregated from the other students. Sudhir of Danapur, Patna said,

> Wherever I sit in the class I face difficulty because the teacher always tells me to sit at the back of the class. He makes the upper caste students sit in the front. The teacher does not let the Dom students sit in the front even if they want to because the headmaster would always be present there and this is how we face discrimination and untouchability in school. The teacher also shows improper behaviour towards us sometimes. I have always been sitting at the back of the classroom.[1]

In some schools of Rajasthan, we have observed that during morning assembly there was a separate row for the children of Valmiki community. In Patna, the scavenging community students are separated in the classroom. Pinky and Rani shared that they were forced to sit behind on the carpet by the teachers.[2] They beat them. This is not all, it is also a

1. Discrimination and Exclusion in Education...Bihar and Jharkhand, p. 110
2. Ibid p. 96

common exercise in some schools where the teacher forces scavenging community students to clean the toilets and sweep the campus. Such cases are very few; in our sample data one such case appeared in the city of Sagar. In Alwar, Rajasthan we found a similar case, Muskan, 11 years old girl student at a Government School stated:

> Teachers make the students clean the school by cutting grass, sweeping, and sometimes even being told to clean the toilet which is done by scavenging community students. Other caste children do only arranging and cleaning furniture in schools.[1]

The children being humble and submissive generally accept the dictates of teachers without any protest. However, we have encountered a case where a Valmiki boy strongly retaliated but at the cost of his dropping out.

> I hardly went to school even for a month as the teacher never taught me and asked me to clean the class. I was made to sit in the corner and usually scolded and beaten if I did not do the homework. One day the teacher was beating me for not doing my homework so in return, I hit the teacher with a brick and broke open his head. Then onwards I dropped out of school.[2]

An Ambedkarite researcher Dhamma Darshan Nigam narrated an incident that he witnessed in Lucknow.[3] Two daughters of a manual scavenger woman, 12 and 15 years of age, were forced to clean the school toilets for quite a long time. They were told by the teacher '*apnakaam karo. Padhkarkekyakaroge?*' (do your work, what will you do with education). Their parents got to know about this when their daughters stopped going to school altogether, due to the harassment and humiliation. When their parents inquired about it in the school, the teacher told them that this is a government school where everybody takes turns to sweep and clean the toilets. However, that was not the case — only the children of the Valmiki community were being given this task and not others. For Republic Day or other cultural events, students of the community were asked to do the cleaning and washing. This is not all; we were also told that in some cases the teacher even asks the scavenging community students to call their parents to school to do the cleaning work.

1. Discrimination and Exclusion ...Uttar Pradesh, Rajasthan, Himachal Pradesh and Haryana p. 134
2. Ibid p. 128
3. https://www.academia.edu/104779592/Our_Society_My_Observation

Discrimination against Parents

Parents from the community have hardly been invited to school for parent-teacher meetings in government schools, but some of the private schools do call them. In most government schools, this meeting is held only on paper. There are, of course, some parents being included in the SMC (School Management Committee) but this is again just a formality. These parents are called once at the beginning of the academic year and their monthly signatures are taken in a blank register in a single go.

Anyhow, in general, if the parents visit a school, their experience is not very different from their visits to any government office where the horrible treatment of poor Dalits is well known. One cannot expect humane treatment from school authorities, or even that a chair would be provided to them. Even if the teachers are humble and humanitarian, they follow the usual norm of keeping a 'respectable' distance from these parents. On the other hand, it is a normal practice for the community parents to be respectful to authorities and remain standing while talking to them. Thus, in both ways, equality in communication and dealings cannot be maintained. Of course, there are no such prescribed customs in dealing with the parents of mainstream society who are provided chairs and dealt with much respect on their visit. Sushila Devi, a mother whose son is studying in a primary school recalled that when she had gone to enroll her children in a nearby government school, the principal asked what community she belonged to. When Sushila Devi replied that she was Dom, the teacher asked her to come four days later.

> After four days, I went to the school for enrolment of the children and greeted the teacher. When I wanted to sit on the chair, the teacher asked "What do you do?" I said that I am in the Municipal Corporation, doing cleaning work. Hearing this he refused to let me sit on the chair.[1]

> In some cases, for instance, in Patna the students shared,

> Whenever there is a cultural program, the school says that all of us have to bring our parents. Our parents come to school and watch cultural programmes. However, the parents of other caste children sit on chairs or benches, while our parents are made to sit on the carpet.[2]

The differential treatment of the parents according to their social status is a normal school practice. The reflection of parents' image falls

1. Discrimination and Exclusion in Education…Bihar and Jharkhand, p. 165.
2. Ibid p. 76.

on the children and in the eyes of teachers, the students whose parents are in white-collar jobs become special while the students with 'unclean' occupational family backgrounds automatically become lowly.

Corporal Punishment

Beating and corporal punishment are anyway very common in India. The teachers also enjoy flogging students despite the RTE Act, which prohibits beating and punishment in schools for any reason. The traditional image of a teacher is that of a strict person bearing no smile on their face. There is a popular saying *'aajshanichar kal itwar, parson haindande ki maar'* (Today is Saturday, tomorrow is Sunday but two days later its punishment day). This is seen implemented in many schools. Sadly, it is accepted as natural and essential even by the parents. Manohar, the father of a Class 4 student, expressed the need for staunch punishment by saying that whenever he visits school he used to tell teachers *'jitana chaho peeto- haddi hamaari, chamdi aapki'* (Beat my son as much as you want to. His bones are ours, the skin is all yours).

However, not every parent supports the merciless beating by teachers and yet, many of them being illiterate have a high regard for the teachers and show respect to them without understanding the motive and ideology of the teacher. A girl student of Patna reported,

> Students from the Dom cluster, including me, were seated at the back of the carpet by the teachers. The teachers did not give us any homework. They used to beat us whenever anybody made any mistake in the class. Once they beat me along with four of my friends and locked us in the toilet.[1]

Such shocking incidents are common all over the nation. Tamil Nadu's Arulswamy, a 16-year-old dropout during his 7th grade said that he felt insulted by his teachers as he was bad in his studies. He was forced to work in the school in front of other students whom he did not like.[2]

In Patna, Vikram recalls an incident where there was a water pot and glass in the teachers' room. Once when he was thirsty, he tried to drink water from there. He was badly beaten by the teacher, who said this is not for the pupils, but for the teachers. In reality, the children of other castes used to drink water from the same pot all the time. So, Vikram went outside to drink water. The teachers always used to look down upon the children

1. Ibid. p. 76
2. Selvaraj Arulnathan SJ, Discrimination and Exclusion... Karnataka, Tamilnadu, Telangana and Andhrapradesh, p.120

from Domkhana. They scolded them and never talked compassionately. For every minute mistake, the teachers beat them up. The children also used to be afraid of them. These teachers, however, behave decently with children belonging to other caste communities. They talked properly with those kids, listened to them attentively, and checked their homework. As a result of such discrimination, there remained no interest to study further and almost 20-25 kids from the Dom caste and the cluster dropped out of the school.[1] In almost all the places, the students shared that selective punishment is common in the classroom. Ultimately, it results in their dropout.

Tactical Discrimination

As mentioned previously, the schools catering exclusively to poor Dalits usually follow 'tactical discrimination' whereby they do not show harshness and rudeness to the students. However, mercy or compassion is not the reason behind this behaviour. It is noted in many schools that nowadays teachers changed their attitudes towards the Dalit students fearing that the issue may get highlighted in the media and land them in trouble. As a result, teachers, in general, are now no longer engaged in the beating of students. Further, due to the rise of the Dalit movement and the stern laws such as the Prevention of Atrocities Act (PoA), the teachers are fearful of punishing Dalit students. Also in some cases, there are violent reactions by the parents and communities against teachers found guilty of beating children. Therefore, to avoid all such troubles, the teachers have developed a "tactical" way out. Now, instead of taking a personal interest in the individual performance of students, and spending time with each student to help them learn, they keep aloof from teaching activities to avoid all troubles. Since the schools are attended by poor Dalits, the teachers do not perceive any moral dilemma in failing to perform their duties. A lady teacher in a government school in Sagar shared:

> Earlier I was very strict towards the students, I was always carrying a stick in my hand and used to punish those students who were insincere and were not studying and understanding the teaching, but nowadays because of RTE, our hands are bound … I feel handcuffed… Moreover, there is also a fear of violent reactions and the implementation of the Atrocities Act. Therefore, to avoid getting into trouble I started to give them more freedom. Why should I waste my time and energy?[2]

1. Discrimination and Exclusion in Education…Bihar and Jharkhand, p. 76-77.
2. Discrimination and Exclusion in Education…Madhya Pradesh and Chhattisgarh, p. 93.

This expression is not confined to one teacher but is very much in acceptance by the wider teaching staff. In all informal discussions with teachers at various schools, most of them are found strongly critical of RTE regulations that restrict beating. It is a firm belief imprinted in the minds of teachers: 'Without beating, students cannot learn. Therefore, if the teachers are stripped of this right, there is no use of teaching!' Such established beliefs make them lose interest in teaching activities. The prominent reason for the teachers' disinterest however, as mentioned above, lies in the fact that children of upper middle class background are no longer opting for these schools and the government schools are increasingly ghettoized by the poor Dalits. This feeling is quite natural for the teachers as traditional religious teachings of mainstream religion prohibit the spread of education to the common masses, especially among the Dalits. The casteist feeling among teachers is easily recognizable in casual discussions, where they often criticize the government policy of caste-based reservation and supply of free textbooks and uniforms to the students. The careless attitude of teachers makes the school system useless. This not only affects the prospects of children but also demoralizes them from continuing their schooling. Mohit, a Class 9 student at a government school in Korba shared:

> I am a regular in my school. I did score quite good marks in the annual exams. Earlier teachers used to be serious in teaching. Now the teachers either remain in the teachers' room or enjoy the sun. They seldom come to class. Even if sometimes they take classes they are not taking any interest in teaching… for the whole day, we are just sitting and chatting with friends in the classroom. Indeed, this attitude of teachers does not hurt those who are not interested in studies but it affects a person like me. What is the use of coming to school daily if there is no one to take a class?[1]

The techniques of 'tactical' discrimination devised by teachers directly result in making the education system futile. In such an environment the students develop negativity against education and prefer to remain absent from school. In addition, even if they are regular in schools, they are not able to learn anything because of the teachers' lethargic and careless attitude. Thus, in either way, it negatively affects the students' engagement with the school system and education.

Sexual Abuse

The poor Dalit students both male as well as female are prone to sexual abuse. Earlier in this chapter, we mentioned a few cases such as

1. Ibid. p. 93.

that of a scavenging community girl Delta Meghwal who was raped and murdered on the campus and also of Ajay Pandole who was sodomised by his Brahmin senior, leading to his suicide. Leading Dalit author Omprakash Valmiki, in his autobiography mentions:

> The ideal image of the teachers that I saw in my childhood has remained indelibly imprinted on my memory. Whenever someone starts talking about a great guru, I remember all those teachers who used to swear about mothers and sisters. They used to fondle good-looking boys and invite them to their homes and sexually abuse them.[1]

In some states, particularly in Haryana, such sexual violence against poor Dalit females and male students is very common. However, most of these cases remain unreported. In the case of females, at least in some instances, such crimes appeared in the media and were noticed somewhat seriously, but the victimization of males has always remained under the carpet. A senior Dalit activist, on condition of anonymity, reported that there are many instances in Haryana and Punjab where boys of the poor Dalit community are forced to act as sexual slaves of the dominant caste youth. In some instances, they are also forced to act in local porn films as gay actors. These local gay porn films are quite popular in the region and had been available in CD form. Nowadays with a change in technology, these films are freely available on mobile phones using various illegal cyber channels. The sexual victimization of Dalit male kids and youth, however, remains under cover and has not come out in public discourse. Even the mainstream or sub-stream Dalit movement is aloof to such a form of victimization. The mental pain and sexual torture suffered by the children and youth could not be healed anyway. Under such conditions, one can imagine the chances of them performing well in their studies.

As mentioned, the sexual victimization of girl students has gained a bit more attention in some cases. This is again more common in Haryana[2] where rapes of Dalit women occur frequently. Cases of sexual harassment have also been discussed in Chapter 6 of this book.

Unsafe Campus

The caste conflict in society is equally visible on campus. States like Haryana, Uttar Pradesh and Bihar where caste violence is more common

1. Omprakash Valmiki, Joothan p. 4.
2. For instance, https://www.nationalheraldindia.com/gender/schoolgirls-in-haryana-allege-daily-harassment-ask-high-court-to-provide-protection

are more prone to it on campus as well. The caste conflict is rife in Haryana, especially between the Jats and the Dalits. In this context, a Valmiki leader of Panipat feels that the dominant castes, the Jats, would not want his community to progress. He adds that in S.D. College, Panipat, there are hardly 2 or 3 boys from the Valmiki Samaj. The Jats abuse them, but Valmiki boys cannot say anything, as Jats are in big numbers, 20-30. The Jat boys are *awara* (hooligans), they do not study, but they never fail. The college president is a Jat, drinks openly in the canteen and troubles girls, but nobody dares to say anything; even the principal is afraid of Jats. Can our boys do this? Never, they will be thrown out of the college. It is very difficult for our boys to continue in college in such an environment.[1]

Amit Kohal shares that he dropped out in Class 11 from Gandhi Memorial Senior Secondary School, Panipat. He feared that the Gujjar boys would beat him up if they got to know that he was a Valmiki. There was an old enmity between these communities; a Gujjar boy was murdered by a Valmiki boy. The other Valmiki boys in the school could hide their caste identity, but he could not lie. He says, 'I stopped going to school out of fear. I did not want any problem for the family.' A similar experience was shared by Dinesh, Vikas, and Aman, three boys from A.C Nagar who went to Kurukshetra College for higher studies and had to drop out. They said that Jats are the majority in the college and have a stronghold. The Valmiki boys kept a distance and they were mistaken to be Biharis and could escape the gaze of the Jat boys. The Valmiki boys lived in constant fear and it affected their studies.[2]

In Bihar, there is frequent conflict between Bhumihars and landless Dalits. This is not all; there is also a conflict between Yadavs and Dalits. Often this comes out in the open on school premises. A Dusadh student shared that in Gaya it was common until a few years ago that Yadav goons used to beat Paswan boys on the campus. He further said 'It stopped to an extent when our leader Ramvilas Paswan built a fraternity with Lalu Prasad Yadav. Though their political friendship came to an end, our relations with Yadavs from then onwards remained peaceful'. Yet, in one case in Gaya, local Yadav goons tried to rape a woman on the school campus during the night. In an interview, a group of Musahar boys informed us that 'Yadav goons once abducted a young girl from some other locality and bought her forcefully to the lonely campus of a school to rape her. However, when her voice for help reached the scavenger youth they immediately

1. Discrimination and Exclusion ...Uttar Pradesh, Rajasthan, Himachal Pradesh and Haryana p. 134.
2. Ibid p. 67.

rushed to the place and rescued her. Though we protected her, after this incident there is fear of retaliation among Musahar kids.'[1]

Schools, especially in Bihar and Jharkhand, are used by miscreants for activities like drinking, gambling etc., after school hours. Broken glass, wine bottles, cards and used condoms are commonly found on the school grounds. The teachers also share that at night the school ground is totally under the control of goons.

Calling caste names

As per the Scheduled Castes and the Scheduled Tribes (Prevention of Atrocities) Act, calling anyone with caste names is punishable. Omprakash Valmiki, in his autobiography mentions how his headmaster thundered loudly '*Abey Chuhre ke*, mother….., where are you hiding… your mother… Go sweep the whole playground… otherwise, I will shove chillies up your ass and throw you out of the school.' Such casteist and atrocious behaviour is still common in many schools. Often this led to the dropout of students from schools, and in higher education such inhuman treatment breaks the Dalit students to an extent that they take the extreme step of committing suicide. Manish Kumar Guddolian, 20 years of age, was pursuing B. Tech. at Indian Institute of Technology (IIT) Roorkee.[2] He was ragged and abused so much by his seniors and fellows that he felt he had no option left other than to commit suicide. He jumped off the 5th floor of his hostel on 6th February 2011 to end his pain and suffering.[3] His father said in an interview 'My son was a brilliant student, but he was targeted by his classmates and seniors, they used to shout *cham-cham-chamar,*[4] whenever they saw him. They made his life hell and ultimately he lost all hope.' Gangamma of Karnataka who completed her SSLC has similar horrid stories. Though she studied in a private school named Kanakadasas High School, she could not continue her studies, because her classmates harassed her for her poor and old clothes. The taunting on caste lines was so much that she discontinued her studies for one year.[5] Rohit, B. Tech student in Guru Jambeshwar University recalling his school days said:

1. Discrimination and Exclusion in Education...Bihar and Jharkhand, p. 146.
2. Manish's father was serving in the Indian Air Force but his uncles are still in the leather work occupation.
3. https://thedeathofmeritinindia.wordpress.com/2011/07/06/the-death-of-merit-manish-kumar-iit-roorkee/
4. Cham-chamis a short form of chamar created by the casteist students.
5. Discrimination and Exclusion...Karnataka, Tamilnadu, Telangana and Andhrapradesh p. 102.

> Everybody in school knew that I am a Bhangi's son, so nobody wanted to even touch me. When everyone was punished, the teacher would slap other children, but not me. I was asked to sit like a rooster in a corner, and she wouldn't touch me. During lunch hour teachers would eat and taste food out of other children's tiffin boxes but would never taste my food. Children would also never eat my food but would share with others. I just stopped asking and sat by myself and had my food in one corner. Many times, if some boy looked messy or dirty, the boys would comment, 'you are looking like a Chura'. I was offended and would wonder why a dirty looking person is called a 'Chura'. Do we look dirty or stink or is it our 'unclean' occupation?[1]

In Shimla, a student of class 7 shared that his class fellows are calling him 'Chuhra' but he was unaware of its meaning. He said:

> Many students used to call me Chuhra. I had not heard this word before so I was unaware. I used to think that they were calling me a rat, as this is the only meaning I knew of Chuha. Later I came to know that it is not a rat but they are calling me by a caste name. This was a strange act. Frankly speaking, I didn't get hurt by this as I know my caste is Balmiki, not Chuhra.[2]

Chandraprakash, a youth of Uttar Pradesh, shared

> While I was a student and even today upper caste boys and some teachers also still address me as 'Saale Chamaar.' On many occasions the victims are unaware of the meaning of caste slurs and hence stay aloof. The perceptive students, however, shared that 'Bhangi, Mehtar, Chamar, Dom etc., has become an abusive slur. Sometimes these are used directly against us but often they are used as abusive slurs within the communication of the dominant caste student community.[3]

During a casual conversation, the words like Chamar, Chuhra, Bhangi, Mehtar became such a lighter abuse that nobody hesitates in using it. Therefore, it is no surprise that the English speaking elite class including movie stars like Salman Khan and Shilpa Shetty, cricket star Yuvraj Singh and TV actress Munmun Dutta picked up 'Bhangi' as a synonym for ugly, bad or dirty.

---

1. Discrimination and Exclusion...Haryana p. 71.
2. Field based information shared by a student in Solan.
3. Ibid p. 207.

Determinants of Friendship

The scavenging community students in mixed community schools are generally found to have limited interaction with their classmates. A separate place located in the back is reserved for them. Children were also found to be comfortable within their caste groups. This seems to be a natural outcome for the reason that those living in the same locality are generally close friends as they spend ample time together. Therefore, their friendship motivates them to sit together even in their classroom. However, along with this natural fraternity of localized friendship, the caste, irrespective of the localities of the students, plays an equally significant role. During the pilot survey, it is observed that when asked about the determinant of friendship the students deny that caste is a factor. However, in casual discussion, it appears that caste is indeed a base of friendship in the classroom. Yet, it is so natural that the students follow this norm without being aware of it. Therefore, to know the truth we adopted a different strategy. Accordingly, in the interview schedule, surveyors first asked each of the respondent students to name four close friends. The immediate follow-up question was about the caste of each of these friends. The answers indicated that in the majority of the cases, the sub-caste or caste was not a determinant factor but the social category of Dalit and non-Dalit group is certainly a factor in each of the friendships. The responses show that Mehtar, Chamar, Dusadh, Dhanuk, Dom, Dumar, etc. could be friends but there is little possibility of friendship between a Dom and Rajput or Chamar and Brahmin. Therefore, more properly speaking the *varna*[1]instead of caste is primarily a basis of friendship among our sample students. Interestingly, in the eyes of teachers also there is no hierarchical difference or graded inequality between Chamar, Mehtar and Dom. For them, all the Dalits are equally downgraded. The casteism within Dalit groups is hardly being expressed on the campus either from the students' side or from the school authorities. We also observed that the teachers in schools also fail to distinguish between the students whose parents are directly involved in 'unclean' occupations or those who are in no way associated with it. The only yardstick for discrimination against the students is the combination of poverty and their position as Dalit. The poor Dalit students thus irrespective of their parents' occupational background and the hierarchical position within the Dalit community are

1. Here we have used to the operation definition of Varna, which means fourfold or five fold division of society in Brahmin, Kshatriya, Vaishya, Shudra and sometimes including the fifth category the Ati-Shudra while the castes (Jatis) are numerous among each of these varnas.

all met with almost the same exclusion and discrimination. This practise reminds us of Ambedkar's view on the Indian psyche 'In India, a man is not a scavenger because of his work. He is a scavenger because of his birth irrespective of the question of whether he does scavenging or not.'[1]

The graded inequality of the various castes among Dalits thus remains the social truth within this community but for the outside world, poor Dalits are equally 'untouchable' irrespective of their caste and engagement in 'clean' and 'unclean' occupations. On the campus, therefore, varna based friendship is an established practice. We cannot forget that it is carried out even in higher studies. The separation of the upper two floors of a hostel for Dalit students in AIIMS Delhi as reported by the Thorat Committee[2] is the continuity of the same social practice. Caste as generally discussed in sociology or common discussion is thus absent on campus. Varna was the only determinant of the fraternity. In higher studies, particularly in the premier educational institutes, the separate identity of SC and ST also gets blurred. The common derogatory term used by the mainstream students against these communities is '*Shiddu*'.[3] Exclusionary and discriminatory practices are equally targeted against them,this brings them closer on the campus and often makes a community. In minuscule instances, there is friendship between the forward castes and Dalit students but these are stray cases practiced with much *care* by both the parties. These opposite social strata of students keep their interaction limited to their campus and public places but seldom visit each other's homes. They are conscious of the social limitations and do not want their dictates to rule over and ruin their friendship. Rahul, a Valmiki student of class 9th in Solan said 'we are smart enough to maintain the friendship.'

> My caste is known to all, so is the occupation of my father and my locality. But as far as friendship is concerned, this doesn't matter. I have good friends among all castes. We share pass-time; we go to films and markets together. Almost every evening we walk and move together on Mall road.[4] There is no question of caste or hierarchy

1. BAWS Vol. 9 p. 293.
2. See Thorat committee report on AIIMS
3. This is a universally popular term against SCs and STs across the nation. Both the Dalits as well as non-Dalit students of the higher education do find its usage common in the campus. However, we have not observed its popularity in schools.
4. The Mall Road is a famous site for evening walks and leisure time for locals and tourists in Solan. During this time entry of vehicles is strictly prohibited to maintain its natural beauty and leisure.

> amongst us. But we know our boundaries, despite being good friends I never go to their house; neither have they come to my home.[1]

However, the case of Roshan Kumar in Patna is just the opposite. After knowing his father's occupation, his classmates dissociate from their friendship. He said,

> My father slaughters pigs and sells the meat. I help him with this work. When my teachers came to know about our trade, they started to maintain distance from us. They don't like to touch us. They won't be drinking water from our hands. Teachers used to say that they don't have any problem with my caste, but they do with the occupation since they don't eat pork. Similarly, when my friends in the school got to know that I slaughter and eat pork, they also started to maintain a distance from me. I had to face a lot of abuse when my father insisted I sell the meat and I refused. I was so furious but went to school. But as I entered the school, they started to say that 'the Dom is here' and ridiculed me. They ridiculed me by asking if I would start the trade (slaughtering pig) there!" I couldn't refrain from hitting the boy who said this and he fell unconscious. Then the headmaster called me and scolded me a lot. He told me that he is going to strike off my name from the register. They dismissed me and sent me home that very day. He never took me back in the rolls even after my parents approached him and begged for his pardon. I have had to stop my studies since then. I didn't even try to enroll in another school. My friends are still studying there.[2]

Yet another unique observation in the field was that, on many occasions, the forward caste students do visit the homes of their scavenging community friends and do accept water and food in their homes without hesitation. There seems to be no existence of purity-pollution customs among them. Yet, this relationship has a strict limitation and self-defined rule. In such cases, it is always the entitlement of forward caste friends to visit their scavenging community friends but never vice-versa. The poor Dalit friend simply cannot visit the homes of their forward caste counterpart. This practice shows that among the younger generation in *some* instances, caste may not matter much but its sanctity continues to hold at a broader level. It is interesting that all such inter-caste friendly relations are confined to males; no case of fraternity between forward caste girls and scavenging girls was found.

1. Discrimination and Exclusion in Education...Himachal Pradesh p. 265.
2. Discrimination and Exclusion in Education...Bihar and Jharkhand p. 165.

Discrimination in Mid-Day Meal

Food and water are the most important determinants of purity and pollution. Dr. Ambedkar has written that during his school days, he was not allowed to fetch water from the common source. This practice still continues in some places, and we have observed such a practice in Rajasthan and Uttar Pradesh. Some children also reported that they had to make way and stand at a distance when forward caste children come to drink water and that 'we do not drink water together'. This is because the Dalits have a polluting and inferior status according to higher castes. However, this treatment is less exposed in the media. It is strictly enforced in those schools where the caste feeling is culturally deep-rooted. The discrimination in mid-day meals is, however, a slightly more exposed practice. A few years back the Times of India reported one such incident from Mandi, Himachal Pradesh:

> Mid-day meals have exposed the fissures between upper castes and Dalits in Seraj valley of Mandi district as in many schools, students have been sitting separately on a caste basis. Sources said that upper caste students have also not been taking mid-day meals from workers belonging to the Dalit community. Sources said that similar discrimination has been continuing in Government Senior Secondary School at Thachi, Government High School at Seri-Batwara, Government Senior Secondary School at Somnachi, Central Primary School at Seri-Batwara, Government Primary School at Tandi, besides many other schools in Seraj valley. Sources said that despite complaints, no strict action has been taken by authorities till now... The majority of schools in Seraj have been facing discrimination and Dalit students are made to feel inferior to others.[1]

A 2014 study by the Indian Institute of Dalit Studies (IIDS) in Uttar Pradesh, Bihar, West Bengal, Jharkhand, Odisha, Chhattisgarh and Madhya Pradesh found that Dalit children were being given markedly less amount of food compared to forward caste children. About 30 percent of Dalit children and parents interviewed said that they were being served a lesser quantity of food, while 14 per cent reported that Dalit children were not allowed to serve food to upper-caste children. Some 20 per cent of the children attended school irregularly and were disinterested in going to school because of such discrimination.[2]A study by the MP Institute

1. https://timesofindia.indiatimes.com/city/shimla/dalit-students-made-to-sit-separately-during-mid-day-meal-in-mandi-school/articleshow/72465065.cms
2. https://www.downtoearth.org.in/news/governance/how-caste-is-marring-mid-day-meals-60898

of Social Science Research, Ujjain, reported that in Narsinghpur, in 17.5% of schools, forward caste children did not eat mid-day meals as the cooks were Dalits. Untouchability was reported within school premises in schools of Betul, Satna, Chhindwara, Burhanpur, Balaghat, Shivpuri, Narshingpur and Hoshangabad. In Satna, forward caste, SC and OBC children sat separately. In Panna, food to Dalit children was being served from a distance. Children of one social group were even getting their plates from home to avoid mixing. In Hoshangabad, girls of the forward castes sat separately from Dalit girls.[1] In our sample study, we also observed the existence of both blatant and subtle forms of discrimination in MDM. It is reported more often in the cities of Alwar, Jaipur, Patna, Sagar, Panipat, Faridabad and Mathura. A Valmiki student from Alwar shared "We were asked to bring our plates for MDM, unlike other students."[2]

> Meanwhile, separate seating is a common practice all across. In most cases, it was not forced but is followed naturally by the students because caste and varna are their basis of friendship. In Patna, in a mixed school with a student population of 150 students, there used to be two rows of children in the midday meal, as ordered by the teacher. The forward caste children sat in one row and children of Dom and Musahar castes sat in another. The latter also reported that they were asked to wash utensils used for cooking. Of course, during washing the purity-impurity and untouchability cease to become an issue.

While speaking with other students and activists, it also emerges that there is a lot of corruption in the implementation of the Government's plans and policies. The quality of food was not very good and, in a few cases, it is not even reaching the needy. This malpractice in many instances led to opposition to this scheme by some quarters. It is especially criticized by middle class Dalit activists who say that it drains a lot of energy and focus of the teachers resulting in the decline in the quality of education in government schools. However, when we shared these views of middle class Dalit activists with the scavenging community students, they were shocked. They said that in their home they have nothing to eat. Their parents work hard to meet the requirements of the family. The MDM is an opportunity for them to fill their stomach. They ask,

1. https://timesofindia.indiatimes.com/india/Caste-gender-biases-blight-mid-day-meal-scheme-in-four-states/articleshow/15347784.cms
2. Discrimination and Exclusion in Education..Haryana, Rajasthan, Uttar Pradesh and Himachal Pradesh, p. 134.

> What is the problem of those who are opposing it? There are many things to be opposed to. Why are they not opposing the opening of private schools? Is it not creating a difference between students? The rich students are going to private schools and we poor are in the government school. Is it not discrimination?[1]

In an interview, Rita, a student in sixth class in Korba says:

> I always take food provided by the school, though not tasty, and served so little. However, I still like the food as most of my friends do. Some girls in my school bring food from home. But they are from rich families (The word 'rich' is often used by the community students for those who are in a comparatively better financial position). How can I bring tiffin from my home? There is no one in my family to prepare food for me in the morning. Instead of remaining hungry for the whole day, the food that is being served to us is a better option. We get *kheer* (pudding) and *poori* too once a week. I am satisfied with the food. Once my teacher told me that some of you (referring to researchers and activists) are opposing the mid-day meal policy. I also heard from someone that some rich people are recommending to the government a ban on midday meals in school on the grounds that it affects the quality of education. But I request you not to take this view. There are indeed some problems and issues with this food, but this is the only option for my friends and me to fight with hunger.[2]

A senior activist of Korba, associated with Safai Karmachari Andolan (SKA) also supported the mid-day meal scheme, and said:

> How can one say that the midday meal disturbs education? The *Sarkari* schools are always known for poor quality education. If you want to improve education, there are several sectors, which could be looked upon. At least our children are getting something to fight against hunger. For middle-class people this could be a distraction from education, but for our community where both mother and father have to leave their home early in the morning, what is the way out? Who will prepare food for the children? The government is doing at least a single good thing for our community's students. But people are opposing it as if our children are fed from their pockets. This opposition is not different from the opposition to the policy of reservation for SCs, STs and OBCs by the forward castes.

1. Discrimination and Exclusion in Education...Madhya Pradesh and Chhattisgarh, p. 99.
2. Ibid. p. 98.

> It is, however, strange that even middle-class Dalits seem to oppose MDM. How can a well-fed man understand the pain of a hungry stomach?[1]

This problem is well addressed by a senior activist from Sagar, who opined that on the one hand, this scheme is useful while on the other side, it is equally true that this scheme has led to lethargy and corruption among teachers. Therefore, instead of taking extreme views, they need to take a middle path. He says:

> Whatever we say in support of MDM, it is a fact that this policy has led to corruption and lethargy among teaching staff, but it is equally true that this is at least providing food to needy students who otherwise will drop out of school. What is the use of quality education if a section of children drop out because of hunger? Therefore, instead of opposing this scheme, an alternate policy must be implemented. There is a need to be more vigilant on this scheme and need to recruit non-teaching staff for its administration. The teachers in any way shall not be asked to manage or administer this activity.[2]

We have observed in Bihar that the food for MDM is being prepared by a central office of an NGO and it is being distributed to all the schools included in its list. This has spared the teaching staff from extra responsibility and prevented corruption at the school level. However, on the question of discrimination, there is no easy policy solution.

Entitlements of Students

The students of government schools irrespective of their castes are provided with free textbooks, school uniforms and mid-day meals under the Right to Free and Compulsory Education Act 2009 (RTE). Apart from this, students belonging to SC, ST, OBC and families engaged in 'unclean' occupations are entitled to a scholarship. There is also provision for hostels for SC and ST students. All the government schools including Navodaya School and Kendriya Vidyalaya which are considered to be quality schools in the government sector have reservation of seats for SC, ST and OBCs. In this study, however, we have found almost negligible presence in KendriyaVidyalayas and even more shockingly, that none of the community members have even heard of Navodaya Vidyalaya. The reason for this is their lack of awareness. As a senior female activist of Sagar, in a personal interview opines,

1. Ibid p. 99.
2. Ibid. p. 100.

The entrance process in Navodaya Vidyalaya is very tough. It requires rigorous preparation and proper guidance. For other Dalit students, it is a little easy as their parents help them in this preparation. But it is not so among the scavenging communities, as their parents are generally illiterate or semi-literate. Moreover, they have no access to employment newspapers or any other source where the dates and process of entrance tests are published. Therefore, there is no question of the community students appearing in this exam. Even if someone fills their forms and asks them to appear in the exams, they cannot compete with other Dalit students, who have comparatively better support than the scavenging community children.

In Kendriya Vidyalayas, only those scavenging communities have access whose parents are sanitation workers in railways, defence or other central government offices.

The RTE act, which also has a provision for providing quality education to the children of marginalized communities, has however failed in providing any measurable support to the children of the scavenging community. More than 99% of our respondents across the nation shared their lack of awareness about the RTE. During the survey, we found only one beneficiary of this act in Gaya, Angad Kumar. He was studying in one of Gaya's elite public schools named Creane School, having got admission under RTE. His mother is working as a sweeper in this school and therefore, out of gratitude, the school authorities took a proactive role in admitting Angad under RTE. Speaking of his school life Angad says:

> My school is very good. Teachers take care of me. I have friends from all walks of life. In the classroom, the school follows a rotation system for seating. This also helps to engage with new friends. But my friendship is limited to them on the school campus only. Neither I visit their home nor do they ever come to my home. I score good marks in exams. In addition, I received a gold medal in a dance competition. I also won a medal in cricket.[1]

This stray case of RTE benefit happened due to the school's proactive role in choosing a child of their staff. Otherwise, this act has not yet reached the scavenging community. The common entitlements such as the supply of free textbooks are also not as effective. We have found that in almost every state the delay in this supply is to such an extent that it reaches the hands of the students after half the session has passed. In such

1. Discrimination and Exclusion in Education...Bihar and Jharkhand p. 171.

cases, the students manage their studies by collecting old books from their senior class students.

In some states like Delhi where there is a policy for free distribution of stationery, it is not executed properly. In other states, there is no such policy. As a result, the students from the vulnerable sections do not have access to necessities like geometrical instruments, atlas, notebooks and other stationery.

Scheduled Caste Status and Scholarship Question

The scavenging community is also facing an identity crisis. They are in the Scheduled Caste category in their native state, but on migrating to a new state for job opportunities, they cease to be SC in that state. Therefore, the inter-state migration snatches away their legal identity. In the absence of caste certificates, they cannot claim their entitlements. Thus, their children in such cases are deprived of scholarships, hostel facilities, and other provisions meant for the SC and ST. However, inter-state migration is very common in this community. During our study, we found that most sanitation workers in Himachal Pradesh are migrants from Haryana and Punjab. In Madhya Pradesh, a large number of scavengers are from Andhra Pradesh, while in Chhattisgarh the scavenging community is largely from the Banda district of Uttar Pradesh. In Bihar and Jharkhand, there are a few migrants from West Bengal. In southern states also there is a lot of inter-state migration. Overall, due to joblessness in native states, the scavenging community is forced to migrate to a new state in search of work. They easily get sanitation jobs in the new states but lose their entitlement to Scheduled Caste benefits. During my fieldwork, I observed many such cases, but two prominent cases worthy of discussion was encountered in Jabalpur and Korba, where there is a huge interstate in-migration of scavengers. In the former case, there are sizeable numbers of Malas and Madigas and a few other Andhraite castes found to be engaged in sanitation work. Most of these people got settled in Jabalpur much before the pre-independence era. While, in Chhattisgarh, the migrant Domars of Uttar Pradesh have opted for sanitation work for their livelihood over the last few decades. The interstate migration ceased their entitlement of Scheduled Castes in these states.

> It is also clarified that a Scheduled Caste/Tribe person who has migrated from the State of origin to some other State for the purpose of seeking education, employment, etc. will be deemed to be a Scheduled Caste/Tribe of the State of his origin and will be entitled

> to derive benefits from the State of origin and not from the State to which he has migrated.[1]

Due to this provision, the most vulnerable and weakest community thus loses all sorts of opportunities. The children are neither entitled to scholarship nor reservation.[2]

Students who are natives of the states are eligible for the scholarship but the process is not easy. Preeti is from Gandhi Colony of Faridabad and has completed her graduation from a government college. She received a post-matric scholarship, which was Rs.14,000 per annum. It was to be electronically transferred to her account. However, many times she could not pay the fees, as the scholarship amount was not transferred on time. On inquiring, the officer would be rude and say that the government has no funds. I hesitated to meet him. The scholarship was handled by a separate teacher, probably an SC, but had been co-opted to middle-class thinking. He would often comment that SC children come to college only for scholarships and not for education. Preeti fervently disagrees and says,

> This is not true, we want to study, we want to take up a respectable job, and we do not want to do our parents' 'unclean' work. However, it is also true that we cannot afford a college education without a scholarship. We keep quiet and tolerate such aspersions as we are helpless.[3]

She added that in the first year, she got Rs. 2,000 to purchase books, but in the second and third years she was not given anything and this affected her studies, as she could not afford to buy books. The attendance record goes to the university and if the attendance is poor, the scholarship amount is reduced and if somebody fails then the scholarship is discontinued. Repeaters do not get a scholarship. Teachers know that we are SC students as they sign our attendance sheet. We have to be regular and perform or else we lose scholarships. Many children dropout because of this reason and many also study for the same reason. There are more SC students in this college. The other castes say that we get admission very easily and the backward castes say that they get more scholarship money than us, they get Rs 400.[4]

---

1. Circular issued by the GoI, Minister of Home Affairs dated February 22, 1985.
2. For details see, Migrant Workers in Sanitation Work: Vulnerabilities of Inter-State Migrants in India, in Labour Migration Post Liberalization Era (eds.) Denzil Fernandes and PO Martin, , Delhi 2019, ISPCK pp. 153-172.
3. Discrimination and Exclusion in Education...Haryana p. 68.
4. Ibid.

The bank also harasses the children and their families. They are made to run around to get the scholarship money. As the families are illiterate and unaware of the banking system, they would often face atrocious treatment. It was shared that the parents had to frequent the bank, losing a day's wage, and children had to miss school. Many would forgo scholarships because of this continuous harassment. According to Mahesh, an active member of an NGO, the policies further exclude the vulnerable groups from education, employment and advancement. He adds, 'Scholarship and free books are of no use, children get it very late, just before the exams.' He said that his niece got admission to a technical institute with a scholarship but during admission, they asked for fees. When she informed the management about the scholarship, they said they had not received any intimation from the government and asked her to pay Rs 40,000, which they could not afford and so she had to give up admission. At the level of public policy, several initiatives have been taken by the government to address social exclusion in education, but in reality, several unofficial factors — the actions of casteist teachers, school management — stop them from gaining access to what they are entitled to.[1]

The case of pre-matric scholarships for the children of those families Engaged in Unclean Occupations is even worse. None of the schools in Bihar and Jharkhand were found to be aware of this scheme. While in other states, where this scheme is known and implemented there are just one or two beneficiaries who appeared in our samples. Those schools that are aware of these schemes say 'Yes, we know and implemented this scheme in our schools but the beneficiary students are unable to produce documentary evidence to avail of this scholarship'. Anyway, the amount of fellowship is just 225 rupees per month for day scholars and 700 rupees per month for hostellers for a period of ten months in a year for students in class I to X. The scholarship amount provided by the government to the SC and ST students is just a drop in the ocean. This amount has neither proved to be an incentive for the students nor is it enough to fulfill their needs. Moreover, due to the castiest attitude of teachers, this scholarship often becomes a way to humiliate the beneficiary student. Narendar Jakhu, a youth belonging to a family engaged in leather tanning in an interview recalled his horrible experience:

> I was in the 9th standard at one government school and at that time Haryana government came out with a policy of scholarships for Dalit students whose family members were engaged in menial/unclean caste-professions like scavenging, leather tanning, etc. The school

1. Ibid p. 68.

> authorities came to our class to prepare the list of such students. But no one stood up except me although there were many Dalit students whose families were still engaged in the 'unclean' profession. The next day, my class teacher who was present when the authorities visited the class, made me stand up in the class and forced me to repeat what my family did for a living. When I told them that we are leather tanners, she started making faces and said in a very humiliating tone, 'You lift dead animals and peel their skins!' After this incident, the attitude of my classmates changed and I was subjected to lots of nasty comments.[1]

The life of scavenging community students is difficult and challenging on campus. The multiple layers of discrimination and exclusion with a stink of poverty and lack of a support system create so many hurdles that very few of them can fight and continue their education. A large chunk of students is bound to discontinue their education, mainly from their middle classes onwards. School education has failed to address issues of self-worth, dignity and livelihoods and therefore undermined students' confidence in education as a vehicle for social mobility.

1. https://roundtableindia.co.in/index.php?option=com_content&view=article&id=2836:narinder-jakhu-i-want-to-motivate-our-students-to-join-universities&catid=119&Itemid=1.

Chapter - 5

Vulnerability and Marginality of Children and Youth

> Educational and occupational attainments are related to the family background rather than talent and ability.
>
> **-Bowels and Gintis**[1]

Stupidity was my innate heritage. Many people were born between the first person in the human race who was biologically my ancestor, but none of them was educated… The result of the lack of education for the generations resulted in their foolishness which filled them with many blind beliefs and stupidity.[2] These opening lines by Professor Tulsiram for introducing himself and his community in his autobiography Murdahiya are enough to understand the innate vulnerability of Dalits who have been outcast from all sorts of mental development and support for centuries. The social and cultural deprivation keeps them marginalized in contemporary times. Data collected from our studies show that children from scavenging communities and other 'unclean' occupational backgrounds are still facing problems at multiple levels. A few of them do not get an opportunity to be admitted in schools, while some get admission but are unable to complete their schooling. There are only a few students who managed to reach college and higher education. Overall, the samples of these studies show that over 15 percent of students never get an opportunity to get admitted in school. In most of the samples, the student dropout rate is as high as 40 percent. This chapter attempts to highlight the background variables that create obstacles for the scavenging communities in achieving success in the field of education.

1. Quoted from M Haralambos& Heald, Sociology: Themes and Perspectives p. 184.
2. Tulasiram, Murdahiya p. 9.

Schooling as an 'Imposed Custom'

The education level of parents in scavenging communities is found to be very low and in many cases, they are essentially illiterate. Therefore, they are oblivious of the meaning of education and its utility. They are unaware of the benefits of education and career prospects and as a result, they do not think of admitting their children to schools. In most cases, because of the pressure either of some drive of the government[1] or in some cases as a trend to follow others, they do admit their children to school. However, admission to schools in such cases has proved to be an 'imposed custom'. This means that the community does not have an inner wish for schooling but is simply following others either due to pressure or as a custom. In such cases, the children equally find this exercise to be meaningless and imposed upon them. There is ample reason for this, as no one in their family, school or elsewhere helps them understand the meaning and importance of schooling. There is a total lack of motivation and support. Therefore, for these children, school going becomes a meaningless exercise and they follow it as a ritual or an imposed custom. On the contrary, the free life of those children and youth of their community who have never been to school or dropout in between inclines the school going children to revolt against the imposed custom of schooling and follow the dropout youths and their lifestyle, which is much more attractive and appealing. Their fashionable and attractive dressing sense, modern haircuts and style and above all their indulgence in pastime activities lure the school-going kids into breaking the imposed custom of school going. As a result, they frequently prefer to remain absent or bunk classes and imitate the lifestyle of their dropout role models. The habit of bunking and absence from schools eventually disrupts their education and results in dropout. This is one of the most common reasons for school dropout among the vulnerable section.

The lack of motivation and guidance both in school and at home or in the community of course plays a prominent role in this. Due to the illiteracy and poor educational status of parents, they are unable to teach their children even in primary classes. The parents are unable to understand scoring and in higher classes, they cannot guide their children to choose the streams of arts, science, and commerce. This badly affects the prospects of children, since the sole responsibility for doing well in school and completing their education lies on their shoulders. The poor educational background of the parents is also responsible for the lack of aspirations in life. This results

1. For instance, *school chaleabhiyan*, where it becomes mandatory for teachers to visit the houses to enroll the children in their schools.

in a kind of aimlessness in the life of the children. There is a lack of goal setting and any dreams or wishes for upward mobility. As observed by an American Sociologist Herbert H. Hyman:

> The kids do not get any support, motivation, and guidance from their parents, as the other students are getting in their homes. The lower-class individuals don't want as much success. He knows he couldn't get it even if he wanted to, and doesn't want what might help him get success.' Thus, the motivation to achieve, whether in school or outside it, will generally be lower for the working class.[1]

School life is anyway not easy for the scavenging community children. As mentioned above, unlike mainstream students, they do not receive any support from their parents. If at all their parents visit the school for parent-teacher meetings, it is almost useless because of their inability to understand the education process. They are completely aloof from the marking system, scoring, etc. The teachers find it uneasy to discuss the progress of their child with the parents. In an interview with a school teacher, she shared:

> We want every student to score good marks. It is a question of our school's reputation. In case a student is not good at studies, we want to guide the parents to repeat his/her board exams session, but the parents at any cost do not like to see their children repeating the same class whether they learn anything or not. Even in the case of assignments, if a child scores lower marks than his previous assignment, it becomes a big issue for parents. For them, their children should score better in each of the consecutive assignments. If the marks are not better than the previous tests, instead of looking into their children's disinterest in studies, they start blaming teachers. Throughout my life (as a teacher) I did not find even a single case where any parent came forward with a request to repeat his child in the same class no matter how weak a student is.[2]

In most cases, the parents hardly participate in parent-teacher meets or other similar activities since they believe that, it is the duty of a teacher to teach students. Once we admit our kid to a school, our responsibility is over.[3]

---

1. American Sociologist Herbert H. Hyman 'The Value Systems of Different Classes.' Referred from Sociology: Themes and Perspectives, Haralambos& Heald, p. 194.
2. Discrimination and Exclusion in Education...Himachal Pradesh, p. 252.
3. One of the common comments appeared in FGDs in all the sample states while data collection.

Therefore, to participate in parent-teacher meets is a burden and 'imposed' exercise on them. If at all they participate in any meetings, due to the lack of awareness and education, teachers find it extremely difficult to explain their views. The teacher further shared:

> In none of the meetings, parents participate. Even if they attend, we cannot discuss their children's performance with them. They are unable to understand the difference between various subjects and the common things like homework, assignments, and projects are not understood by them. The only thing they understand is 'pass' or 'fail'.[1]

When the above view of a teacher was put before a community, the parents replied the same. They said:

> It is true we rarely go to parent-teacher meets etc. We do not understand why teachers call us to show our child's progress. It is their (teacher's) duty to teach our children. We are illiterate (a word frequently used by the community members even if they had primary school education). How can we understand the test and exam system? The copies of mark sheets that are being displayed to us have no meaning to us.

In this blame game, one cannot ignore that there is complete silence on the part of teachers on motivating the students and guiding them for their future. The life of a poor child on campus is like a boat without a sailor. The lethargic attitude of teachers is not an act of simple laziness or negligence, but as has been discussed in Chapter 4 of this book it is a well designed strategy to maintain the status quo in society. The separate schooling system — convent and International schools for the elite class and government schools for proletariat class — especially after the 1990s is a strategic attempt to widen the gulf between rich and poor, which in Indian society is synonymous with forward castes and Dalits. A French sociologist Pierre Bourdieu (1930-2002) has taken a clear stand on this system. He says that a major role of the education system is the social function of elimination.

> This involves the elimination of members of the working class from higher levels of education. It is accomplished in two ways: by examination failure and by self-elimination. Due to their relative lack of dominant culture, working-class students are more likely to fail examinations, which prevent them from entering higher education. However, their decision to vacate the system of their own volition

1. Discrimination an Exclusion in Education...Himachal Pradesh p. 252.

> accounts for a higher proportion of elimination. They know the dice are loaded against them. Their attitudes towards education are shaped by 'objective conditions' and these attitudes will continue 'as long as real chances of success are slim.'[1]

Bourdieu has also coined the term cultural capital, and explains cultural deprivation as one of the causes for the poor class lagging behind in education.

Cultural Deprivation

Every act of a child is a reflection of her family values and culture. Children of better-off families get access to learn soft skills of communication, etiquette, and behaviour. This learning helps them to develop a good image before outsiders and it particularly supports in creating their positive image before the teachers, other school authorities, and fellow schoolmates. These children naturally receive better treatment in their schools and outer world. However, the opposite is true for children of scavenging and allied communities. The parents' poor education and lack of cultural capital result in their inability to teach proper soft skills to their children. This affects the image of children both in school and outside. The lack of etiquette and behaviour affects the prospects of children on campus. These students are branded with a negative image and are unable to develop friendships beyond their community.

The limitation of their acceptance by outsiders is the result of what is called 'cultural deprivation' — a term coined by Bourdieu— who defined it as 'the difference in attitudes towards education between the working and middle classes.'[2] The first aspect of cultural deprivation is intellectual development. He said that working-class parents are less likely to give their children educational toys, books, and other activities that foster thinking and reasoning, due to not being able to afford them or not realising their importance. This affects the intellectual development of the children, possibly resulting in them being disadvantaged when starting school, compared to middle-class children.[3]The cultural deprivation is further accentuated by a lack of a balanced diet which is the result of their poverty. These deprivations affect the development of their brain to a great extent.[4] However, apart from limited intellectual development,

1. Haralambos and Heald, Sociology: Themes and Perspectives p. 216.
2. https://workingclassandachievement.weebly.com/cultural-deprivation.html
3. Ibid
4. Elizabeth L Prado, Kathryn G Dewey, Nutrition and brain development in early life, Nutrition Reviews, Volume 72, Issue 4, 1 April 2014.

cultural deprivation also impacts many other aspects of human life. As mentioned above, the scavenging community students also lack soft skills which hamper extending their friendship beyond their caste-class circle. This equally affects their relationship with their teachers. The dressing sense and mannerisms of the scavenging community children look different from others. The difference in dress is of course again a result of poverty. It is true that in an attempt to bridge the gap between students, the school administration, irrespective of being government-owned or private, follows an essential norm of school uniform for all its students. It is certainly a good measure to reduce the gap between rich and poor. However, in practice, the poor students, despite having similar-looking uniforms, lack proper ironing and washing facilities, making them look shabby and unclean. This results in a visible difference between the two different sets of students. The scavenging community again becomes identifiable for their poor care of school uniforms.

Another visible difference also appears in the form of hygiene habits. Some of the poor class students are not in the habit of having a daily bath and other basic neatness habits. These marked differences also instigate the teacher to behave differently with them. The lack of care and tidiness of the scavenging community students is, however, not for cultural reasons but due to practical problems such as the unavailability of water, and their parents' work hours which start early in the morning and conflict with the start of school hours. The absence of parents in this crucial hour also often results in the late coming of children to school. Sometimes they are also not able to bring their lunch with them and have to remain hungry during school hours. Overall, these students are deprived of adequate care and support. With the introduction of the mid-day meal scheme, at least none of the children remains hungry in the schools. The biggest beneficiaries of this scheme are the scavenging community students. This scheme however has been vehemently opposed by the middle class as they believe that it has resulted in lowering the quality of education in government schools.[1]

Labelling of the Students

A famous philosopher Ralph Waldo Emerson says 'a man is what he thinks about all day long.'[2] Similarly, in recent days Rhonda Byrne,the author of the famous book 'The Secret', said 'If you can think about what

1. This issue is discussed in detail in chapter 4 of this book.
2. https://www.goodreads.com/quotes/541463-a-man-is-what-he-thinks-about-all-day-long

you want in your mind, and make that your dominant thought, you *will* bring it into your life.[1]' Centuries ago, the Buddha equally stressed the power of the mind by saying 'Mind precedes all mental states. Mind is their chief; they are all mind-wrought. If with an impure mind, a person speaks or acts, suffering follows him like the wheel that follows the foot of the ox. While if with a pure mind, a person speaks or acts happiness follows him like his never-departing shadow.'[2] Obviously, the mind plays the biggest role in human development and individual success. However, for the development of the mind to be positive and creative there is a consistent need for motivation and support. This is available in abundance to the children of upper-class families. Their parents, relatives, teachers, friends, and all those who came in their contact are always supportive and motivating them. As a result, they continue the legacy of their parents. However, as discussed in the previous chapters the children of scavenging communities seldom receive any motivation. Instead, they are continuously demoralised and demotivated in the school and elsewhere. The teachers in school do not miss any opportunity to brand them negatively and think them to be worthless in schools. In discussions and interviews with the children across all the sample cities, they responded that 'for us *gadha, ullu, nalayak, nakabil, bewkoof, moorkh* (slangs for stupid) are being used by teachers and classmates.' They are always prone to labelling. The impact of these terms has a long-lasting effect on the children. If we believe the above-mentioned quotations of the Buddha, Emerson and Rhonda Byrne, then there shall not be a doubt that the continuous usage of these negative labels ultimately results in developing negative attitudes towards themselves and they began to feel that they are really stupid and worthless. This further decreases their ability and capacity and eventually, they become so. The impact of labelling on Dalit students however has yet not become a topic of study in Indian academia. However, elsewhere, sociologists studied the impact of labelling on students. For instance, French and American sociologists, Cicourel and Kitsuse said, 'the pupils labelled may lead to further deviance on the part of their attempt to resolve the problems. They may feel being discriminated against and may defiantly respond to deviance by consciously committing deviant acts. Finally, they may seek out others with similar problems, that is those who have been similarly labelled. From their interaction, a deviant subculture may develop, a subculture which, positively sanctions deviance. Those involved will then tend to see themselves in terms of

1. The Secret, p. 9, Atria Books, New York, November 2006.
2. The Dhammapada source: https://www.accesstoinsight.org/tipitaka/kn/dhp/dhp.01.budd.html

the deviant label.'[1] David Hargreaves further explained that'the pupils labelled as troublemakers tended to seek out each other's company and within their own group award high status to those who broke the school rules.'[2] This exactly happened to the scavenging community students in schools, as they used to form a ghetto and there began a competition among them to break the rules and regulations of the schools. Apart from other problems the group of negative-minded students (they are made negative by their teacher by labelling) late coming, bunking class and absenteeism, at last leads to their discontinuation and dropping out of school. If one of their close friends opt to drop out the other friends lose their interest in schooling and they too prefer to discontinue schooling. There is also another reason for it. The students of scavenging families find school unfriendly, therefore, daily school-going is itself challenging for them. However, in the case of their close friendship with students of their socio-economic background, there develops a little hope and support. If for any reason this close friend drops out of school, there is no choice left before another close friend but to discontinue schooling. In most of the discussions with dropout students, this appears to be a responsible factor. Gita of Patna is one such example. She had a close friend, Radha, who discontinued her studies because of some reason. This makes Gita uncomfortable in school. She felt lonely and lost. Recalling this incident, she says

> I was left alone in the school. There was no one in my class with whom I can sit and talk. The teachers, who always make fun of me and my friend Radha, then began to say, "schooling is not for you, we know that you people take admissions in schools but you cannot complete it. You, garbage picker, have less mind. Why you are wasting time in school." Such comments are common in my school. I was feeling depressed and alone. At last, I discontinued my school. I was at least relieved from the tension. I do not know whether education helps the poor or not but schools are certainly not for us.[3]

This is one of the most common background variables of dropout yet this factor cannot be captured in a structured interview format for the reason that the immediate reason in most such cases is loss of interest. Unfortunately, the researchers do not trace the story behind this. The case of Rohini who discontinued her study after 8th class is similar, she said:

1. Sociology: Themes and Perspectives p. 213.
2. Ibid p. 213.
3. Field based information.

> I was studying in Government Girls School, Gaya. I was almost regular in school, but whenever there is any urgency or need at home, I used to stay at home. Going to school was a meaningless exercise for me as the teachers hardly teach in the class. We all girls used to chat in the classroom. This was our daily routine. I used to enjoy this initially but someday later one of my close friends stopped going to school. Thus I used to get bored in school and felt alone in the school. There was none in my school with whom I could talk with ease. I am not saying that I was not having talking relations with others, but it was just a formal relationship. I could hardly share any personal problems or feelings with them. As a result, I became used to sitting aloof in a corner. I can't mix with other students because their behaviour was not cordial to me. It was a very difficult situation and I never faced such loneliness in my life. Therefore, the only way out was to remain absent from school and I stopped going to school. None in my family asked for any reason for this. Ultimately, I dropped out of school.[1]

Class Difference between Teacher and Student

In government schools, the teachers are receiving a good amount of salary. This salary structure draws the middle class and rich people to opt for a teaching job in government schools. This is especially true in cities where the middle class and rich people find this job more comfortable also because this job doesn't demand extra office hours. During fieldwork in the selected sample, it was observed that there were some teachers whose children are studying in Western countries to pursue their higher education. In many cases, the husbands of lady teachers are found to hold good positions in government or private sectors. Overall, the creamy class is predominantly visible in the teaching services.

While on the other side, the striking opposite is the student community in the government schools. They are increasingly ghettoized with students from poor Dalit communities. This sharp difference between teachers and students has resulted in the creation of a vacuum between the two. The language spoken by the teachers and the dialects and slang used by the children is different to such an extent that both of them are unable to understand each other. During teaching, if queries emerged due to linguistic differences or because of their inability to understand the concept. It remains unaddressed. The poor students being unable to clear their doubts emerged in the classroom. Moreover, there is no outside

1. Discrimination and Exclusion in Education…Bihar and Jharkhand, p. 54.

support like a private tutor or seniors available to them where they can clear their doubts. They have no option other than to carry the doubts in their minds. This obstructs them to move further. As the Buddha said that the unresolved doubts are one of the biggest stumbling blocks in achieving success.[1] The doubts thus prove detrimental to the life of the students. The continuous crediting of such doubts in the mind of the children results in a demoralizing effect and dissociates them from school activities. This ultimately results in a loss of interest in education that finally results in their dropping out of school.

Low Accumulation of Pre-school knowledge

In the existing system of schooling, admission to primary school starts at the age of five years in class first. This is considered to be a common starting point for the marathon of education. However, this is merely a belief. There are different starting points for the pupils of different caste-class groups. For a child of a middle-class background, formal education starts with a nursery, which is followed by KG 1 and KG 2. But for a poor student, there are only Balwadi and Anganwadi. In these government-sponsored pre-schools, low-paid and untrained semi-literate Anganwadi workers share the responsibilities of taking care of the kids. On the contrary, in the nurseries and KGs, there are well-educated and Montessori trained teachers. Their teaching skills, knowledge sharing, motivation and support build a solid foundation for the students to get launched successfully in the future field of education. The educational aids, toys and types of equipment used by these children also make education interesting and help in shaping their minds to be more active, alert and sharp. The upper-class students receive equally good treatment in their schools. Therefore, for them, there is little difference between school and home. The language, vocabulary and culture reflecting the upper-class cultural values are common at both places. Moreover, the love and care from the teachers and other school authorities develop a sense of bonding. The wide range of peers from similar class-caste backgrounds gives more confidence and develops attachment towards schooling. These factors contribute to ensuring their daily presence in the school. Therefore, they enjoy their school life. There is no question of absence and dropping out for them. However, the opposite is the case of poor Dalit students that lead to their apathy towards school and their foundation remains weak. In this regard, Bourdieu rightly said that 'the success of all school education

1. According to the Buddha, doubt is one among the five hindrances that are sensual desire, ill will, sloth, restlessness, and doubt.

depends fundamentally on the education previously accomplished in the earlier years of life.'[1] This early education is abundantly available to upper-class children but the poor are deprived of it.

The absence of pre-schooling for poor children results in a shaky and poor foundation for handling the load of education in the future. They find it difficult to understand the teaching in the classroom due to the lack of preparation. It is no surprise that, if at all these pupils get a chance to be admitted to elite private schools under the RTE Act, they struggle to cope because the starting line for their education is markedly much behind compared to the mainstream students. Meanwhile, in government schools, well-known issues such as poor teacher-student ratio, involvement of teachers in various governmental surveys and duties, poor infrastructure and above all, insensitivity towards students and prevailing caste prejudices on campus tend to hamper the bonding between the poor students and schooling.[2]

Lack of Sharing of School Issues in the Family and Vice-versa

Sharing is one of the easiest ways of releasing tension. It also helps in making relations strong. The prerequisite of sharing is mutual trust and the ability to understand the sharer's issue. In the case of children of the mainstream community, it is easy for them to share school issues in their homes. This sharing not only helps in removing school tensions but also helps them in getting suggestions to overcome problems and to get motivated for education. However, the opposite is the case of students of the scavenging community. The low education level of their parents puts a hurdle before them to communicate with them the school events. Unlike the mainstream children who can share their difficulties, achievements, joys and failure in their families, the children of the sanitation worker community have to keep all the school issues to themselves. Their parents, being illiterate, do not understand the meaning of grades in exams such as A+, B, C, etc. The one thing that they understand is 'pass' or 'fail', which in the modern educational system hardly has any meaning. Therefore, the students are unable to share their performance with their parents whether they are doing well in school or not.

Even in case of any humorous or joyous moment of school, the community children are unable to share with their parents, as they cannot understand even humour or joke. A primary student of Shimla narrated

1. M Haralambos& Heald, Sociology: Themes and Perspectives, p. 216.
2. These issues are discussed in details in chapter 8 of this book.

such a case to me. He said that once a teacher asked in our class the name of our country. 'To which a student whose village was Mandi immediately stood up and answered 'Mandi.'[1]In the whole class,there was laughter as it was known to all that the name of our country is India. This incident becomes such a matter of laughter that they even shared it with their families. But when I shared this incident with my parents, they remained silent. Because for them it was not at all a strange answer but it was a correct answer as in their view country means the village. This is the level of understanding of my parents. How can I share any moments with them?' The poor Dalit students cannot share any matter of laughter, joke or a serious matter with their parents or the matter of choice of the stream of Science, Arts and Commerce after the 10th class. Apart from the lack of understanding by the parents, there is one more reason for the non-sharing of school issues. This is because of the busy schedule of the parents. Moreover, the lifestyle and culture of the scavenging community are so different from the mainstream that they cannot share these happy and sad moments with their mainstream classmates. Thus, the scavenging community students also remain aloof in the schools and have to keep their school life and home life strictly separate which ultimately results in a 'lack of interest'. Finally, the discontinuation of school is the easiest way out for them.

The lack of sharing is two-sided, the parents also do not like to share their struggles and difficulties with their children. In the city of Sagar, in an interview, a Head Cashier of a reputed bank shared how he began his career as a Sweeper in the same branch but with his continuous efforts cleared the departmental exams and ultimately reached the position of Head Cashier. He shared that after clearing his first exam of the cashier, he was transferred to a branch of a neighbouring town. He said, "It was the joyous and happiest moment of my life. I never dreamt before that I could become a clerk or cashier in the bank for I used to think that sweeping is my job. However, when I went to join the new branch the ugly truth of discrimination appeared before me. I faced a bit of trouble in the new branch but the bigger problem is that no one is ready to rent me a place to stay because of my caste."

When asked whether he shared this experience with his children. He said, 'no I do not want to expose the ugly truth of caste discrimination to them. His son, who completed his BE, is jobless and has taken admission in B. Lib. Course, is aloof about social awareness. The community in

1. Mandi is a town in Himachal Pradesh

general lacks sharing in the family and is unable to link their struggles with the life and struggle of Dr. Ambedkar as it is a culture of Ambedkarite-Dalits where the personal struggles are always related to the experience of their great leader. Due to the lack of inspiration and motivation within the family and community, using Dalit icons also played an equal role in diverting their attention from education. The families, in general, are found to be defunct, where sharing between family members is missing. The struggles and achievements of both parents and children become an individual experience.

Need to Engage in Earning Activities

The poor earnings of parents create a lot of problems for the children. To share the burden of their parents in fulfilling the basic needs of the family, children are bound to engage in income-generating work at a tender age. There are many options for them such as working in hotels, assisting in bicycle or mechanical repair shops, and so on. However, the easiest available work for them is rag-picking which is again 'unclean' work in the eyes of majoritarian society. The students involved in it face double disadvantages. Firstly, due to their direct involvement in an 'unclean' occupation, they are treated as untouchables by their peers and teachers. Secondly, the task of rag-picking also results in late coming or being absent from school. This is because, on many occasions, the kids have to go to work early in the morning which is also their school time. Often when there is any event or special call to collect the garbage, the concerned child has to attend to the task or face a financial loss. These factors again disrupt their studies and the ultimate outcome is their discontinuation and dropping out. Mohit a student of class 6th in Korba, Chhattisgarh narrated:

> My father is working on a contract in Nagar Nigam. My mother is also working as a Sweeper. None of them has permanent employment. Our family income is so low that we are unable to meet our family expenses. As a consequence, I am bound to seek income. I have started working in the garage as an assistant. I did not have any experience but my master was kind enough to provide me with an opportunity. I used to earn two thousand rupees a month. I was happy with it. However, I was just a part-time worker. I have to be in school for the other half. A few days later my mechanic got a full-timer boy who used to work for the whole day on a similar wage. As a result, he asked me to discontinue my work. Now I am engaged in rag-picking. This work is comparatively manageable with schooling. Though, I

have often been late in reaching the school. Sometimes when I get more work I have to remain absent from school.[1]

In most cases, the children are bound to discontinue schooling and drop out for the sake of earning. As mentioned, these students also face discrimination in their school on account of their part-time occupation which is considered 'unclean' and filthy by others. Rohit, a student of 9th class in Shimla narrated his story:

> I used to help my parents with their work in cleaning drains and sweeping streets. One day my classmates saw me doing this work. Then after that they began to tease me in school by saying *'jo sadak pe Bhangi hain wo school main kaise sangi hai'* (One who is Sweeper in the street, how he can be our companion in the school). They made me feel very disappointed. I broke down. But I consoled myself and went to them and asked, 'Is it not a duty of a child to help his parents?' I was not sure that this would change their hearts but to my surprise, those students realized their mistake and started behaving well with me.[2]

Shimla and Solan in Himachal Pradesh are found to be relatively more liberal in caste practices than the rest of India.[3] This is probably why Rohit gets acceptance among his peers. However, the students involved in scavenging elsewhere are not so lucky and remain excluded by their classmates.

Impact of Parents' Involvement in Hazardous Occupations

It is often believed that with the enactment of Prohibition of Employment as Manual Scavengers and their Rehabilitation Act 2013, manual scavenging is banned in India. However, this is not true. Firstly, while there are many states, Himachal Pradesh for instance, which have declared zero presence of manual scavengers; it is true only on paper. There are a noticeable number of manual scavengers in this state but for reasons best known to administrators, they are not listed as such. Secondly, this Act has not banned manual scavenging but has only restricted it with some rules and regulations. Practically speaking this work is prohibited nowhere. Even manual cleaning of septic tanks, which requires entry of a scavenger into a tank filled with human excreta as deep as 10-20 feet, is not

1. Field-based information from Korba, Chhattisgarh.
2. Discrimination and Exclusion...Himachal Pradesh pp. 264-265.
3. See, Discrimination and Exclusion in Education. Uttar Pradesh, Rajasthan, Himachal Pradesh and Haryana.

prohibited under this Act; rather it is allowed with a few safety measures. In practice, even safety gear is not provided to manual scavengers. This work is performed in broad daylight without any fear of punishment for those responsible from any authority.

It has also been observed that coal fields, SECL (South Eastern Coal Fields Limited) Korba for instance, are issuing tenders for cleaning septic tanks. The railways continued to be one of the biggest employers of manual scavengers despite the passage of the Act and the introduction of bio-toilet facilities for the simple reason that leakages and poor fittings routinely result in dirt on the tracks. As already discussed in one of the previous chapters, the common habit of throwing *bidis*, cigarettes, tobacco pouches, and matchsticks into the bio-toilets also creates problems for sanitation workers. Further, the widespread lack of civic sense, which results in spitting, urination, and even defecation in some cases is equally responsible for making railway tracks filthy. There is no mechanical solution available for cleaning the tracks and manual scavenging continues to be engaged.

In urban areas, door-to-door garbage collection is often the responsibility of Municipal Corporations but sometimes remains with private garbage collectors. In both cases, it results in manual scavenging. The collection of garbage in the case of private services results in holding the garbage overhead or on the shoulder in a carry bag. In an interview, a garbage collector in Shimla shared 'earlier we used to carry human waste on our heads but now we are carrying the dirt, often human shit, on our shoulder.'[1] Seepage in these bags exposes the workers to direct contact with house waste, which in some cases also includes kids' excreta, menstrual waste, and other filth. In the case of ownership of this task by the municipality, which often uses a mechanical vehicle for collecting garbage, the matter, however, doesn't end with collection. The disposal of all the collected waste at the mass disposal site requires a prior classification in bio-degradable and non-degradable types. This exercise needs manual intervention for the reason that it directly needs the involvement of hands in separating these types of wastes. Further, whenever there is garbage dumped at any place it becomes difficult for the garbage collector to clean

1. In the hilly region garbage vans cannot be used easily therefore carrying the garbage on the shoulder is more common. This is also common elsewhere in plain areas, where door-to-door garbage collection takes place. In this case also the garbage collector has to put the garbage bag on his shoulder until he disposes of it in his cart. However, in hilly tracts, in most of the cases, the garbage bag remains on the shoulder of the worker until he reaches the dump station.

up. Even at the disposal centres, when garbage heaps up, they jump on it for flattening it. In both these activities, the broken pieces of glass and sharp metals including blades and knives often injure the workers' feet and hands badly. Cleaning open drains or smaller septic tanks is equally disgusting and risky. In all sorts of manual scavenging, skin disease is very common. The hands of manual scavengers become infected to such an extent that the outer layers of skin erode permanently and the delicate pink inner layers of skin are exposed. This skin is so light and thin that an infected person cannot have a handshake with others.[1] Thus, the scavenging work turns one into an untouchable permanently.

Quite naturally the family members of such workers, especially their children, face exclusion and discrimination in society. The teachers and wider student community being part of the same society observe the same customary practices of exclusion and discrimination on campus against the children of manual scavengers. Apart from the psychological and religious and customary discriminations met in school life, the biggest shock in many instances is the death of their fathers. This is often the result of diseases or regular liquor intake. The underlying reason, in either case, is their involvement in manual scavenging. A death in the family, especially of the parents, results in the children dropping out of school.

Poor Health of the Children and Parents

The youth of the community engaged in scavenging are known for their muscular figure and rowdiness. In many cities, the most notorious elements are believed to be men of this community. Pork, being the well-known staple diet of the community, adds weight to the belief in the physical strength of the youth. However, these beliefs proved to be just a myth. Many cases of malnutrition were visibly observable, and it is a common ailment in the scavenging community. In a study by Beck and Darokar (2005), the common diseases that they reported to have suffered include (a) skin disorders, (b) communicable diseases, (c) respiratory disorders, and (d) diminishing vision.[2] It has been observed that, whether pork-eating or otherwise, the community in general and its children, in particular, are weak and lacking in stamina. There are various reasons for this. As discussed in Chapter 3, due to cleanliness drives, pig rearing is increasingly banned in many places, and the scavenging community there no longer has access to pork. Their poor financial situation does

1. This is my personal observation in Solan.
2. See, Avatthi Ramaiah's Health Status of Dalits in India, EPW, October 24, 2015, Vol. I, No. 43.

not allow them to have any substitute and thus the problem of anemia and malnutrition is increasingly becoming common among them. The deficiency is not restricted to children; adults are also generally found to be physically weak. The absence of pork in the diet could be one reason, but the fact is that the community is deficient in a balanced diet anyway, either vegetarian or non-vegetarian.[1] However, another reason for this weakness, as mentioned by one social leader of the community, is the growing habit of drinking. He says:

> I am not sure how liquor affects the upper class, but in the case of our community, the intake of local liquor (regularly and in large quantities) negatively affects our people.[2]

These reasons apart, the primary reason is that those who are directly involved in manual scavenging work and door-to-door garbage collection are always at risk of skin infections and respiratory diseases. A female respondent who works as a Sweeper in the Army cantonment of Shimla describes the situation of manual scavenging in the following words:

> Our boys have to climb down into septic tanks to clean them.... It is true that in some places machines are being used to clean it but even that doesn't solve the problem. The tanks are so full of dirt that even after sucking from the machine, the walls and the top of the tanks remain stuck with human waste. To clean these walls our boys have to get inside the tanks and remove the dirt with their own hands... no gloves or headgears are provided to them.[3]

Such inhuman work directly affects the health of these individuals who are bound to be infected with skin ailments, respiratory disorders, and migraines. Many of these diseases are communicable and easily passed on to family members. The children in the family are thus always susceptible to disease. These infections accentuate their exclusion in schools. Overall their performance in school goes down and also results in absenteeism and dropouts.

Negative Impact of Parents' Occupation

Sanitation work is deemed to be the lowest occupation and this impact the children of those who are involved in it. The parents' engagement in

1. This is well discussed in chapter 3.
2. Discrimination and Exclusion...Himachal Pradesh p. 258.
3. This issue is discussed in detail in Discrimination and Exclusion in Education: A Study of the Children of Household Associated with "Unclean" Occupations of Madhya Pradesh and Chhattisgarh.

public places often breaks the confidence of children and compels them to keep a distance from other students. This results in their absenteeism and dropping out of schooling. We have encountered such cases in almost all the sample cities; one such is the case in Haryana where Rohit, a student of class 7in a private school, narrated:

> My classmates know that my father is in MCF (Municipal Corporation of Faridabad), and they saw my father sweeping the road. I felt ashamed when they told me. I hesitate to mix around freely with others, and my performance has gone down. My father has been called several times to school for cleaning the toilets. The teachers also sometimes call the parents of other children for other work. But the task of cleaning remains with the parents of children belonging to an 'unclean' occupation.[1]

Like Rohit, many other children feel a loss of self-worth when their background is disclosed. It worsens when they are branded as 'poor performers' or 'not fit to study.' This drains their self-esteem and the desire to continue with their studies. One could understand the plight of such children in mainstream society. A Valmiki youth who is active in the politics of Himachal Pradesh says:

> When a child in school sees his father or mother working as a sweeper on a road or Kothi, he feels ashamed. He cannot be normal with his peers at that time. Some of the general students also tease him in such a situation. This affects our children very much. Parents' engagement in sanitation work plays a major role in their dropping out.[2]

The Children of Sweepers Working in Schools

In each school, there is a position of Sweeper to clean the school's premises including toilets. The exceptions are low-budget government and private schools where these daily tasks are outsourced to contract Sweepers. In both cases, when the children of these Sweepers study in the same school, quite naturally these children get branded as the son or daughter of the Sweeper, and thus lose their independent identity. The peers and teachers link them with their parents' occupation, and these children are seen as lowly and unworthy. This is one of the psychological pressures that the children of Sweepers working in a school face. Another problem is of course practical in nature as discussed earlier. The low

1. Renuka Ramanujam, Discrimination and Exclusion...Haryana p. 72.
2. Discrimination and Exclusion...Himachal Pradesh p. 264.

salary or daily wage of the Sweepers, makes it extremely difficult for them to take material care of their families, and as a result, their children suffer.

However, in many cases, one particular benefit is found to be received by the children of these parents. In many states, their children are recipients of the facility of admission under the RTE (Right to Education) Act, without having to bear the admission fee, tuition fee or any other miscellaneous expense of schooling. This Act was introduced in the Parliament to make unaffordable quality education accessible to poor students. I have encountered one such beneficiary in Gaya, where a son of a mother who is working as a Sweeper in the city's elite school was found to be admitted under RTE. This happened because the principal of the schools personally knows the parents hence they find it easy to help them with this provision.[1] One is not sure how far such beneficiary students can access quality education in the long run. Within the limited time of implementation of RTE, its implications are yet to be assessed.

1. See Discrimination and Exclusion in Education...Bihar and Jharkhand p. 171.

Chapter - 6

Triple Discrimination: Caste, Class, and Gender

> A school environment that may be acceptable to boys may be hostile to girls. The physical and sexual violence against women that is common in many societies is reflected in the school environment in a number of countries. Physical abuse and abduction are not only a major violation of girls' basic human rights, but they also present a major practical constraint in getting to school. Parents feel a duty to protect their daughters and may decide to keep them at home if they feel the school is too far away. Violence against girls and women has been identified as a key barrier to girls' education.
>
> **--Department for International Development Report 2005**[1]

The female children and youth of scavenging communities share the problems faced by their male counterparts, but gender-related issues often accentuate their vulnerability. The bane of challenges that emerge both from within the family and the outside world badly affects their prospects. The stigma and poverty of the community is compounded by the inferior status of females in the wider society. The girls are also highly susceptible to sexual violence in the vicinity of dominant castes in their regions. Life, at home or outside, is even more challenging for them than their male counterparts.

The Problem in Accessing Education

As far as school-going kids are concerned, it is somewhat surprising

1. Quoted from a DFID report, 'Girls' Education: Towards Betterment of All. https://www2.ohchr.org/english/issues/development/docs/girlseducation.pdf

that the dropout rate for girls is lower than boys based on data available for the scavenging community students. For instance, a study for Haryana suggests that the total dropout rate is higher among male children (62.2%) and lower for female children (37.8%).[1] In Jharkhand, the male dropout rate is 40% while for females it is 24.7%.[2] In Madhya Pradesh, it is 42% for males and 36% for females.[3]These data points appear to show a positive side of the picture.

However, the reality is the opposite. The reason for lower dropout rates among girls in all the studies is mainly because the girls are married off at a young age. This often results in their migration to a new place. Therefore, such girls cannot become the data in any surveys on educational status. During any data collection on education status, the target of a researcher is children, classified into three categories—ongoing, continuing and dropout or discontinuing education. However, those girls in families, who are married ata younger age and migrate to their in-law's houses, remain out of the scope of research data and they do not become part of a sample. This reality was captured in an FGD with community members in Haryana. The actual percentage of dropouts and discontinuation of girls could be known only when apart from data from unmarried children, women of a certain age group are also taken as the sample of any research on educational status.

Early marriage, and child marriage in some cases, still survives as a common practice among scavenging communities, especially in Haryana, Uttar Pradesh, Rajasthan and other states. This practice affects the prospects of both male and female children. However, in the case of a male, there is a possibility of continuing with the education for the reason that despite financial pressure and family obligations, he remains in the same place – city, town, or village. Therefore, it is easy for him to continue his studies and he is also free from the household chores such as cooking, washing, etc. However, in the case of girls, the burden is two-fold. Firstly, as discussed above, owing to prevailing patriarchal norms she has to move to her in-laws' house after marriage. This automatically breaks her attendance at the school which is located near her parents' home. Secondly, even if she is married off in the same city and vicinity, the household chores of taking care of her in-laws, homemaking, cooking, etc. do not allow her to continue schooling. Above all, the

1. Discrimination and Exclusion in Education…Uttar Pradesh, Rajasthan, Himachal Pradesh and Haryana.
2. Discrimination and Exclusion in Education in Bihar and Jharkhand.
3. Discrimination and Exclusion in Education in Madhya Pradesh and Chhattisgarh.

customary beliefs and patriarchal mindset against female education always puts barriers before girls, especially in those communities that do not understand the importance of education. Early marriage ruins all possibility of continuation of education and results in dropping out of school or discontinuation of study. During my fieldwork, I met Ranjana, a fifteen year old girl in the Samalkha village of Haryana. She always used to be a topper in her class and was very much inclined towards education. However, she shared:

> In our settlement, early marriage is very common. I wanted to study more and get into higher education. I always dream of becoming an officer but I know that my parents will hardly allow me to study for one or two more years. I am saying so because it is our prevailing custom. You cannot see even a single college-going girl in our community.

The above comment also proved to be statistically correct as in our sample from this village we did not get a single college-going girl.

Dowry

The problem of child marriage and early marriage is however restricted to a few states only but the custom of dowry is quite popular among the scavenging communities across the states. In most cases, it is claimed that this does not result from a demand from the bridegroom's family but is more a token of love for the beloved daughter from her parents. A decade or two ago, a motorbikewas a much more popular dowry item apart from the other relatively expensive household items. However, in recent years, it has been replaced with a car. The newlywed couples with dowry become an owner of a four-wheeler irrespective of whether a parking facility is available to them or not. Only extremely poor families are unable to gift a car or motorbike in their marriages, but even in these cases, dowry in other forms is quite high. A senior activist of Safai Karmachari Andolan (SKA), shared:

> The girl's parents are so keen to give four-wheelers as dowry that they do not even bother whether there is any space for parking available in the bridegroom's house or not!... In many cases, poor and unemployed men were given cars but they did not even have space to park, leave aside their ability to maintain it. They have no choice but to keep it in the open near their small house or park it at some friend's house. Whether the poor man has money for fuel is not the concern of the girl's family. But in any condition, this man is not allowed to

sell this (because the girl's family will not let him do so) as it is a gift marking the prestige of the girl's family.[1]

In Jabalpur, we observed one more evil custom related to marriage: a married sister of the bridegroom also has the right to claim any item from the dowry of her brother. In some cases, the greed of the sister creates trouble in the marriage, and she even demands the most expensive items such as a motorbike or car which often results in a family feud.

Nevertheless, in the dowry custom, the girl's family feels proud in gifting the car and other expensive items. In reality, this affects the position of a girl within the family since she is always considered a burden. In their eyes, she is *parayadhan* (other's property). This evil custom affects the education of a girl child since parents, instead of investing in their daughter's education, prefer to save money for her marriage.

Inheritance of Manual Scavenging

It is more challenging for girls to break the caste rules. In many cities the task of manual scavenging transfers from mother-in-law to her daughter-in-law. Irrespective of fact whether the daughter-in-law has any experience of this task or not. In many instances, the daughter-in-law, who even if totally unaware of this task, is forced to engage in manual scavenging. Women's participation in sanitation work, however, in all the sectors is at par with their male counterparts. Yet, some of the tasks, for instance, cleaning of septic tanks by entering inside them, are indeed male-centric. But the effect of these occupations in the form of skin diseases and other health disorders are not restricted to males but almost equally shared by the family members. Yet there are some exceptions however, in both cases, wives of the scavengers are prone to skin diseases and other communicable diseases. The bigger impact on their lives, however, occurs with the death of a male relative in the sewerage. This is irreparable damage to their personal life. In such a case, the responsibility of the family suddenly falls on the shoulder of the woman. In the absence of any option of occupation, the easiest available source of income in most such cases is to perform the work on behalf of regular sanitation workers but at much lower wages. This option is often available to them as a proxy worker in place of a regular sanitation worker employed in the government sector. Much against common knowledge that the dominant caste persons when they get into permanent service of sweepers in government sectors do employ scavengers from traditional scavenging communities, it is

1. Discrimination and Exclusion in Education…Madhya Pradesh and Chhattisgarh, p. 114.

equally true that a large number of Sweepers employed as permanent staff do follow the same system by employing the vulnerable persons such as young widows in their place.[1] Anyway, in case of the sudden death of the father, children's education is affected.

Denial of Admission in Schools

One of the biggest challenges in the life of the girl child is that, in many instances, she is deprived of education. Quite often, girls are not even admitted to school because of household responsibilities and patriarchal values. The parents believe education for girls is unnecessary and wasteful. A girl of fourteen years, who never got the opportunity to enter school narrated:

> My parents collect garbage. Father sometimes also does the work of cleaning. I also used to collect garbage. My family has financial problems. I used to look after my house when my parents used to go to collect garbage. I also used to babysit my younger siblings. My parents never sent us to study, never got us admitted to the school. When I was 7 years old and told my mother that I also wanted to study, she asked what I would do after studying? Girls in our community are not allowed to study and also in my family girls do not study.[2]

A Dom caste girl Julie Kumari was in tears while narrating her story. She once used to go to school with other girls of the Dusadh caste but discontinued her education. She shared that nobody in her family supported her in school going. Even her maternal grandparents never wanted to let their children study. She said:

> My parents opposed and beat me. They used to ask me what I would do after studying. They said it is better if I collect some garbage instead, so that we earn some money at least. Today if someone asks me to read and write our name, I feel very bad. I cannot even write my name. Whenever I have to visit a doctor, I cannot read the board hung outside the clinics to find the right doctor. I ask other people what is written and then I go.[3]

Patriarchal values among the victims' families are not the only cause that restricts them from being admitted to schools. There is ample evidence that even if parents try to admit their daughters in schools, the

1. See Chapter 7 'Challenges Within the Community' of this book for details.
2. Discrimination and Exclusion in Education…Bihar and Jharkhand, p. 60.
3. Ibid. p. 60.

school authorities deny them admission. As discussed in the previous chapter, in the state of Bihar, it is not uncommon to deny admission to poor Dalit students, both girls and boys.

The Problem of School-going Girls

In many parts of the country, there are girls being admitted to schools. But they are also burdened with the responsibilities of the family. In this tussle, education becomes secondary while household responsibilities become their main liability.

Household Chores

The children, both female and male, of the poor community have a set of responsibilities on their young shoulders. This is anobligation as their parents are engaged in various income-generating activities both at normal times and at odd hours. The boys in the family are seen bringing ration, firewood, and other necessities for the home. On many occasions, these activities disturb their study at home. However, for girls, there is a lot more trouble. In most households cooking and other household activities become their daily responsibility. This is more so because the mother of the family has to leave home for work at cooking time. Cooking in almost every household with female members is a female-centric responsibility. Washing utensils and clothes, sweeping and cleaning are also established feminine household tasks, and in all these tasks, the involvement of daughters is usually higher than the mother. With these responsibilities draining a lot of their time and energy, the girl children cannot concentrate on their studies and eventually drop out of school.

Sibling care

As said earlier, the work participation rate of women in sanitation work is quite high. Therefore, the responsibility of taking care of younger siblings in most of the cases becomes the prime responsibility of the elder sister. In the case of a newborn, the responsibility becomes her burden. In the beginning, the elder daughter tries to manage the responsibilities with the discontinuation of her classes and attempts to manage both school and household chores. Soon, however, caring for the newborn sibling becomes her full-fledged responsibility. Even during the day time, she is bound to take care of her younger siblings with the continued absence from school, and this eventually leads to her dropping out of school. The matter doesn't stop here as an individual case because such dropouts of girls are a trend in the community. This practice became an established norm in the scavenging communities and all families follow the same model. The sacrifice of the eldest girl in the family is the outcome of the lack of family planning by parents, and lack of resources for alternative childcare arrangements. This badly affects the career prospects of elder siblings in general and girls in particular.

One such case is of Ravina, the eldest among three siblings. Her father and mother both are working as contract workers in the Municipal Corporation. The total family income is between Rs. 5000-7000 per month. Apart from this, they earn some amount through piggery, but this earning comes only once or twice a year. Ravina's school was not far from their home. She left school because she had to take care of her younger sister as both her mother and father were working and there was no elder person at home to look after the younger kid. Initially, it was not a planned step to disband the studies, but a one-day absence from school as requested by her mother later became a regular exercise. The continued absence from school and discontinuation ultimately led to her dropping out of school. She said:

> I never thought that I would drop out of school. Both parents had to leave the house early in the morning and I had a newborn sister… Neither of the parents was able to take care of her as they were going out to work. It was thus my responsibility to take care of Gudiya (younger sibling). This became a regular practice which ultimately led to my dropping out of school. However, my other friends were regular in school, but I know that many of them also sooner or later left school for the same reason.[1]

A similar reason for dropout emerged during an interview with Raju Manjaria, a father of five children (two daughters and three sons). He is a contract worker engaged in the cleaning of chambers and drains. He said:

> My wife was also working in the Municipal Corporation. There was no one at home to take care of household chores. I admitted my daughters to schools and they were regular in attending. Our family income was very low and I got into debt. Further, when my son was born it became an additional responsibility for us. My wife had to leave home early in the morning. Therefore, my daughters used to take care of my son. This resulted in their absence from the schools that ultimately led to their dropping out of school.[2]

1. Discrimination and Exclusion in Education…Madhya Pradesh and Chhattisgarh p. 110.
2. Ibid. p. 109.

In a few exceptions, there are cases where an elder brother has dropped out of school due to the responsibility of newborn siblings in the family. However, it is much more common in the case of the elder sister, where the household chores and responsibilities of her siblings become her sole responsibility. In general, the female child becomes the victim.

Unavailability of Sanitation Facilities and Health issues

Poverty is the main cause of weakness and poor health in the community. It is further amplified by the limited space and absence of sports facilities and other recreational activities. The poor health and frequent occurrence of fever and other ailments result in absence from school. In the case of girls, menstruation is an added trouble. Brighouse and Unterhalter have noted how the lack of toilets and water in schools has a greater impact on girls' attendance.[1] Schools lack toilets and sanitation facilities and hence there is no private space for them to change the napkin. The body aches and weakness during these days also compel them to remain absent during this duration. In interviews with school-going girls, a common response is 'During *bimari*(menstrual period) I do not go to school.' In almost all the Hindi-speaking states, the girls prefer to use *bimari* or *tabiyatkharabhona* as a code or an expression for the menstrual cycle.[2]

The toilets, if there are at all, are poorly constructed, improperly maintained and lack water supply. These could somehow be used for urination perhaps but cannot be used for any other purpose. In the interviews with boys, most of the respondents claimed to urinate in open places rather than in the toilets due to their improper maintenance. In some cases, it is thought of as a show of manliness by them. For girls, there is no question of showing off by urinating in the open. However, the female investigator responded that 'urination in the open is equally common among girls because the toilets in schools are dirty and unusable. There is no water facility and maintenance. Urination in the open thus becomes more hygienic than using the dirty toilets.' In all the schools, there are separate toilets for teachers. During our visits, it was observed that these toilets are often kept locked to ensure that they could not be used by the students.

1. Brighouse, Harry&Unterhalter, Elaine. (2010). Education for primary goods or for capabilities?. 10.1017/CBO9780511810916.009.
2. In my initial discussion, I was not able to decode the meaning of this phrase but a female field Investigator assisting me in data collection, expressed the meaning of this code to me.

Apart from the lack of infrastructure, the taboo on menses is an added trouble for the girls. A student in Dhanbad narrated her sorrow:

> At that time I used to have severe stomach cramps. I did not go to school for two days. But when I resumed going to school, because of the bad condition of the washroom we had many problems. I thought that from next month I will take leave for five days. Time passed, I did not go to school for five days and when I resumed going to school the boys had deciphered the reason for my missing school. The boys started shaming me for my condition in front of other boys and girls. I was in tears and went on to complain to the teacher. The teacher called me with my parents to school the next day and also called the boy with his parents. After coming back home, I explained the situation to my mother and she stood by me. She told my father about this and he also agreed to go to school with us the next day. The next day I reached the school with my parents on time. The boy did not bring his parents. The teacher talked to me and my parents while maintaining a distance, and also scolded the boy. The teacher warned the boy and said if the complaint comes again he will be thrown out of the school. And the teacher blamed me for this problem in front of my parents, saying that I came to school all dolled up. Listening to all this, I and my friends did not feel good.[1]

Poverty also constrains the girls from using sanitary pads, which forces them to stay at home during the menstrual period. The schools have no provision for the distribution of sanitary pads to girls even in case of emergency. All these motivate the girls to remain absent from school, and such discontinuity often results in them becoming dropouts.[2]

Eve-Teasing and Sexual Violence

In Chapter 4, we reported a disgusting incident at a school in Madhya Pradesh where two women teachers of dominant castes forcibly stripped two girls in a classroom in front of male students. This is one of the reported incidents, but such cases are common on various occasions. There are reports in the media where male teachers were found to be guilty of molestation and forcible sexual acts against the girl students. During the field survey, my team, however, did not hear of such acts. One of the reasons is that the victims in many cases experience depression and do not feel at ease in sharing such experiences. However, a study

1. Personal Interview conducted by field investigator in Dhanbad.
2. Sevanti Patel, Tribal Girl Education: Prospects and Problems, Women's Link,Indian Social Institute, New Delhi, January-March 2007, pp. 32-33.

conducted in Tripura by Sibnath Deb and Kerryyann Walsh shows that, in their sample of 160 girl students, 29 or 18.1 % of girls faced sexual violence or molestation.[1]

The reported cases of molestation in our study were outside the campus, on the way to and back from school. This is quite common in Haryana, which is a state infamous for rape and atrocities on Dalits. Many girls complained that they feel unsafe while going to school as the dominant caste Jat boys are always ready to create a nuisance for them. The parents also believe that it is not safe to send girls to school after puberty. Some boys wait outside the girls' school, to follow and tease the girls when they head home after school. Such incidents are commonplace.[2]

A Dalit girl living in Manana village of Samalkha district complained, '*Ghar se bahar nikalte hi Jat ladke mujh echedte hain, main school se waapi saat ihun toh mera raasta rokte hain.* (As soon as I leave my house, Jat boys eve-tease and verbally harass me. On my way back from school, they block my way)'.[3] In a discussion with a scavenging women's group, a woman said:

> It is not safe to send girls to school after puberty. The boys wait outside the girls' school; they follow and tease the girls after the school gets over and they trouble them on the way. Many such incidents have occurred.[4]

Safety concern of girl is shared also by a District Education Officer of Panipat:

> The parents are reluctant to send their girls to school because of safety reasons, especially grown-up girls. There are lots of complaints about girls being teased on their way back from school. The fathers and brothers are therefore not in favour of sending their girls/sisters to school. They fear that if something happens to them, the family will get a bad name.[5]

However, the lack of safety for girls is not an issue restricted to Haryana. The other states also reported such incidents in their localities. For instance, in Karnataka, Sowmyalatha, a 14-year-old girl child from

1. https://journals.sagepub.com/doi/10.1177/0143034311425225
2. Discrimination and Exclusion...Haryana p. 59.
3. Baseline survey of CRY 2014 referred fromExclusion and Discrimination... Haryana p. 32.
4. Ibid, p. 60.
5. Ibid, p. 74.

the Mera community was one such victim. In her case, it was the male teachers in the school who took advantage of her, leading to her dropping outof school.

> I had been tortured a lot because of the caste I belong to. I had a lot of pain and frustration. I discussed all the issues at home with my parents. They started weeping. The only thing that they then said to me is that not to go to school.[1]

In most such cases, the poor parents feel helpless and lonely. They do not have support from anyone to challenge the culprit teachers. The culprits on the other hand are very confident because of the vulnerability of poor Dalit girls. The sexual attacks on both girls and boys are directly impeding their education. However, due to a lack of material evidence in many cases, they go unreported and unpunished. Both reported and unreported incidents of sexual violence result in the discontinuation of studies and dropouts.

Unavailability of Schools for Higher Classes

In some instances, students are forced to discontinue their studies because of the unavailability of girls' schools for higher classes. Phoola, a girl from Mastipur, Bodhgaya is one such example. She is the eldest of five siblings.She has three younger brothers and one sister. She discontinued her study after Class 8. She says,

> I did my schooling at Mahabodhi School but I was also admitted to a government primary school. The reason for this is that Mahabodhi School was not recognized by the government so I took admission in a government school to get a mark sheet and transfer certificate. I rarely attended the government school but was a regular in Mahabodhi School. My school was very good; we had cultural events, sports day and other celebrations besides study. I participated in dance and singing competitions. The school was not charging any fees and I used to get uniforms from the school. I did not get textbooks from the school but this was not an issue since I used to get this from my government school. However, there was often a delay in supply but I was not alone who was facing this problem, there were a lot of other students who too were facing this problem. We used to get full cooperation from the teachers. Most of the students are from the same or similar caste and occupational background. I have a friendship with all. My parents wanted me to be admitted to another school

1. Exclusion and Discrimination in Education: A study of Southern States p. 67.

after 8th class as this was the highest class in Mahabodhi School. My mother even took me to Government Girls School to admit me in 9th class. But the teacher informed us that the date of admission is over. We were late in going there because my family went to attend a marriage ceremony of my close relative in a neighbouring village. When we came back, the time of admission was over. The teacher, while refusing my admission on grounds of late admission, however, said that in the next session admission is possible provided I submit the form before the due date. However, since my parents are illiterate and hard workers they do not get time for my admission in the next session. I too became more relaxed and was involved in household chores. It is especially my responsibility to take care of my younger siblings, therefore, I also dropped the idea of getting admission. As a result, I discontinued my education after 8th class.[1]

The unavailability of schools for higher classes is more prominent in Bodhgaya. The children get free and quality education until their secondary classes from the Buddhist missionary schools but since most of these schools have classes only up to secondary, they discontinue their studies afterwards.

Discrimination and untouchability on campus

Students from the scavenging community are almost routinely subjected to discrimination in schools. We have discussed these cases earlier in this book, particularly in Chapter 4. However, some specific cases against girls also came up during data collection. In a focus group discussion with the girls in Haryana, we were told that children from scavenging occupational backgrounds were restricted in opting for popular subjects and they were given unpopular subjects like home science. Jyoti from Class 9 shared that she wanted to opt for Computer Science, but the teacher told her that the seats were filled already. There are around twenty girls from the scavenger colony but none is enrolled in computer science. Members of this group are humiliated precisely because they are from scavenging community. 'We are considered dull and slow learners by the teachers and are therefore not given the course of our choice.'[2]

The girls of other communities do not behave properly with children from scavenging occupation households. Referring to the attitude of dominant caste girls, the Valmiki girls of Haryana shared:

1. Discrimination and Exclusion in Education…Bihar and Jharkhand p. 59.
2. Discrimination and Exclusion...Haryana p. 70.

> They are rude; they do not help in work or share notes. They are arrogant and think that they are better than us.They also make fun of our Valmiki Diwas and the procession. We are made to feel inferior. We do not like to tell others in the class about our parents' occupation, as we also do not like our parents' work.[1]

Within the student community, the scavenging community faces much exclusion. This becomes more acute among girls for two reasons. First, compared to males, the psychology of socio-religiosity is found to be dominant among females. This obligates the dominant caste girl to practice untouchability against Dalit girls. Such feeling is not as dominant amongst the males, therefore, the friendship across caste lines including fraternity between forward-castes and scavenging caste students is sometimes prevalent if not often observed on the campus. For instance, a Valmiki student of Sagar narrated that he has friends from all castes and he shared a close friendship with Brahmins. Similarly, there is a Valmiki boy in Solan who has comfortable relations with his Brahmin classmates. However, in both these cases, the Valmiki boys know their limits and seldom visit the homes of their Brahmin friends. In some cases, however, the Valmiki boys also shared that their Brahmin and other forward castes friends do not hesitate to eat food and snacks in their home but do not invite the Valmiki boys home as their parents are not as liberal as they are. Anyhow, in most cases, commensality is not a big issue among males. However, among the girls, this is still a strictly surviving feature. In none of the interviews, any scavenging caste girl shared that they have visited the homes of the forward castes or shared food with them.

The second reason for the conflict and strict bordering on caste lines amongst girls is the pattern of admissions. The boys tend to be separated on caste lines in the choice of schools - forward caste boys are mostly in private schools while the poor Dalit boys are mostly in government schools. This trend, observed more prominently in Haryana, restricts the inter-caste relations among the boys. However, as we have already discussed, the middle-class parents of dominant and forward castes do not prefer to invest equally in girls' education and tend to admit their daughters in government schools which cater to all classes of students, including a large number of Dalit girls. As a result, girls' schools in most of the cases, especially in Haryana, have become more heterogeneous and inclusive in terms of admission. The negative aspect of this mixing is that the scavenging girls in these schools are more prone to caste-based victimization by their peers.

1. Ibid, p. 70.

In certain government schools, when children reach school, they are made to clean the class, wash utensils, etc. The parents ask a basic question: how can a child feel like studying when she is made to do cleaning work the moment she enters school? Most of her enthusiasm is lost by the time the teacher starts to teach. There are cases in government schools where the teachers arrive late, around 11 am, and begin to check students' uniforms, nails, shoes, etc. If a child is shabbily dressed, the teacher sends her back home to take a bath and by the time the student returns the school day is mostly over.[1]There are some instances of a regular practice, where the teachers do not hesitate to assign the task of cleaning toilets to the scavenging community girl students.

There is also a practice in some schools where the students of scavenging castes are asked to bring their own plates for the mid-day meal. The humiliation is not restricted to the student community.The same was observed among teachers as well if at all there is any teacher from the scavenging caste. They too feel the humiliation. Sunita Nidania, a government teacher in Alwar said, *sab nafrat kartein hain* (everybody hates us), and narrated:

> Once my colleague pointed a finger towards a student from the scavenger community who had come shabbily dressed to school, and said *'haathlagane ko bi man nahikartainkebacchon ko' (*do not even feel like touching their children). I understood that she was referring to my community as unclean.[2]

The caste slur is common in schools. It breaks the confidence of the students and paves the way for their becoming dropouts. Rubi of Bihar narrated her pain:

> I dropped out of school after finishing class IV, the main reason for which was that I was called Domni by the students in school. On winning any competition in school, I would get beaten up by the students and they would snatch the prize. During the mid-day meal, I would have to bring my plate, and if my plate touched some other student's plate, she would start fighting with me. On complaining to the teacher, she would only scold me. That is why three of us girls from Domkhana dropped out of school together. When we went to another school for enrollment, the school began to ask for the report card. Since I did not have it, I couldn't get the enrollment done in school again. My father also said 'Let it be, if your name is not being

1. Discrimination and Exclusion in Education...Rajasthan p. 116.
2. Ibid. p. 133.

written (as enrolled), then leave it, what will you do with all the education? You have studied till the time your name was there. No need to study more.'[1]

Some girl students shared that in school they are not allowed to drink water from a common tap. One such case was shared by Poonam from Patna.She and her fellow pupils from Domkhana weren't allowed to drink from the only tap installed in the school. If they try to do so, the teachers scold and beat them. Even in the midday meals, Poonam and pupils from lowly castes were forced to sit behind the others. The same pattern of discrimination was also visible during prayer and parade, where pupils from Poonam's cluster were made to stand behind in the queue. The teachers beat and punish the pupils even for minute mistakes, which discourages them from speaking in the classroom. Out of fear of punishment, Poonam didn't go to school at times. Poonam and her fellow pupils from the cluster do not complain to the headmaster, as the headmaster would rather punish the pupils instead of heeding to their complaints. In another case, a girl student Simran reported:

> Students from the Dom cluster, including me, were seated at the back of the carpet by the teachers. Teachers didn't give us any homework. They used to beat us whenever any mistake was made in the class. Once they beat me along with four of my friends and locked us up in the toilet. During the midday meal, four pupils from Dom and Mestar (Mehtar) caste were often made to eat from a single plate, whereas every pupil from other castes used to get a separate plate.[2]

In many schools, the students of scavenger community are asked to clean the classroom and to get involved in menial works. A girl student shares,

> There were 150 children from many castes. But the menial work was assigned only to them coming from Domkhana. In the school, my teacher would make me sweep and clean the school.In fact, he would tell other students in the school, "Make Deepa clean the school. "You clean very well. Your father also does the same work, he too cleans very well". I had thought of changing my school but could not go to another school seeing the economic condition at home. My teachers and friends never behaved properly. The teacher would always ask me to sit at the back during the class and my friends would say that I have not taken a bath and worn clean clothes and I do not look good.

1. Discrimination and Exclusion in Education…Bihar and Jharkhand, p. 54-55.
2. Ibid p. 50.

> The teacher would pick up some issue and beat me with a stick in front of my friends and would teach students from other communities with love and care and would never beat them up. I did not inform my teachers on dropping out. When I told them this at home, they said who will take care of the family, and because of this, they told me that in school the teacher always beats you up, does not want to teach children coming from poor families, so you work and contribute tothe family. Children from our village hence dropped out of school and began to get involved in work, for example, rag picking, masonry and cleaning work.[1]

As we have mentioned in Chapter 4, none of the parents of scavenging communities and poor Dalits are invited to Parent Teacher Meet or on the occasion of any school functions. Simran of Patna, shared that "Our parents were never invited to the parents-teachers meetings. They were invited only once at the Republic Day function. Other than that, they weren't asked. It's been 3 years since Simran dropped out, but her parents haven't made up their minds to enroll her in some other school. Many kids in her cluster have dropped out due to fear of beatings. Moreover, they weren't keen to study. Their interest in studies waned due to disappointment. But you talk to us gently, so now I want to study."[2]

There is no motivation, no support but hurdles are omniscient whether it is family, community, school, or elsewhere. The scavenging community girls face triple discrimination at the intersection of caste, class and gender, and oppression both outside and within the community and family due to customary practices. Being the marginalized among the marginalized, their problems seem insurmountable and it is a struggle for them to stay hopeful. Under these conditions, the few among them who manage to reach higher studies and achieve occupational mobility are miraculous exceptions.

1. Ibid, pp. 52-53.
2. Ibid, p. 160.

Chapter - 7

Challenges within the Community

> A person, whose mind is not free, though he is not in chains, is a slave. One, whose mind is not free, though he is not in jail, is a prisoner. One, whose mind is not free, though he is alive, is dead. Freedom of mind is the proof of one's existence. What is the proof, then, to judge that the flame of mental freedom is not extinguished from a person? To whom can we say that his mind is free? I call him free who with consciousness awake, realises his rights, responsibilities, and duties; he who is not a slave of circumstances, and is always bent upon changing them in his favour, I call him free. One who is not a slave of usage, customs, and traditions, or of the teachings because they are brought down from the ancestors; one whose flame of reason is not extinguished—I call him a free man.
>
> **-Dr Babasaheb Ambedkar[1]**

We have discussed various factors and causes of the marginalization of the scavenging community in the previous chapters, which are important reasons and push factors for their vulnerability. There is not the slightest doubt that if these issues are properly addressed and the State acts in the spirit of the Constitution *that envisages humanitarian and egalitarian values and justice in all its forms,* there will be a substantial change in the situation. However, due to the lack of social democracy, the philosophy of the Constitution is far from being implemented. Among the scavenging community, the lack of education and awareness further resulted in adhering to those cultural traits, values and social practices which are putting hurdles in the development of the community.

1. Ambedkar in his address 'What Path to Salvation' delivered at Bombay Presidency Conference, 31st May 1936, Bombay. Ref. BAWS Vol. 17, Part III, p. 128.

These values often resulted in opting for them the status-quo ideology. Unlike other Dalits who drew their inspiration from Ambedkar, it is observed that the scavenging community is resistant to change and closed eyes on any revolutionary ideology. The acceptance of Karma philosophy as divine and unchanging which teaches that one is born into a lower caste due to his bad actions in his past lives is well established in their mind. These conservative thoughts are resisting them to accept social change and occupational mobility. During informal interviews when we discuss with them about the pitiable work condition of scavenging and their low treatment in society and put an argument, why are you still continuing with your traditional caste occupation while almost all the other castes left their ancestral occupations, the answer as one logically expects is not lack of opportunity and support but their immediate response is 'if we will not do scavenging who will do?' This straightforward and simple-looking answer is not received in one particular area or city but the answer is the same across all the sample cities from where we have collected our data. The reason for unanimity of shouldering the responsibility of scavenging on their heads irrespective of their language, caste and region is nothing but an invisible string of Karma philosophy which is so deeply rooted in their minds that they all are stitched with a belief that they are born for this task and therefore not susceptible to any change. Therefore, to counter the caste system, whenever any progressive institution or individual opens an employment opportunity in sanitation work for an open category, which is otherwise reserved only for traditional scavenging communities, the first and foremost opposition comes only from the scavenging communities, saying that this is our traditional occupation and cannot be shared with others. However, those castes which are treated as 'pure' and are in the upper level of social hierarchy also come to the forefront to oppose such a move as it happened in Ahmedabad, when the Human Development and Research Centre, issued an advertisement for the posts of sanitation workers stating that preference would be given to general categories. The Rajputs, Muslim Saiyyads and other privileged castes took violent actions to mark their protest.[1] The similar attempt by both opposing groups suggests that the status quo is liked not only by the beneficiaries of the caste system but it is equally wanted by the victims of this system.

Socio-Political Ideology of the Community

Indians, in general, are known for their festivities and celebrations.

1. https://timesofindia.indiatimes.com/city/ahmedabad/xaviers-ngo-seeks-toilet-cleaners-from-gen-category/articleshow/52876770.cms

The Hindus have festivals almost every fortnight where singing and dancing are a normal part of the celebration. These rituals are generally not consuming their time and energy to a level as to disturb their business, job and study of their children. The middle-class Hindus are clever enough to mark a borderline between their devotion and practical lives. While on the other hand, among depressed classes, there is no such division. The celebrations and festivities play a larger role in their life. This is probably because for them music and entertainment are the only way out to release their tension and to overcome their depression. The excellence in music and singing can be seen among the depressed communities globally for instance among blacks and Afro-Americans. The Dalits in India do share similar skills. There is a popular proverb in Maharashtra and southern Madhya Pradesh in Marathi and Hindi:

'Brahmin ke ghar gyaan, Kunbi ke ghar dhaan aur
Mahar ke ghar gaan'[1]

(Knowledge is a part of Brahmins life, the house of the agrarian caste (*Kunbi*) is filled with grains and in Mahar (One of the Dalit castes) houses one will get songs). The singing which includes music also, however, is not limited to the Mahars alone, as mentioned in the above proverb. The other Dalit castes such as Mangs and Pariahs are excellent drumbeaters and instrumentalists. This quality is equally seen in the scavenging castes, which are also fond of music and dance. This community has produced legendry classical musicians, for instance, *Shehnai* maestro Bismillah Khan, singer Uma Devi who is still remembered for her legendary Bollywood song *'Afsaana likh rahi hun dile bekaraar ka, ankhone me aansu bharke tere intazar ka.'* A famous Sufi singer of international repute, Anand Raj Anand, gave his voice to many popular Bollywood songs. The popular pop singers Daler Mehandi and his brother Mikka Singh belonged to Mirasi, a Dalit caste. Also, among the common persons, there is a wide range of people of this community excelled in the field of music and dance. I have encountered a few music players even in smaller cities like Jabalpur and Sagar who are part of a team of a Hindu Bhakti music group that is performing even abroad including the countries like the USA and other Western countries, especially during *Nau-Ratri* (A nine or ten-night celebrations of Goddess Durga).

These successful artists are however one side of the coin; on the hind side, there is complete darkness. The involvement of youth and children

1. This popular proverb in Maharashtra and southern Madhya Pradesh is also referred by Eleanor Zelliot in her book 'From Untouchable to Dalit.'

in music and dance often deprives their attention to their studies and on many occasions, too much involvement in such activities also results in their discontinuation and dropping out from schooling. In this regard, festivals play an addendum. The scavenging communities had too much involvement in Hindu festivals and rituals, especially at the time of *Nau-Ratri* and *Ganesh-Puja* which lasted for ten days. The other major and more important community celebration is Valmiki Jayanti which is celebrated to such a grand level that it takes about a month for the preparation. This celebration drains all the energy and money of the community. The special puja of a community goddess Mashani Devi and other community festivals require a sacrifice of pig and a community feast.[1] These festivals and rituals bring much financial burden to the concerned families. The preparation of these festivals and rituals requires an absence of children and youth from their schools and colleges. The relatives, close or distant living either in proximity or far off places or other cities and towns, have to attend and participate in such festivals. This compulsory presence further extends their absence and discontinuation from schools and colleges. The involvement in dance and festivities also demands youth and children to be fashionable and attractive. This is visible in the dressing sense and hairstyles of youth who are found having modern hair cut in the style of Bollywood stars and seen roaming in colourful and modern dresses. This is of course a result of continuous watching of films and songs both on television and in theatres. This habit further takes up their precious time and money which otherwise could be utilized for study and developing mental ability.

Another impact of the deep involvement with Hindu festivities is the community's association and involvement in right-wing Hindutva politics. These celebrations become a meeting point of the two hierarchical opposite groups. The community being socially depressed and outcasts find such participation a useful remedy to come out of their inferiority complex. However, these meetings drive the youth of the community to join right-wing groups such as Bajrang Dal, Vishwa Hindu Parishad (VHP), Rashtriya Swayamsevak Sangh (RSS), etc. Their entry into these groups ends up making them foot soldiers of these groups. However, those among them having leadership qualities are given the position of lower rank in the BJP. This is a uniform pattern across India. During our field work across states, we found a close political bond between right-wing Hindu forces and scavenging communities. In some cities, the BJP

1. Field based information collected during FGD with community members at Sonipat.

leaders played an effective role in settling them by providing *pattas*. Saraswati Shishu Mandir, the school run by RSS, is always ready to cater to the education of the children. The functional role of rightwing forces quite naturally creates a bond with them. While it is equally true that Ambedkarites, Leftists and other progressive groups despite their empathy for the scavenging communities are unable to provide them any such support. As a result, the scavenging community is always ready to become foot soldiers of the right-wing organizations. We have seen in the recent past how the youth of scavenging communities participated in the Babri Mosque demolition and many of them, including Dalits of Hindutva ideology and Tribals, did participate in Gujarat riots targeted against the Muslims. This process is not just a one-day outburst but this is made possible only with the consistent efforts of right-wing organizations. The process of drawing the scavenging and other marginal Dalits into right-wing politics is also discussed well by Vijay Prashad in his book 'Untouchable Freedom'. The practical aspect of this linkage is also described and well documented in the autobiographical notes of Bhanwar Meghwanshi which is published under the title 'I could not be Hindu.' He writes:

> I heard a lot about weapons being stored in the basements of mosques" and that getting rid of the Babri Masjid was like "a second battle for independence.[1]

The emotional involvement of scavenging communities in the right-wing Hindu nationalist movement naturally urges them to sacrifice their career and education for the sake of the making of the Hindu nation. As propaganda, Hindutva preachers go to any extent and portray atheist revolutionaries, like Bhagat Singh, as right-wing revolutionaries. Their volunteers even convey to the community that Ambedkar was an admirer of Hindutva ideology and was against Muslims. The sacrifice and struggles of these great leaders for the alleged cause of Hindutva drive youth to become members of these organizations. With these inspirations, they become ready to sacrifice their careers for the sake of the Hindu nation. However, as happened in the case of Meghwanshi, they end up being badly utilized in Hindutva politics. Of course, in this process, they get out of the process of education.

The Hinduization of scavenging communities however is not a new phenomenon of the 90s as popularly believed, but it started as a reaction

1. This reference is quoted from Christophe Jaffrelot's review on this book on the wire https://thewire.in/books/book-review-bhanwar-meghwanshi-i-could-not-be-a-hindu

against foreign missionaries in Christianizing Dalits during British rule in India. The Shuddhi movement and slogan of 'go back to Vedas' are popular cries for the Hinduization of Indians, particularly the Dalits, who being outcastes were more susceptible to conversion. Bhagwan Das in his popular book *'Main Bhangi Hun'* and his booklet '*Balimiki Jayanti aur Bhangi Jaatiyan'* provided details of the attempts of Arya Samaj in Hinduization of scavenging communities. He particularly described a cunning and crafty attempt of a Brahmin Amichand Sharma, who created a myth of Valmiki as a seer of Lalbegis.[1] According to him, the community otherwise werefollowers of Islam through their devotion to a Sufi saint Lal Pir. This astute approach of right-wing Hindu nationalists succeeded in adopting the author of the legendary book Ramayana, Valmiki, as the forefather of Lalbegis. In later days, most of the scavengers had forgotten their real identities and started adopting the title of Valmiki to show or claim their lineage with Sage Valmiki. Some of the Lalbegis just followed the community while many adopted this title as a process of imitation[2]or what is popularly called Sanskritization to claim higher ritual status among the Hindus. Yet, in contrast to the theory of Srinivas, the Sanskritization hardly helped them in elevating their social status but it certainly resulted in remaining at the margin and eased only to become foot soldiers of Hindu politics. With time, many other scavenging castes did adopt the Valmiki title and identity and attempted to elevate their social status within their community. This of course proved worthy to some as within scavenging communities the 'Valmiki' title beganto be held with special respect. Therefore, it is no surprise that many other individuals of scavenging castes other than Lalbegis also started adopting the Valmiki title. I encountered one such case at Sagar, where a Dom migrant of Uttar Pradesh after earning a bachelor's degree in Law embraced the Valmiki title in an attempt to show his distinct and higher identity than other Doms of the city, who are still into scavenging. This attempt may have succeeded in making his special identity within his community however, in the wider Hindu or Indian community, this title is hardly considered with higher esteem but remain branded with the 'scavenger' identity. Therefore, it is no surprise that many occupationally mobile individuals, instead of carrying their traditional surnames or the Valmiki adopted casteless surnames.

---

1. Lalbegi is the original name of the castes who now begun to identify them as Valmiki.
2. Dr Ambedkar in his seminal essay 'Castes in India' refers the adoption of 'higher' caste rituals by the 'lower' castes as imitation. This process is later termed as Sanskritization by MN Srinivas.

Imitation of Hindu Clanship

One of the more unexplored facts in the scavenging community is that within the traditional castes engaged in 'unclean' occupation, there is a lot of caste conflict. The Valmikis or erstwhile Lalbegis are considered to be ritually superior to other traditional castes. Valmiki, which is generally treated as inferior in mainstream society, keeps a ritually higher meaning among the scavenging community. The occupationally mobile and well-educated Dumar and Domars do often use this title to claim their superior status within the scavenging community, which is otherwise adopted largely by the Lalbegis. Describing this practice, a senior activist of SKA shared that Valmiki is no more linked to a particular caste of Lalbegi. Nowadays whichever caste among scavengers wanted to claim superior status they do use the Valmiki title. This becomes an attractive title in the scavenging community. More and more individuals have adopted this title and are believed to earn better ritual status than the rest of the community.

There is also another option adopted by a prominent scavenging community Domar. They, instead of Valmiki, claim themselves to be descendants of an ancient Sage Sudarshan, whose name was mentioned in Mahabharat. This belief was developed a little later than the Valmikization of Lalbegis and Bhangis. It was popularized among the Domars that they all believe to be the descendants of this Brahmin sage. The community readily accepted this belief to eliminate the burden of impurity and low caste stature which they are facing at the hands of caste-Hindus. Therefore, the temples of Sudarshan appear to be common in all the Domar localities. Similar to Valmikis, the Domar do observe Hindu festivals including Sudarshan Jayanti with much faith and rituals. The fate of this attempt is, however, similar to that of the Valmikization of Lalbegis. The Dumars, as a result, became foot soldiers of Hindu politics and thus began to lose their access and entitlements in the field of education.

One of the negative impacts of the Hinduization of scavenging communities is that by imitating Hindus, they are getting drifted away from the Ambedkarite-Dalits, thus they are losing their opportunity for occupational mobility and the possibility of accessing education. They also lose their awareness of social and political rights. As a result of the pride in a false identity, their focus is shifted from the struggle for human rights to Sanskritization or Hinduization which ends up making them the foot soldiers of Hindutva.

Tussle and Transition in Political Philosophy

The Hinduization of the scavenging caste has done much harm to the scavenging communities, however, it has drawn little attention from academicians. Yet, an even more, ignored issue in this subject that affected the fate of the community, is the impact of the Ambedkar-Gandhi debate on caste and untouchability. During the pre-independence era, the sole attention of Congress and Gandhi was to oust British rule and set up a sovereign and independent India. This was of course the need of the time as the country was ruled by Britishers. However, opposite to this approach Ambedkar started his struggle. With his personal experience and observation, he came out with a feeling that untouchability and casteism are worse than political slavery. Both Ambedkar's and Gandhi's approaches could go together but eventually, they got overlapped when both the groups placed their demand before the British regime. Ambedkar presented his argument through his report to the Simon Commission and he participated in all the three round table conferences held during 1930, 1931 and 1932 representing the Dalit community. The demands of Ambedkar were more genuine and humanistic, and also less harmful to British rule therefore, the British government started showing positive signals for the Dalit issues. In the third roundtable conference, the British government also accepted Ambedkar's demand for a separate electorate for Dalits. This demand was not anti-national in any way (as projected by Congress of that time) for the reason that the government had equally supported and accepted the demands of religious minority groups such as Muslims, Sikhs, and others, which were in a much better position than the Dalits and was well accepted by Congress. However, the moment the British government accepted the Dalit demand,it became a bone of contention between Congress and Dalits.

Congress sharply reacted and forcibly protested against the Dalit representation. The separate representation of Dalits (Depressed Class) was taken as a challenge to the leadership of the Congress, who otherwise was claiming the leadership of all the communities including that of Dalits. Therefore, Gandhi in his attempt to reclaim the leadership of Dalits, began to oppose their separate representation.

The Congress was no doubt a mainstream party and it was supported by the corporate houses and dominant castes. The Dalits on the other hand had no backup and banking. The only source they have is their hope and trust in the leadership of Ambedkar. The Congress with strong monetary funding and the charismatic leadership of Gandhi helped in breaking and wooing the loyalty of many Dalits. The Dalits at that time got divided into two groups and a sharp difference emerged between them. The castes such as Mahar, Dusadh, Jatav, Mala, etc. of militant nature which was already a backbone of Ambedkar's struggle kept their allegiance intact with Ambedkar. While the submissive castes such as Bhangi, Mehtar, Chamar, Mang, and others joined the chores of Gandhi, who had coined a special term Harijan for them. They were so keen to adopt this Hinduite title that there occurs a struggle between some of these castes to grab the 'Harijan' title. This was of course against the wish of Gandhi who formulated this term as an umbrella to cover the whole Dalit community.

In Gujarat, which is the home state of Gandhi, this title is successfully taken by Bhangis. This was easy for them since Gandhi himself was sharing his affection and attachment to this community. The scavengers of Gujarat were also inspired by Gandhi's politics. However, the scavengers of Haryana were not so lucky in staking this claim. Their immediate competitors were the Chamar, who were equally attached to Gandhi and Congress but being located in a ritually higher position than the Bhangis, they had better access to Gandhi and Congress. Therefore, they grabbed the Harijan title for themselves and did not give its access to Haryana's Bhangis.[1] As a consequence, the Bhangis of Haryana were deprived of this title and it gets attached to the Chamars. During our fieldwork, we have observed that still in Haryana, the Harijan is exclusively used by the Chamars while the Bhangis use Valmiki or other customary titles for them. Any way this conflict was limited to this area alone. In the rest of the area, it is well-accepted by the scavenging communities.

The attraction towards the Harijan title was quite close to the process of Sanskritization. Therefore, like any other Sanskritist attempt, it has drawn the attention of many Dalits, who with much hope adopted this term. The result of this approach was, however, not different from Valmikization and Sudarshanization of scavenging castes. Those castes which got attracted towards Harijanism, whether the Bhangis or Chamars remained at the mercy of spiritual elevation and ended up developing attachment towards their caste occupation as a sacred and spiritual act. On the contrary, those Dalits, who accepted Ambedkarite militancy and dared to revolt against their traditional caste occupations, have achieved remarkable progress in the field of education and succeeded in receiving their entitlements.

1. Even at present the Chamars of Haryana use Harijan for them while the scavenging castes use their Valmiki or their original caste identities. This is my observation in the field survey.

The remnants of Gandhism are still affecting a section of Dalits for instance, the Valmikis of Sagar, who celebrate Gandhi Jayanti at par with their Valmiki Jayanti celebration. Being too much involved in this celebration they used to devote their one month of time and energy to this function. This of course resulted in diverting the attention of youth from their studies. Moreover, this philosophy also made them believe that scavenging is a sacred and noble caste occupation. A senior activist and associate of Safai Karmachari Andolan (SKA), in his interview, shared:

> My grandfather was a staunch Gandhian and a devoted activist of Congress. He had a close link with Gandhiji. On two occasions when Gandhiji visited Sagar,before meeting any other Congress leader and activist, he first visited my grandfather. He also shared the dais with him on both occasions. The humble gestures of Gandhiji really attracted our community towards the Congress. We were much away from Ambedkarism. Moreover, as an impact of Gandhiji's direct approach and special treatment to my grandfather, the other contemporary local leaders of Congress also had great regard for my grandfather who was of course a true idealist as he has never been after name and fame in Congress politics. I used to hear many stories of his greatness since my childhood. But equally true is the fact that the local Congress activists and leaders used my grandfather and my community for their politics. Many petty Congressmen grabbed a higher position in the party and electoral politics. Their family and communities have harvested the crop reaped by my grandfather but at the end of the day, neither my grandfather nor my community got anything in return. From my childhood onwards I have also followed the footsteps of my grandfather. Our community used to have the Gandhi Jayanti celebration as a big event comparable only to Valmiki Jayanti. We children and youth used to spend our entire month in its preparation. But when I grew up I realized the futility of this grand celebration. It used to drain all our energy and time. We Valmiki children and youth used to work day and night to make it colourful and attractive. Of course, this requires a long absence from school and bunking of classes. But the 'upper' caste Gandhians were very smart. They used to spend their extra money for this celebration but none of their children and youth had been directly engaged in any sort of preparation. In the celebration politics also we are losers.[1]

The scavenging communities in the pre-independence era and early post-independence period were much inclined towards Gandhi's ideology

1. Personal Interview during Field work.

and accepted Harijan identity with pride and spiritual flavour. However, parallel to this they have also adopted the Sanskritic identities of Valmiki and Sudarshan supplemented by right-wing political forces. Initially, there was no conflict between 'Harijan' and 'Valmiki-Sudarshan' identities. For the reason that Valmiki-Sudarshan identity aims to keep the community in the fold of Hinduism and to put a barrier before Christian missionaries. This is a more socio-cultural attempt than the political one of 'Harijan'. The socio-cultural attempt of Valmikization-Sudarsanization has invisible political agenda of making these communities votaries of the Congress. However, after the death of Gandhi and later with the downfall of the Congress party in the '90s, the right-wing groups explored the possibility of taking this socio-cultural agenda a step ahead in fulfilling its political desire of creating 'Hindutva Bharat'. The scavenging communities who were already devoted to the Hindutva ideology easily got into a trap of communal politics. However, as we have discussed earlier, both these ideological efforts succeeded in keeping the community away from accessing their entitlements and restricted their participation in the field of education and career-making.

The Jamadari System

It is a known fact that scavenging castes are most vulnerable and at the bottom of the margin even among Dalits. Often the phrase 'Dalits among Dalits' is used for them.[1] The reason for this is that those castes among Dalits who traditionally consider themselves better in hierarchy and are at a higher social scale in graded inequality did practice untouchability and show their cultural dominance over scavenging communities.[2] The Jatavs in western Uttar Pradesh, Chamars in almost all the states, the Mahars of Maharashtra, Madhya Pradesh and other adjoining states, the Dusadhs in Bihar, the Malas in Andhra Pradesh[3] and Telangana are few such castes that do show their cultural and political hegemony over the traditional scavenging castes. As discussed in Chapter 3 in Tamil Nadu such intra-caste conflict appears between the Pallars and Parayars

1. For instance see, D. Shyam babu's 'Caste and Class among the Dalits' in Dalit Studies in Edited by Ramnarayan S. Rawat and K. Satyanarayana ISBN electronic: 978-0-8223-7431-2 2016. AlsoJoseph's Xavier book Excluded and Victimized City Makers: Economic, Social and Cultural Rights of Dalits and Dalits, Shanlax publications.
2. See for instance, Ronki Ram "Internal Caste Cleavages among Dalits in Punjab." *Economic and Political Weekly*, vol. 52, no. 3, 2017, pp. 54–57.
3. Balagopal, K. "Justice for Dalits among Dalits: All the Ghosts Resurface." *Economic and Political Weekly*, vol. 40, no. 29, 2005, pp. 3128–33.

on one side and Arunthatiyars or Adi-Andhra on the other. These two SC castes as in the case of most of the other states have benefitted due to reservation much more than the Arunthathiyars. The Adi-Andhras in some instances are even exploited by the moneylenders from other Scheduled Castes.[1]In some states for instance, like Haryana, Bihar and Andhra Pradesh, there is an attempt to bridge this gap by introducing categorization of reservation for SCs into A and B groups,where group A represents the most unprivileged castes of SCs and group B includes those castes that attained comparative occupational mobility and progress. Probably Punjab was the first state to introduce this sub-categorization in 1975 to secure the share of Mazhbi Sikhs and Balmikis both engaged mainly in scavenging and allied occupations.[2] However, in academic as well as other discussions, the issue of intra-caste tension and the struggle of scavenging communities did not gain much attention. The Jamadari system is one such. The term Jamadar is often used as a common term for a sanitation worker and sometimes even for the whole community engaged in sanitary works. However, this is a false understanding. This word in actuality has a special meaning and it is a position reserved for a contractor, who is employing and monitoring sanitary workers under him. This position was designed and came into existence with the establishment of scavenging as a municipal service during the British period.[3] The sanitation work then appeared in the form of public sanitation under a contract system. The British rulers initially gave contracts to the heads of the scavenging communities to clean and collect garbage from public places and private spaces. These heads or contractors were known as Jamadars. This practice continued in municipalities even after decades of independence. While in some instances, such as government offices, including railways, sanitation workers had been recruited as permanent government staff,in municipalities, however, the contract system under Jamadari remained in practice for a longer period. Under this system, a wholesome amount was paid to the Jamadar to get the work done instead of individual wages to the sanitation workers.

Later in independent India, the system continued but instead of the wholesome amount being paid to Jamadar, it was given to him to

1. Joseph's Xavier 'Excluded and Victimized City Makers: Economic, Social and Cultural Rights of Dalits and Dalits' p. 192.
2. Himabindu M., Policy And Politics of Sub-Categorization of Scheduled Caste Reservations In India: A Social Justice Perspective, The Indian Journal of Political Science Vol. LXXV, No. 4, October-December, 2014, pp. 641-654 (ISSN NO. 0019-5510)
3. See Vijay Prashad's 'Untouchable Freedom'.

distribute to the sanitation workers in the form of salaries by undertaking their thumb impression or signature. The Jamadar with the ownership right to distribute salary got full control over distribution. He used to distribute salaries on his whims and fancies by producing forged signatures and thumb impressions. This was certainly an oppressive and corrupt practice where the wage of a sanitary worker was decided by a Jamadar although he was receiving the full amount of salary of each worker by the municipality. In this oppressive system, the oppressor and oppressed belonged to the same caste and often of the same sub-caste. The Jamadar was getting rich at the expense of poor sanitation workers. This was a tyrannical system where the poor sanitation workers' earnings depended to be at the mercy of a Jamadar. This arrangement was creating a class difference between the workers and the contractors, who otherwise both belonged to the same community. This system was continued in many municipalities till the decade of late 80s. As a result, it has created a wide gulf between the poor and rich of the same castes. In an interview during fieldwork, a senior activist of SKA (Safai Karmachari Aandolan) in Sagar shared:

> I was observing this system since my childhood. I used to see our people standing in a group on a day of payment to wait for Jamadar, who sometimes come on time but often at his whims and fancies. He used to carry bundles of rupees with him in his bag. He then asks all the workers to wait and call their names one by one. The Jamadar used to take their thumb impressions on his register and pay them the money individually. This payment was not fixed. The amount was decided by him. In case of less payment when one asks the reason,the Jamadar responds by pointing out to his absence on some days and late comings as the reasons. The workers were aware that they are not paid exactly what their salary was. But they were helpless. There was no authority where they can complain against this injustice. The Jamadar was a known wrestler of our community. His dominant voice and physical stature created fear in the mind of poor scavengers. They dare not challenge his corruption. The situation was miserable. I disliked this act from my childhood and decided that by hook or crook I will stop this oppressive and unjust system. When I grew up, I discussed this matter with friends. We all wereschool-going and many of them are sons of the scavengers who were being paid at the mercy of the Jamadar. Naturally, there was also a personal angle. So, we decided to follow a militant approach. A group of these boys waited for the day of the distribution of wages. When Jamadar came with

the bag and began to open his register for attendance, they jumped on him and robbed his bag and fled away from the spot on a motorbike. They covered their faces so they were not recognized by the Jamadar. His goons were also unable to catch them. It became big news in the city. A case was registered at the police station. On the other hand, workers protested before the municipality office demanding early release of their salaries. The officials then realized that it is no safer to give lumpsum money to Jamadar and then after that, they changed the style and began to distribute the salary of the scavengers from their office with proper paperwork. This was a big relief to workers as in this formal process no one was able to take undue advantage and the workers and their salaries are no more decided by the whims and fancies of the Jamadar and from then onwards they began to receive the actual amount.

When this system was ended and municipalities took over the responsibility of recruitment and distribution of salaries in their hands, the proper distribution of salaries through a perfect official mechanism resulted in the well-being of the workers and a positive change appeared in the community. This continued over two decades. However, sadly this did not last long. With the introduction of privatization in the sanitation sector, the sanitation workers returned to their pitiable condition.

The Class Difference among Scavenging Castes

We have discussed earlier that the scavenging communities like any other communities whether an oppressed-depressed community or mainstream community is not homogenous in terms of their caste and class. There is ample ground for this phenomenon. The major reason for the class difference in contemporary society mainly appeared due to the nature of employment. For instance, those employed as Sweepers in the government sector in the pre-90s are regular employees in the respective departments. Their salary is much better along with their entitlement to provident funds (PF), health insurance, and the facilities of government quarters, pension, and many other social security benefits. Their salaries are four-five times higher than those of sanitation workers employed under contract. On many occasions, it is observed that many members of the same family get a chance to be employed regularly in government sectors. In such a case, the family income reaches as high as one lakh rupees a month or even more. Such families have been found to be living in a big and beautiful house with all sorts of luxuries and comforts which is a natural outcome of their higher income. In most of the cases, these people were found to claim to be Brahmanic but hold scavenging caste-linked identities of Valmiki and Sudarshan with pride. This mixed identity favours them in two ways.First, it keeps their hereditary caste occupation intact with their families while the usage of the names of age-old Brahmin sages as their ancestors helps them to claim their position in Hindu society. Secondly, these upper crusts of Valmikis being better in financial status also favour them to attain the leadership of SafaiKaramachari Unions. This brings about their closeness to mainstream political leaders and government officials. This connection helps them to grab the permanent post of a sweeper in municipal corporations. These union leaders being affluent in the community, however, seldom perform the work themselves. They instead hire a proxy worker at much lower wages. This is easy and unchallengeable since the tasks are being performed in public places rather than in an office. Therefore, none of the officials could notice or object to this malpractice. The sitting worker thus draws their full salaries as a regular staff but pays only a meagre sum of rupees to the actual worker. The proxy workers are the poor and most marginalized among the scavengers. This proxy work setting continues until the retirement of these permanent employees. There is no hope left for the proxy workers in this arrangement and she or he remains at the mercy of this regular employee throughout her or his life.

We have come across many such cases during our field study. In one such case, a poor widow of the Bhuinyaa caste at Gaya was seen performing the duty in place of a regular sanitation worker who is the wife of the president of Maha-Dalit cell of the ruling party belonging to the same sub-caste. Such cases are common in almost all cities and towns. It becomes more common when an influential person of traditional scavenging castes gets the contract of sanitation work. In such a case, the close relatives of this person easily become sanitation workers on paper to draw their full salaries, while as usual their work is performed by the poor workers of their caste. This practice results in the widening of the gulf between rich and poor of the same caste. The poorest sanitation worker is always at the receiving end. In such a case the education of their children is bound to be affected.

Another sad impact of this system is that in the long run, both the proxy worker and actual worker remained under the trap of sanitation work. The actual workers have no escape from the job because of their poverty while the workers on paper also remained associated with scavenging because of their identity as sanitation workers. In this exercise, they both keep the tag of the sanitation worker intact. In this exercise, the community thus, by and large, seems to remain associated with scavenging. The labeling of sanitation tasks with the community also results in branding of the students of—Bhangi, Mehtar, Musahar, Dom, Domar, Dumar,etc—as 'untouchables' on the campus. This label continues even if an individual comes out of the scavenging occupation because their upward mobility is seen parallel with those well-off scavengers who took the services of proxy workers for their work. This corrupt practice therefore apart from being atrocious to the poor scavengers also helps in sustaining the caste identity intact with the traditional scavenging castes.

The occupational mobility of a few individuals is no doubt a positive sign of development in the community. But we have no data in social science on the occupational mobility of the traditional scavenging castes. This is mainly because being occupationally mobile most of these families have moved to posh localities, which is usually beyond the purview of any field research on scavenging. The upward mobility and migration to general or posh localities quite naturally resulted in their breakup with the scavenging mass. However, as far as the claim for privilege is concerned, it is common for this class, like any other occupational mobile Dalits, to claim their Scheduled Caste status. Yet, it is observed that, in general, the mobile scavenging castes have little connection with the other Dalits and they seldom become a part of the Dalit movement. They are on the other side as previously mentioned and are also cut off from their roots. Such an attempt is well narrated in a Hindi story 'Andhad' by a famous Dalit author Omprakash Valmiki, where an occupational mobile individual Sukdu Lal of scavenging caste tries to shed his caste identity by adopting a new name S Lal and was even successful in getting his identity hidden from neighbours of his posh locality. He did this to avoid any negative connotation among his children as he raised them with much care so that they should not get exposed to their roots. Another eminent Dalit writer Suraj Pal Chauhan in his story 'Ghaate ka Sauda' describes how an occupational mobile rich Dori Lal of scavenging caste adopted a new identity to claim equal status with his neighbours of the forward-caste background until he was exposed and was forced to sell his bungalow of 10-12 lakhs in a posh locality for just 6 lakhs.

These Dalit stories are samples of much prevalent hidden desire of the occupationally mobile Dalits, particularly of scavenging castes, to get rid of their negative social identity. In most cases, these occupational mobile groups are just a reaper of the benefits of caste-based reservation without bothering to perform their duties towards their community and in the Dalit movement. A senior activist shared that in Bhopal there is a group of occupational mobile Valmikis, who used to organize an annual gathering of their people. This used to be a grand event where all the senior officials and bureaucrats of Valmiki castes come together. They also invite political leaders of dominant castes as their guests. But this is a closed group of the occupational mobile Valmikis. There is no presence of common Valmikis in it. The organizers also make sure that their caste identity is not visible in this event even though it is known to all. This is a new endogamous group emerging among the occupational mobile individuals of scavenging castes with a higher cultural and economic ranking than the rest of the scavenging communities. It is a common practice among them to hide their caste identities by adopting caste-less surnames or even putting the traditional surnames of Brahmin, Thakur, and Bania such as Gaur, Chauhan, Gohil, Singh, Goyal, etc. Of course, some of these surnames are also traditionally common in both scavenging castes as well as among the forward castes. But the usage of these surnames anyway helps the occupational mobile scavengers to come out of what is believed to be negative and low caste stature. On the other side, there are a few individuals, like Bhagwan Das and others, who after achieving occupational mobility remained faithful to the Dalit movement.

The scavengers, in general, at present are divided into four main categories.The first is still in the traditional caste occupation. Secondly, there are those who have moved out of the caste occupation but owing to their political connections remain in touch with this occupation by appointing the proxy workers of their caste community. Thirdly, there are those who completely moved out of the caste occupation and created a secular space for them. Fourthly, as mentioned in Chapter 3, there are those individuals and castes, and tribes, who are erstwhile not associated with scavenging but fell into this occupation due to a variety of reasons.

The most miserable and vulnerable among them is of course those who are still into this occupation irrespective of their castes, traditional scavenging caste, other Dalits and tribals who fell into this occupation. As we have discussed in Chapter2,they become most vulnerable. They are unable to claim their so-called ritual superiority over traditional scavengers mainly because of their poor strength. The migrant scavengers often fall into the lowest grade of petty scavenging occupations like manhole cleaning and rag picking and daily wage services.

The liberal nature of the economy proved to be a burden to the working class in general but for the sanitation workers, it affects them even more. Their monthly salary is reduced to the range of 4000 to 9000 but the work hours are not restricted to eight hours but extend even to fourteen hours a day. The atrocious nature of tasks generally prevents the local scavenging castes to enter into it but as said above the migrants, mainly inter-state migrants, being most vulnerable and without any means of livelihood and social security fall into this trap. The manhole cleaners and other manual scavengers do come under this category. These new entrants are the most pitiable among the sanitation workers, both in terms of their poor financial status and minimum citizenship rights. They used to struggle for basic identities like ration cards, aadhaar cards, voter cards and documents like caste-certificates. In the absence of any proper habitation, they are bound to seek refuge in temporary slums located in the cities or at fringes. The scavenging caste thus on the one hand is still largely into traditional slums and temporary slums but some of them also reached the status to get their accommodations in government quarters, general settlements and even posh localities. The loss of connecting link between these two classes and the master-servant relations in the case of proxy worker arrangement prevents the community to get united and fight against the age-old customary practices and their exclusion and discrimination in the wider society.

The rich class among the scavenging castes as discussed above is cut off from her roots and engaged in their material and socio-spiritual comforts while the poor among them become the worst victim of economic and social exploitation. While interviewing a group of Valmiki children in Shimla, when a question about their parent's occupation was asked, the children started saying loudly '*mere papa clerk hain, mere papa airmen hain, mere papa dukandaarhain, mere papa court me vakil hain*'etc.. (My papa is a clerk, my papa is an airman in the Air Force, my papa is a shopkeeper, my papa is a lawyer in a court, etc.) But a girl of 6 years of age remained silent. When I asked the same question to her then also she remained silent. But within seconds other children who described various occupations of their parents in loud voices, shouted in one voice '*iski mummy to hotelon main jhadulagatihai ...hahaha*' (Her Mother sweeps in hotels...laughter). This observation narrates the petty state of children whose parents are still in sanitation work even among the scavenging community. If the children of scavengers are ridiculed by those children who just enter in the lower range of occupational mobility,one can understand the vulnerabilities of the scavengers' children in society.

Liquor Manufacturing and Drunkenness

The meagre salary, undefined work hours, strenuous and hazardous tasks and extremely poor habitation lead the scavenger community to be in depression and stress. In the absence of any support system, the immediate solution is none other than to engage in intoxicants. Indigenous liquor is quite commonly available among the community. The habit of drinking indigenous liquor is common in this community. It is well known that liquor sale and manufacturing is banned in the Bihar state. Yet, liquor making continues as a traditional caste occupation of Musahars and they continued with this profession. Their customers include not only their own caste men and other Dalits but individuals of Rajput, Yadav, Kurmi and other dominant and backward castes. Many times, there have been police raids conducted in various settlements. 40 year old Nagina Manjhi, who is a bootlegger inindigenous liquor, says that before the prohibition, her income was a fraction of what she earns today after prohibition in Bihar. When the police conducted raids, they fled the scene. Or when arrested, they start brewing again after the release. Since there is a strict liquor ban imposed in the state, the sellers are punished brutally by the police. However, after each such raid, the work of liquor-makingregains normalcy within a short period.[1]

The prohibition of liquor in Bihar is a recent step, but such demands also emerged during the making of the Constitution. Many leaders during that time also supported the ban but Ambedkar was against this ban. For the reason that any ban cannot restrict the manufacturing and sales of liquor as the consumers will pave the way out. He said, "Prohibition (*On liquor*) is sheer madness. Its progress must not only be arrested but must be immediately abolished. It has produced more evils than those it was intended to stop. The manufacture of liquor has become a cottage industry. Formerly only men drank liquor. Now women and children also drink because liquor is manufactured in every home in the presence of women and children. It has produced more crime and the worst soil of demoralisation of the lower classes."[2]

This prophecy was seen to be true in Bihar. The habit of drinking is also common among females but compared to males the drunkard females are less in number. The habit of drinking is developed even among children at the age of 13-14 years onwards. This indigenous liquor is heavily intoxicated thus it results in many more problems for its users. The habit of consuming liquor by most of the family members across age and gender and the impact of customers' visits to purchase the liquor

1. Discrimination and Exclusion in Education ...Bihar and Jharkhand p. 145.
2. BAWS Vol. 17 part 1 p. 398.

creates a negative impact on children and hampers their attention from their study. Ramesh a dropout of sixth class said,

> Liquor making was my family occupation. My father was an expert in making liquor. His liquor was especially liked by the people. He had customers of all castes, the Yadav, Kurmi, Bhumihar and others. He never faced any sort of discrimination but this business adversely affected me and my siblings. My elder sisters studied only unto the fourth and fifth class respectively. They were married off at fourteen. At that time, I didn't realize why my parents were keen to marry them. But now I understand. The customers' intention towards them was not good. Early marriage was thus a tactic to avoid any untoward incident towards them. Because of this business, I was also not able to concentrate on my studies. I dropped out in the sixth class and began to help my father in this profession. Now he is no more. I am independently handling this work.[1]

The condition of Musahars, however, continued to be deplorable. They are engaged mostly in scavenging and some of them are also involved in liquor making. In fact, due to the official ban on the manufacturing and sale of liquor, there is a tremendous rise in the manufacturing and sale of indigenous liquor, especially in slums. The ban on liquor thus created more problems for the community rather than making them good citizens as envisaged by the Bihar government. A Gandhian social activist Karu ji of Gaya shared:

> In Bihar, you can find liquor for sale in every slum. The Musahars are experts in liquor making. They continue to manufacture and sell it in their bastis. Their customers include men from all castes, the Rajputs, Kurmis, Brahmins, etc. These customers do not hesitate to drink the liquor at the Musahar seller's home. There is no casteism while drinking! There are also Kalar (an OBC caste) who are manufacturing and selling liquor illegally. But the customers always prefer Musahar's liquor over them. However, as far as earning is concerned, you can see many rich among Kalars, but the Musahar liquor makers continued to be at lower income levels. The reason is, Kalar being a business community, has an art of savings and investment but the poor Musahars completely lack the skill of financial management. Therefore, despite their higher earnings they are not able to save money.[2]

1. Ibid, p. 145.
2. Personal interview.

Due to the selling of liquor at home, the family life of the seller gets disturbed. Some customers often come regularly with bad intentions. The modesty of vulnerable family members is always at risk. The children in the family and especially the girl child and other female members are prone to sexual abuse. In some cases, the male child also faces such attacks. Even when there are no such incidents, the environment of the house and the neighbouring area which sells liquor is not conducive for study. There are also frequent fights between customers and also sometimes with the sellers. Overall, the environment is never conducive for the children. Their education is bound to be affected by this. The seller on the other hand is under much pressure. In case of any wrong behaviour including the attempt of misbehavior of the customers against his female relatives or in any other case, they do not raise their voice against them but are bound to remain silent for the reason that their business is illegal and therefore any sort of report to a police station could result in heavy punishments. This illegal business adversely affects the prospects of their children.

Otherwise also as observed in all the selected settlements across India, in the evening,the roaming of drunkard males is a common scene. While among the youth and adolescents chewing tobacco and cigarette smoking is common. The children, especially those engaged in rag picking, are seen smelling whiteners for their intoxication. While interviewing seniors and children, they readily accepted it as their regular practice but none in any slums admitted to the use of drugs. This, however, does not mean that there may not be any drug abuse in the community. Possibly, due to the fear of getting exposed, they are hiding their habits. However, secondary sources such as interviews of rag pickers and scavengers in mainstream media for instance, in Doordarshan[1] proves that drug addiction is common among the slum dwellers. Such habits of parents make them irresponsible in performing their family duties while among children such habits distract them from their education and schooling.

Rampant Violence and Abusive Language in Settlements

The illiteracy and poor education of parents also result in their poor soft skills, rough communication and rude language. Abusive slurs frequently appear in their communication both within the community and also inside the family. In Shimla, a teacher shared 'the slum students not

1. During 80's the Doordarshan mainly during the break of Sunday films used to show program against drug addiction where the interviews of drug addicts of Delhi slums mainly engaged rag picking seen claiming their drug addiction.

only use abusive wordson the campus, but they do not hesitate to use it in our presence. It is true that none of the students directly abused any teacher but when we cross their settlement, while coming and going to school, we do hear the abuse in a louder voice. It is not just a coincidence but I know they are deliberately abusing to hurt us'.

Playing music and TV in high pitch, shouting nonsense, use of abuse is a very common act of day-to-day life. It is common among all walks of life of slum dwellers, whether elder, middle age, youth women or children. Abusive language and quarrelingare also a normal practice of both genders. It is more common among women, who being engaged in family affairs and household works, are bound to be affected by other dwellers mainly on account of their engagement in water collection from a common source. The competition in accessing water and sharing of common space which is very limited in slums often results in quarrels and fights. Moreover, raids of police against suspects of theft, murder or other big or petty crime are much common, irrespective of the fact whether the culprit belonged to the slum or an outsider. The slums are often branded as a colony of criminals. The negative identity is so strongly attached to the slum dwellers that it continues to hound their children even in the schools. In case of theft or losing any stuff of children, in the eyes of school authorities, the first suspect is the students from slums. Soin the case of a fight between students, if one is from the slum, the teacher believes the slum student to be a culprit no matter who is responsible.

The quarrels are not only male-centric but it is more common among women and sometimes it is also cross-gender. When a quarrel starts, women generally take a leading position. With their full voice,they shout and abuse the opponents with all patriarchal expressions. In case the opponent is a male, the woman doesn't hesitate tothreaten him with all sorts of abuse against him and also does not forget to add abuses against his mother, sister or daughter. This drama occurs in such a high pitch that none can concentrate on work. In the case of a quarrel among men, the fight involves the same sort of abuses, but it doesn't restrict merely to verbal abuses, iron rods, swords, *guptis* (an indigenous weapon), lathis and even pistols come into the scene.

The fights are not only between different castes and sub-castes, but it occurs even among relatives and family members. In Jabalpur, one of the respondents, who happened to be a political leader of the BJP, had such violent fights with his uncles. This leader is a known criminal and a 'history sheeter'. But his son is studying in a high-quality private school.

The fights and quarrels distract his son's study therefore he had left his ancestral home and got settled in a new locality in a rented house. In this case, because of a better financial position and special concern for his son, this man shifted to a new secular colony. But in other families, leaving the slums and moving to a new locality is not possible. This leads to distraction from the study and ultimately results in their becoming dropouts.

Domestic Violence

Domestic violence is rampant in settlements. There are many reasons behind it, such as illiteracy, patriarchal mental setup, liquor intake, depression, tension, financial insecurity, ill-treatment by others and sexual frustration. These reasons drive males to show their anger and masculinity over their wives. The case of violence in the form of wife-beating is very common in the localities. In the evening time, the husbands are usually drunk and thus lose their conscience, which often results in fighting and abusive attitude towards their wives. There are some families where domestic violence is a daily affair. The fight and beating of the wife happens in front of the children. The boys, who are usually attached to their mothers more than their fathers, have to remain mute spectators. But this silence breaks them down very much. Moreover, in such conditions, it is not possible for the children to study or to complete their home assignments. These affect their behaviour in school and negatively results in their poor performance. Sunil, an Engineering student of Dumar caste in Jabalpur told:

> Alcoholism and domestic violence are interlinked and both are common in my basti. There are only a few homes in our basti like mine, which are exceptions otherwise it is a common practice…This is the reason that my father always instructs me not to mix with others. In some families, the fighting and violence are so rampant and loud that it is not just restricted within the walls of their house. Sometimes it goes to such an extent that family members need hospitalization… In some cases, the matter reaches to an extent that the wives have to leave their homes along with their children… You can easily assume that in such an environment how a child can focus on his studies.[1]

Though domestic violence results in the dropping out of male students in general. But often it gives a positive push to girl students to study hard so that they do not get into the trap of such a situation. This violence

1. Discrimination and Exclusion in Education…Madhya Pradesh and Chhattisgarh pp. 111-112.

develops a sense of insecurity in the minds of girls. It teaches them that if they remained uneducated and unemployed (like their mothers); they too have to meet with the same treatment at the hands of their future husbands. This negative treatment of the mothers is an encouraging factor for girls to study hard and to stand on their own feet. It is, therefore, no surprise that compared to boys, the girls are doing well in their studies and their dropout ratio is lower than the boys. However, one can understand how difficult it is for them to maintain their focus on studies in such an environment.

Social Customs and Ritualistic Practices

Caste is not operated naturally but it has many instruments and tools for its maintenance and management. In north India, especially in Haryana and western Uttar Pradesh, Khap is one such popular institution among the Jats and a few other dominant castes. In the rest of the states, in place of Khaps, the jati-Panchayats are serving as tools for the mechanism of caste. This institution is strongly patriarchal and conservative, established with the sole aim to preserve and perpetuate the institution of caste and the caste system. This also controls the liberty of individuals. In it, there is the provision of severe punishments such as social boycotts, and fines both in cash and kind. Sometimes the jati-panchayats also do not hesitate in passing a death sentence against whom they believe as the culprit, and on some occasions, it even orders mass rape of an alleged culprit. [1]The jati-panchayats are unconstitutional. Yet, it is so powerful and active that none of the individuals candare to challenge its functioning. This is the only surviving institution that played a role within the community to continue the existence of caste.

The Jati-panchayats function more strictly amongst the dominant castes, among the Dalits it is less functional. We have observed in the recent past that among some Dalit caste groups such as the Mahar, Jatav, Chamar, etc., it has become quite dysfunctional, particularly, with their conversion to Buddhism. The converted caste developed their religious committees to govern their religious and social issues. Moreover, new socio-political groups such as SamataSainik Dal, The Buddhist Society of India, Republican Party of India, BSP, BAMCEF, Bhim Army, M21, etc. have also provided to an extent parallel regulating bodies.

Therefore, this development rooted out their old caste panchayats to a great extent. Yet, even if there is a reminiscent of jati-panchayat in some

1. For instance see, https://theprint.in/politics/rohtak-honour-killing-dalit-man-not-allowed-at-jat-wifes-funeral-over-fears-of-backlash/97240/

form or other, it has lost its power of dictating any rules or norms over the community being challenged by the newly created socio-political units discussed above. The reason behind this is that all these new units and organizations have their leaflets, and magazines to spread their views and mission, which is openly and harshly criticizing Brahmanic tradition and values and the caste system. Moreover, with the change in technology, the use of social media channels, such as Youtube channels, Facebook groups, e-groups, WhatsApp and telegram groups, their use is rampant where both organizations' and individuals' voice is being raised against Brahmanism, caste and the practise of untouchability. These issues are anti-caste in nature. Therefore, the jati-panchayat (if at all it is in existence) carries the power to dictate its terms to the community. This does not, however, mean that the Dalit community altogether comes out of traditionalism and caste practices. Yet, the development and growth of various new socio-cultural and political organizations mentioned above reduced the possibility of any dictates of a sole voice among them. Thus, a sort of democracy emerged in them. These Dalits, therefore, lacked a single voice, as we often listen from the castes such as Jats, Gujjars, Rajputs, etc., which are governed by their respective jati-panchayats. Further, education and urbanization of the Dalit community also played a bigger role in reducing the conservative caste ideological approach among them to a great extent. However, it does not mean that these Dalits became caste-less or developed anti-caste characteristics among themselves. Endogamy —which is the root cause of genesis and maintaining the caste—is still in existence among the castes that are claiming to be Ambedkarite or Buddhist. But it is equally true that the intensity of endogamy and the practices of caste rules has to a great extent also become challenging among them. There is also the frequent occurrence of cases of inter-caste marriages, which is often well accepted by these communities, unlike the dictates of dominant castes that frequently resulted in what is popularly called 'honour' killings. One cannot ignore the feeble but straightforward approach of some of the Ambedkarite-Buddhist groups, for instance, the efforts of Punjab Buddhist Society,[1] which is spreading awareness among its followers through their monthly magazine *'Bauddha Dharma Pracharak'* to break the caste-endogamy and to follow inter-caste marriages as a normal practice and a revolutionary move to establish Ambedkar's vision of annihilation of caste and to establish social equity. Such attempts are very few in the movement yet at least openness to accept inter-caste marriage among a small section of Ambedkarites is a unique and revolutionary move that

1. See the matrionial ads published in Hindi monthly magazine Bauddha Dharma Pracharak.

none other social group wished to accept even in the present century. At least these castes do not act gruesome like Khaps and jati-panchayats in cases of inter-caste marriages.

However, the case of scavenging castes is diametrically opposite to Ambedkarite-Dalit castes. The jati-panchayat among scavenging castes in most of the cases are in full swing. As per tradition, this is a five bench judge consisting of five elder males. Like the judges of other dominant castes, these panches also act and behave in their dictating terms. Being illiterate, conservative, and unaware of socio-political developments, their approach is narrow, patriarchal, and casteist in nature. There are strict warnings and punishments against any bid of inter-caste marriage. Yet, compared to dominant castes there is little liberality found in this jati-panchayat,for instance, in the case of inter-caste marriage. There is no physical assault on the 'culprit' neither there is any killing in the name of honour but such marriages are duly accepted by the jati-panchayat after giving a penalty to the concerned family. They are often asked that it be paid in the form of a mass ceremonial feast, in which pork and liquor are essential. Apart from this, the accused also had to pay a small sum of money in the range of 100-500 rupees individually to all the five bench judges of the jati-panchayat and special food and liquor for them. In recent years, however, there is a substantial increase in this fine upto 50,000-100,000 rupees in some places. The poor accused in such a case, falls under the debt trap. This not only results in their lifelong financial insecurity but also affects the prospects of education for their children. In Korba, Chhattisgarh, we have observed the working of Jati Panchayat of Domar caste. The panches in these cases are also active in SKA, where they do share their modern views against the system, while in the panchayat they become equally conservative as others. They have strict rules and regulations to prevent the occurrence of inter-caste marriages in their community. The jati-panchayat is continuously serving well in most of the scavenging castes to maintain the conservatism and patriarchy, yet there is also serious opposition to it in some cities and among some castes. One such successful attempt is noticed in Sagar, wherein in the decade of the 80s, the panch system was quite strong and influential. Remembering those days, a senior social activist and leader said:

> The panches were the elders of the communities. Quite obviously, they used to be illiterate and traditional in thinking. This is also because at that time the literacy level and awareness in our community was very low. These panches were a reflection of our community. Many of our people especially the middle-aged were under their influence.

However, we the hot-blood youth have much modern and rational thinking. We were fed up with these old men and their dictates. They used to consider themselves as supreme and judge of our community. Their power kept on growing and it reached a level that they started behaving like dictators. During marriage ceremonies, the panches have a special role. They were called by the bride or bridegroom's family to inform them about the marriage. This is followed by lunch for them consisting of pork and liquor. This ceremony was not simple but created a lot of trouble for the family. The panches used to have a long discussion within them and thereafter they give their final command for the marriage. The food being served to them was eaten by them in large quantities but this was not enough for them and they also used to carry the food to their homes. This is somehow acceptable but a bigger problem used to occur on marriage day. On this occasion, the panches were again called as special invitees. The family used to greet and serve them with much respect and honour. These panches then start their discussion about the marriage customs but it became so common in those days that instead of providing an immediate green signal for the marriage ceremony, they began to put their arguments which turned into a hot debate between them. Even they used to recall the issues of discontent that emerged during the previous marriage ceremony. And they began to fight among themselves. They were so highly respected at that time that until they stop their fighting and have their dinner, none of the guests could eat the food. Even the children remained hungry till that time. Often their fights continued till late at night. Their power and ego were so tremendous that on many occasions the guest used to leave the marriage ceremony without having any food. That resulted in the wastage of food in large quantities. Such an attitude was disliked by all. Initially, many middle-aged people supported these acts for the sake of our caste tradition. But many of them sooner or later got disgruntled with the dictatorship of the panches. We the youth then developed enough courage to challenge them. To our surprise when we challenged them openly during a marriage ceremony where they were creating a scene,almost all of the guests and families of both bride and bridegroom supported us and asked them to immediately stop the drama. They became frightened. They even feared that we may kill them on the spot or beat them badly,probably, because of the anger we had against them. Our one such effort resulted in the complete end of the jati-panchayat and panch system in our community. Then onwards there is no presence of any panch in our community.[1]

Nowadays with the active presence of Safai Karmachari Aandolan (SKA) in cities and towns,there is a substantial change in the situation. The presence of SKA has to an extent modernized the community and made them aware of Dr. Ambedkar and his mission. Yet in a few places, the problem is still static because the Panches of the community are playing a dubious role as discussed in the case of Korba city. Within the community they are Panches but they also assumed the union leadership of the sanitation community. Therefore, they continue to dictate their patriarchal and conservative ideology to the community in its private affairs but they do claim a rights-based approach in fighting with the management and state. The dual approach of these leaders is helping the community in a limited way but on the other hand, it is depriving the community of modernization and accepting a liberal and humanistic ideology.

Extravagance in Marriage and Other Ceremonies

The ceremonies on the occasion of birth, marriage, death, and other events of an individual life are common events in social life. Human beings are social animals and have little option to dissociate from this. In many cases, these ceremonies and rites are so rigid and expensive that one has to borrow or credit money for them. This practice is very common among Hindus. The ill impacts of such ceremonies are well highlighted in the writings of many eminent authors. Prem Chand in his first novel 'Seva-Sadan', for instance, raised the ill impacts of dowry and extravagancies in the marriage ceremony. Apart from such customs, the Hindus at one time not even hesitated in practicing the inhuman Sati-System. However, such customs were limited among the caste Hindus. On the contrary, the Dalits were to an extent better in their social customs. At least among them dowry, sati, enforced widowhood, and extravagancies in rituals were unknown. The patriarchy among Dalits was a little less atrocious than their dominant caste counterparts.

However, in recent years when the division between Dalits and 'upper' caste Hindus has reduced drastically, especially in urban India,it has resulted in developing harmony in the society. This proves to be a positive step towards humanism, yet one cannot ignore that on the other side it has bought a strong negative impact on Dalit culture. As a consequence

1. Personal Interview with Mr Pavan Valmiki.

of alleged fraternity with the caste Hindus, the Dalits increasingly started imitating the customs and culture of the Hindus. The customs of dowry and extravagancies in rituals have now become a normal part of Dalit life. This tendency is more prevalent among scavenging and allied castes. This is possibly an attempt in the process of Sanskritisation to claim their ritual hierarchy in society. Many of these scavenging castes are claimed to be the descendants of the dominant castes such as Rajputs and Jats. Therefore, it is no surprise to see their habits and culture being developed in the same pattern. The projection of masculinity in form of body-building and wrestling, indulgence in gambling and liquor, and keeping a veil for the women are some of the practices followed by scavenging communities that bring them closer to the dominant castes. However, such practices are creating a wider cultural difference with the other Dalit castes. An essential serving of pork and liquor to community members at any event or celebration is putting extra weight into their pockets. However, with increased participation of the forward caste colleagues and friends in the celebrations such as marriage, etc., the scavenging community has started a new method of dual celebrations. The first one is internal in nature and is limited exclusively to the caste community, where the customary celebration is done. While in the open celebration where friends and colleagues from diverse caste communities have been invited, the celebration is done professionally. This party is organized in big marriage lawns and food is being prepared and served by the professionals. The reason for choosing a professional caterer and marriage lawns is two-fold.First, it fulfills the internal desire of the organiser to show off their status to all. This approach seems to be a negative one to some, but for the community depressed over centuries with a blot of untouchability, this show-off is a psychological remedy to come out of their mental trauma and depression and to develop a feeling that 'yes we are also on par with other castes'. The second reason for this professional hiring of services is to assure to the other castes that there is no fear of getting polluted in having food in this celebration. It is observed that in such marriage parties' people from all walks of life and with a hierarchical superior social background and also those in higher official positions do participate without any hesitation. Such a wide range of participation including rich and poor, Brahmins and scavengers, under the same roof of marriage lawn, as said above helps in developing the confidence of the organisers as being equal to others. This could be a good therapy for getting out of the feeling of lowliness and depression. However, such an event needs a large sum of money. The concerned family, therefore, has no option other than to credit loans from private individuals at a very high rate of compounding interest. The one-day event of a show-off and attempt to earn mental confidence of being ‘equal’ and ‘acceptable’ to all results in making them trapped in debt for their whole life. The worst sufferer of this is the children as their parents,who are not able to spend on their education and other needs.

The dowry system which is discussed in detail in Chapter 6 also proves detrimental to the prospect of girls’ education. Apart from the dowry and marriage celebrations, the community’s too much involvement in other functions is still on which is enough to hamper the education of children. Describing this problem, a female activist of SKA says:

> Apart from marriages, the birth ceremony is equally attractive and expensive in the Valmiki Community which is also conducted on marriage lawns. Thousands of community people and colleagues and friends of other castes are invited. This ceremony is also expensive and attractive, where community people gather with beautiful attires. This function again requires a lot of money that ultimately results in falling in a debt trap. Besides these ceremonies, events such as Balmiki Jayanti in the case of Valmiki caste and Sudarshan Jayanti in the case of Domars and Dumars, Durga Puja, and other Hindu festivals are adding to financial burdens. Moreover, the communities are also deeply involved in materialistic comforts which leads them into a debt trap and divert their attention from studies and good thoughts and keeps them away from social movements and awareness, which results in their continuance with the same occupational works.

One more important observation in marriage celebrations and also other cultural and social festivals is the duration of its celebration. It generally lasts as long as between the range of six to fifteen days. Some of the pujas and celebrations take even a month. The important rituals in these pujas are to be performed by relatives, such as sister, brother, uncle, son-in-law, daughter-in-law, etc. For each of these relatives, the role is well defined therefore their presence is a must on this occasion. In the olden times, such rituals were not affecting the life of the relatives to a much higher degree because at that time there was enough time available to all. But with the urbanization, migration, schooling, and nature of jobs, participation in such festivals or celebrations means discontinuation from schools or colleges and offices for this period. Moreover, the time of travel from their home town to their relative’s home is an added problem. This negatively affects the prospects of education of the young ones. We have observed across India, that participation of the family in rituals and rites also appears to be one of the prominent causes of discontinuation and dropout of children from schools. In many cases, the dropout students narrated that due to festivals and celebrations of their close relations, their education gets discontinued.

Celebration in Death Ceremony

Death is an event of sadness and pain. It is believed that the custom of death-feast is designed to help the grieving family to come out of the pain of their lost family member. This is a ritual where food is served to friends and relatives. This seems to be a positive custom. It has been observed across caste-class lines but practically this custom has taken an evil shape and it is proving a challenge to the family of the deceased. It is no surprise as a positive reaction many castes and individuals passed a resolution against the death-feast.[1] The government of Rajasthan, in the year 1960 had brought the Prevention of Mrityu-Bhoj Act. The Jat panchayat of Rajasthan also passed a resolution against it. The political leader with a modern outlook, for instance, the then Chief Minister of Madhya Pradesh Digvijay Singh himself disregarded this custom and revolted against it on the eve of the death of his wife. He straightforwardly refused to offer death-feast. There is thus a growing discontent and opposition against it. However, the scavenging community, in particular, is ritually much strict in the observance of death-feast. The sad part is that the expenses for this ceremony are also on par with the marriage ceremony celebration. Referring to the extravagance and uselessness of this custom a senior activist and reformer of the community shared:

> The death-feast among Valmikis is not different from a marriage celebration. The participants among Valmiki people, especially young girls and boys, wear fashionable dresses and put on makeup. The feast is organized at marriage lawns and the menu served is also not different from marriage parties. All the friends and colleagues of different castes are been invited to this feast. I can see the expression of other caste guests in this program. They are naturally developing queries in their mind, how come a poor Valmiki afford such an extravagant death festival? I don't know whether they get an answer to their question but I being from the community know that a personal loan with compound interest is the source of this celebration. I tried and in fact, keep on trying to make my community aware of this

1. See for instance, the Jat Panchayat of Rajasthan passed a resolution against death-feast https://english.newstracklive.com/news/jaat-mahapanchayat-put-ban-on-mrityubhoj-child-marriage-and-intoxication-mc23-nu764-ta321-1144161-1.html

> evil custom but very few understand. Extravagance and show-off have become a part of Valmiki culture. Our people are showing more interest in celebrations but hardly put any effort into educating their children and youth.

These enormous expenses for marriage, birth, death and other ceremonies not only result in financial loss but often make other castes envious. Sometimes such celebrationslower the empathy from the other communities therefore when an individual or a group wants sincerely to help guide and motivate the students in education or otherwise, they feel shockedby such extravagance. A senior activist of SKA narrates:

In the Police department, there was a man from the Valmiki caste working as a peon. He was allotted the duty to serve as the Superintendent of Police. The SP was kind to him and often granted, his leaves and other facilities. He was also helping him in all his difficulties. But things changed when there was a marriage in his family. This marriage was organized in one of the city's costliest party plots. The quality and standard of the ceremony were extremely good and the amount spent on this function was visible to all. The crackers of thousands of rupees were burnt in the function and much money was spent on lighting and decorations. He had invited all his staff to that function. But when the staff saw the extravagance in that function, from the next day onwards their behaviour towards him changed. He lost all the empathy and sympathy from the staff. As SP was also transferred to some other place the senior police staff didn't take any time in shifting him to office-bound duties.

This was not a strange case. The extravagances and materialistic lifestyles of communities withdraw the attention of NGOs and social activists to work for this community. A social activist of the Valmiki community ridicules these customs and says that the genuine social reformers and activists start thinking that if these families can spend so much money on such ceremonies, why do they count financial constraints in parting education to their children? How can these two opposite things go together? Such thoughtsdivert the attention of other communities and activists to work for the upliftment of this community.

Apart from a lack of financial planning and extravagance, the lack of application of family planning measures also badly affects the prospects of the family.

The Family Size

It is a well-established principle in management that to perfectly run any unit or organization there is a need for a perfect number of human resources. Either less number of human resources or higher number creates a problem in achieving the goal. Similarly, the country as a unit also needs a perfect balance in the human population for its development. We have seen that well-developed nations, for instance, the USA, USSR,[1] and most of the other developed nations have a balanced human population. The countries, such as China, which was at one time believed to be one of the backward nations was underdeveloped mainly because of its high population. As a response to this problem, China strictly introduced the single child policy across the nation. A study on the impact of the one-child policy in China reveals that the One-Child Policy (OCP) exerted a positive and significant impact on the educational attainment of Chinese migrants to the U.S. compared to other East Asian migrants in the same period. The magnitudes are meaningful in that, for men, the post-OCP increase of .75 of a year of education substantially narrows the education gap between migrants from China and their 12 other East Asian migrant counterparts.[2] The positive impact of small family size is well recognized in India, therefore in the year 1970, the Government of India under the regime of Indira Gandhi came up with a policy of forced sterilization which, however, had its disadvantages and ill effects due to improper implementation.[3] Yet the positive impact of this drive resulted in the balancing of the population to some extent. Later, the government brought a change in its stand and suggested a cafeteria policy by way of letting the couple choose to adopt any suitable means of contraception to control family size. Some of the state governments, such as the southern states and Madhya Pradesh, brought a strict ordinance that government jobs and eligibility of fighting in Panchayat elections will no longer be available to a person having more than two children. Such rules have bought some positive changes in the scenario. The people have begun to observe family planning measures to some extent.

There is no doubt that within the family, its size plays a major role in accessing and distributing resources. It becomes more important when there is a limitation of resources. It also impacts the children's education, as is well observed by Marteleto who finds that the children in larger families from both pre-and post-fertility decline cohorts are disadvantaged compared to children in smaller families – that is, even with other factors

1. Earstwhile name of Russia which was federation of many states. This was one of the most developed nations of the world at one time and was in cold war with USA.
2. http://ftp.iza.org/dp9196.pdf
3. http://www.bbc.com/news/world-asia-india-30040790

accounted for, the negative association of family size and educational outcomes persists in the younger cohort. This persistence of the negative effect of family size after fertility decline suggests that children in larger families in the younger cohort are seriously disadvantaged and should be targeted in policies that aim to increase both enrollment rates and educational attainment.[1]

The families engaged in scavenging and allied occupations on the other hand are found unaware of family planning measures. The average family size in the community is in the range of six or eight members. During interviews particularly with the male heads of families, it is common to notice that they even forget the names of their children. Quite obviously the classes in which they are studying are hardly known to their father. At present, it is a pattern that most of the parents are engaged in a contract job or petty private sector. They are low-paid workers. Moreover, a big problem with scavenging is that it requires leaving home early in the morning. This proved to hurt school-going children. However, in some cases, it is observed that with some adjustment of time, the mother of the family can manage the issue. But things get out of her control with the arrival of a newborn in the family. Sadly, most scavenging communities like any other poor and marginal communities are unaware of any family planning measures.

Another negative impact of the large family size on children across gender is that they do not get their own private space for their recreational activities and study. The absence of individual space prevents them to study and complete school assignments at home. The disturbance caused by the presence of siblings, and private and public conversation of parents is causing much disturbance. It is not at all conducive for school-going children. Further, the arrival of both local and outstation guests adds more trouble to their privacy. A fifteen year old girl Khushboo shared:

> You can see we do not have any space for our private affairs. I heard and also saw in films that the upper-class kids have a separate room for them. In our home, leave alonea separate room, we do not have even a separate corner. Our family members are doing all our household chores and other work in the same room. This naturally causes disturbance in my study. I found my classroom to be a better place to study than at home. But there is a limitation of the schools. I

1. Family Size, Demographic Change, and Educational Attainment: The Case of Brazil Leticia Marteleto https://www.psc.isr.umich.edu/pubs/pdf/rr05-584.pdf

> can't use my classroom for my study outside school hours. Anyhow, I am adjusting my studies at home also but whenever any guest either local or my relatives from outstation do come to our home, I can't study or complete my homework then. My teacher who is otherwise kind and serious gets angry at me whenever I am not able to complete the home assignments. I know there is no way out. We are five siblings naturally each of us and also our parents are struggling with the same issue.[1]

Thirdly, the high number of children in a family makes parents irresponsible towards their family obligations. They are unable to pay individual attention to their children. As discussed earlier it is strange but a common observation that the fathers in such cases are even unable to remember the names of their children. The children are left out without any proper care and support. The family size also results in a disturbance of the family budget and as an immediate result, the family suffers from malnutrition. The financial burden on parents compels the children to engage in gainful employment at the earliest. Many of the children in such cases take up the work of rag-picking or get work in shops or houses. It is a common practice especially observed in the state government schools of Chhattisgarh that almost each of the students are engaged in some sort of part-time work after school hours. The extra responsibility not only drains their energy but also diverts their concentration from their studies. They are unable to perform home assignments and do self-study at home. This often results in their becoming dropouts. Fifteen years old Raju of Korba narrates:

> When I was in the fourth class. My family condition compelled me to work in a shop. I used to help a tea seller after my school hours. It was a good experience for me as I was able to manage both my school studies and my work together. Things were moving well for the year. But a few days later a new boy of the same age joined the tea stall. He was not studying in any school therefore he was able to devote his service from early morning till late hours. The tea seller then asked me to discontinue my work since he got a full-timer. Then I joined a mechanic shop. Here also my school was coming as a barrier for my work. The mechanic uncle was kind to me and once he suggested leaving school altogether and joining his shop as a full-timer. He also promised to raise my salary. I accepted the offer and left my schooling in between. I think it was my right decision I have

1. Personal Interview during Field work.

no regrets because those of my friends who continued their schooling have all dropped out in later days.[1]

Debt Trap

Financial crises are a quite common phenomenon in Indian society, especially among the poor and lower-middle-class families. This is one of the known reasons behind the dropout of students. However, it is observed that in many cases the real cause of poverty is not simply the low income of the households. There are many families engaged in scavenging works whose outward appearance of communities doesn't generally reflect their poor condition. There are a number of respondents who seem to be enjoying materialistic pleasures and comforts. LCD TVs, motorbikes, fridges, coolers, and other furnishing items are quite commonly visible in most houses. Yet in reality, the families are found to be under tremendous financial pressure and in debt. There are several cultural reasons behind this problem.The scavenging communities irrespective of their caste background strongly believe and practice the culture of showing off as discussed above probably to come out of a feeling of being lowly and depressed. However, the long term impact is the debt trap.

Graded Inequality within the Scavenging Castes

Another issue within scavenging and allied communities is the persistence of graded inequality within their castes and sub-castes. This practice seems to be stranger but being a practitioner of the caste system. Observance of graded inequality until its last step is a natural outcome. The Valmikis consider them ritually higher than other scavenging castes. They consider castes like Dom to be of lower rank and lacked morality. In a discussion with a Valmiki respondent at Sagar, he commented:

> We the Lalbegis are known for our morality. In our caste, we do practice strict gotra exogamy for five generations. This is a unique practice of Lalbegis. No other castes including the Brahmins bother to follow this. If at all they follow gotra exogamy only of their father and mother's side. But we are strict in gotra exogamy. But you see these Doms. They have no such moral values. They are lowly. They never consider gotra exogamy in their marriage. [2]

Many such ill wills against the Domarare popular amongst the Lalbegis, who are largely claiming Valmiki identity. Interestingly, the

1. Field based interview.
2. Interview during Field work.

same person sharing his negative and casteist views against Domar also shared how he and his family faced discrimination and untouchability from her neighbour, a Basor (A caste involved in the Bamboo making). He said, 'that Basor woman was so casteist that she doesn't allow us to fill our water pot before her from a common public tap. If we do so she used to wash the tap with 4-5 buckets of water.' The practice of untouchability is not a unique phenomenon. It is carried out in many places. At one time in southern Madhya Pradesh especially in Betul district, the Chamar caste which was at one time fully involved in leatherwork including scanning and tanning did discriminate against the Mahar as untouchable, who were not employed in any 'unclean' occupations.[1]

One such interesting case is the case of Musahars in Bihar. This caste at present is one of the most vulnerable castes among Dalits. Many projects are being run by the state and NGOs exclusively for the Musahars. This caste is facing acute malnutrition and poverty. At one time they were the outcasts engaged in rat-hunting. Later they began to engage as skilled agrarian labour. Possibly being associated with 'clean' work of agrarian labour the Musahar were at a higher grade than the Rajaks (the Dhobis), who were involved in the cleaning of dirty clothes. The Musahars used to treat Dhobis as 'untouchable' and forbid them to accept food and water from them. However, with the change of time, Rajaks earned better financial status and many of them attained upward occupational mobility. On the other side, due to distress in agrarian work, the Musahars are forced to migrate to urban centres, where there is no work available for them. Their skills in agriculture become useless in cities. Being jobless they got involved in scavenging and allied occupations. Yet, even in distress, the traditional Musahars continued to observe the caste rules against occupationally mobile Rajaks. On the contrary, Rajaks being better in both financial and social status in new settings do keep their distance fromMusahars both on practical grounds of being better settled in the city as well as with their reverse caste-hatred[2] against the Musahars on account of being treated untouchables by them. Thus, the Musahars at present are witnessing both social and economic depression. Moreover, due to a lack of socio-political awareness, the Musahars are quite distant from the Dalit movement. Emergence of Jeetan Ram Manjhi, a Musahar leader in ruling JD(U) was offered the post of Chief Minister of Bihar for

1. A senior Ambedkarite shared this piece of information.
2. Reverse caste-hatred used to describe the reaction of the oppressed and discriminated castes against the oppressor castes. A hatred of occupationally mobile Dalits against Brahmin caste is also termed as reverse caste-hatred.

a short term. This also helped the community to be a part of right-wing politics. His political outfit Hindustani Awam Morcha (HAM) was the partner of the ruling JD(U)-BJP coalition in the state.

A famous Advocate Bhagwan Das, who hails from one of the scavenging communities Khakrob of Himachal Pradesh writes:

> The Sweepers and scavengers of UP and Bihar are no better. The Balmikis, a recently adopted name in replacement of Chuhra and Lalbegis, look down upon the Helas, Dhanuks, Domars, Rawats and Hans. They observe untouchability like any other so-called high caste men.[1]

The extent of graded inequality within scavenging castes is not restricted to Bihar or other northern states but is ubiquitously found in every state. One such inter-caste discrimination is reported to me by Ambedkarite Researcher Dhamma Darshan Nigam associated with SKA, referred one such incident:

> In June 2017, I was on fieldwork in the Sanchi district of Madhya Pradesh on behalf of SafaiKaramchariAndolan. We were staying at a community organizer's place in Sanchi, Madhya Pradesh. In the afternoon, we went to the houses of the women around the community and told them that we are having a meeting on the problems of the community in the evening. Almost all the women we spoke to, had arrived on time. By laying a tarpaulin, we had requested everyone to sit. But I realized that they were not sitting together. When I asked for the reason, one of the women says that *ham inkichaukhat pe nahibaithate* (we do not sit on their doorstep) shockingly the woman who shared this belonged to the Domar caste. This incident opened up my eyes. I being a Dalit, was sometimes critical of the Dalit movement that it had not paid enough attention to the question of scavenging. Also, sometimes I did join the chorus that the scavenging castes are Dalit among Dalits. However, this incident was an eye-opener. I realized that there is equal casteism and graded inequality within scavenging communities as it exists between any other set of castes.[2]

Due to the efforts of some Dalit organizations, such as the Safai Karmachari Aandolan (SKA) and a few others, many scavenging castes are now coming into the fold of the Dalit movement. We have observed

1. Collected Works Bhagwan Das Vol 2 ed. Shura Darapuri Dalit Today Prakashan, Luknow 2010, p. 122.
2. https://www.newsclick.in/we-sit-doorpost-sanitation-castes-untouchability-within

that in some places, for instance at Sagar, many of the Valmikis keep the portrait of Dr. Ambedkar in their homes. In Haryana, Chhattisgarh, and elsewhere, there is increased participation of scavenging castes in the Dalit movement. It is a fact that if more individuals and more new castes do join the movement it becomes stronger and effective in claiming their entitlements.

The prevalent socio-cultural practices among the scavenging communities play an important role in maintaining their backwardness and immobility. It is also affecting the prospects of their future generation. The graded inequality which is the structured outcome of the caste system is equally filtered down to the scavenging community and infected them to the extent that the practice and mindset of low and high have got well-established among them. The scavenging castes on account of their various and diverse castes and sub-castes are divided into a vertical structure. The hierarchical division followed by the customary philosophy and backward socio-religious and political philosophy not only keeps the community in darkness but is putting hindrances in their supposed unionization to access their rights and entitlements. The community will be in a better position to call for accountability on the part of the state, authorities, and educational institutions to improve the educational status of their children.

Chapter - 8

Responsibility of a Responsible Government

> There are very few countries in the world where there may be said to prevail so many social evils as has been the case in India. Law is a means by which society from time to time repairs its ills in order to affect its conservation.
>
> **-Dr Babasaheb Ambedkar**[1]

We have discussed various reasons for the marginality and vulnerability of the scavenging and allied communities. As neutral observers, we have not only discussed the external factors but also discussed those features and peculiarities of the community that keep them immobile and reduce the opportunities to access their rights and entitlements. It needs to be mentioned that whatever the main reason for this backwardness, it is the duty and responsibility of the state to check and correct the problem. In this regard, it is worth mentioning that the Constitution of India is a tremendous achievement for the vulnerable and marginal sections as it puts an end to discrimination, injustice, and exclusion in any form and paves the way to establish an egalitarian society based on justice and liberty. Article 17 of the Indian Constitution is the legislation that abolishes the practice of untouchability in any form. Article 15 states that no citizen shall be subject to 'any disability, liability, restriction or condition' based on religion, race, caste, sex, and place of birth. Their access to public properties like shops, restaurants, and entertainment hubs should not be restricted on grounds of religion or caste. This article also guarantees special provisions for women, children, and socially disadvantaged classes. While Article 46 says 'the State shall

1. BAWS Vol. 6, p. 262.

promote with special care the educational and economic interests of the weaker sections of the people, and, in particular, of the Scheduled Castes and the Scheduled Tribes, and shall protect them from social injustice and all forms of exploitation.'

These measures, particularly the protective discrimination policy of reservation to Dalits and tribes in employment and education, have helped in rooting democracy firmly in India. Quite obviously the real meaning of reservation is representation.[1] This provision has made a revolutionary change in the lives of many marginal castes and tribes. Many Dalits have achieved upward occupational mobility to the extent that some castes came out of their traditional caste occupations *en masse*. Even among the traditional scavenging community, many individuals make their presence felt in higher education, bureaucracy and in other sectors. Later, parliamentary interventions such as the introduction and enactment of the Right of Children to Free and Compulsory Education Act (RTE) 2009, also ensured the reach of quality education to a section of poor, Dalits, and Adivasis and has promised to build a better environment to ensure education for all.[2] The Mid-Day-Meal schemes played a pivotal role in retaining students in schools.[3] Further, the pre-matric and post-matric scholarships, and the Rajiv Gandhi Fellowship for M.Phil. and Ph.D. students are playing a commendable role in spreading education among them.[4]

Yet, in hindsight, sanitation work continues to be a fixed occupation of a few castes that have traditionally been associated with 'unclean' occupations. Even worse is the fact that with the passage of time those marginal castes and tribes which were not associated with scavenging and allied services also fall into this occupation. The castes, such as Musahar and Kori, fall into sanitation occupations which were otherwise associated with other sorts of traditional occupations.[5] A section of Chamar, Dusadh and tribals such as Hadi, Gond, Kharia, Oraon also fall into this

1. For detail understanding of reservation see, EWS: The Quota to End All Quotas, The Shared Mirror 2021.
2 https://dsel.education.gov.in/rte
3. Study of Impact of Mid-Day Meal (MDM) Programme on School Enrolment & Retention, August 2014 State Council for Educational Research & Training (SCERT), Chhattisgarh The Director, State Council for Educational Research & Training (SCERT), Shankar Nagar, Raipur, Chhattisgarh – 492007, p. 55.
4. There is as such no study available on the impact of RGNF but based on personal observation its impact is visible is in all the central as well as state universities where a sizeable number of Dalit students are seen directly benefitted.
5. Discussed in chapter 1 of this book.

occupation.[1] In some parts, a negligible presence of general castes is also found in this occupation but this shall not be a matter of serious concern because on the one hand, such presence gives a positive signal that the caste system is diminishing while on the other hand, this feeble presence owing to a number of reasons, such as sympathy and support of their caste men, is unable to bind these workers and their heirs permanently into this trap, as it is the case of Dalits and tribals.

The downward occupational mobility of certain Dalits and tribals after the enforcement of more than 70 years of the Constitution should be a serious question before the Dalit movement, particularly for those castes which are acclaimed to be the flag bearers of Ambedkarism and the Dalit movement, and which firmly advocate occupational mobility and getting out of traditional caste occupations.[2] It is equally serious concern as to why the tribes which at one time were out of the caste structures, are now falling to the lowest rung in the caste hierarchy and graded inequality.

A few radical thinkers, like Anand Teltumbde, for instance, put the blame on the Constitution for all such problems.[3]In his view, it is a bourgeois document prepared under the direction of feudal forces to preserve the *status quo*. However, such a charge is futile and baseless because we can also not ignore the tremendous achievements of the Dalits and Tribals after the enactment of the Constitution. These achievements disprove Teltumbde's observations. The real reason for such a situation is not the Constitution but its poor implementation. Ambedkar's last speech in the Constituent Assembly offers deeper insights to understand the problem:

> The third thing we must do is not to be content with mere political democracy. We must make our political democracy a social democracy as well. Political democracy cannot last unless there lies at the base of it social democracy.[4]

He then explained the meaning of social democracy which he says recognizes liberty, equality, and fraternity as the principles of life. He further said:

---

1. Ibid.
2. In each states there are one or two castes among Dalits that are seen active in Dalit movement while rest of the Dalit communites remain passive. For instance, in Bihar the Dusadh, in Uttar Pradesh it is Jatav and Chamar, in Madhya Pradesh it Mahar and Chamar and in Maharashtra, the Mahar is prominent flag bearer of Dalit movements while remaining Dalit communities are passive.
3. Anand Teltumbde frequently repeated this statement in his talks and delivery address.
4. Writing & Speeches of Dr. Babasaheb Ambedkar Vol. 13 p. 1215.

> On the 26th of January 1950, we are going to enter into a life of contradictions. In politics, we will have equality and in social and economic life we will have inequality. In politics, we will be recognizing the principle of one man one vote, and one vote one value. In our social and economic life, we shall, by reason of our social and economic structure, continue to deny the principle of one man one value. How long shall we continue to live this life of contradictions? How long shall we continue to deny equality in our social and economic life? If we continue to deny it for long, we will do so only by putting our political democracy in peril.[1]

This contradiction was seen in the foundation of our Parliament from the beginning. Most of the members of Parliament belonged to the socio-economic elite class. The other public representatives in state assemblies and elsewhere belonged to the dominant castes. The bureaucracy and judiciary were always in control of the social elite. Moreover, the process of enactment of the Constitution rested on the shoulders of those whose social, religious, and political ideologies were diametrically opposite to the spirit of the Constitution. This contradiction between their social and political life results in the slow and ineffective implementation of the Constitution. Therefore, change in society is much slower than expected. One of the honest comments about this situation was uttered by former Prime Minister Rajiv Gandhi on his visit to the drought-affected Kalahandi district of Odisha. He said, 'of every rupee spent by the government, only 15 paise reached the intended beneficiary'.[2]Similar is the fate of our constitutional measures. However, there was a positive change that appeared during the short-lived regime of VP Singh government, when apart from other positive measures, the Scheduled Caste, and Scheduled Tribe (Prevention of Atrocities) Act, 1989 was passed. The Dalit leader Ram Vilas Paswan was instrumental in introducing this law. In later years, more subsequent and targetedlegal action in favour of the scavenging community was taken during the Congress rule in the name of 'The Employment of Manual Scavengers and Construction of Dry Latrines (Prohibition) Act, 1993'. This provided for the prohibition of the employment of manual scavengers as well as the construction or continuance of dry latrines. It also provided for the regulation of construction and maintenance of water-seal latrines and for matters

1. Ibid p. 1216.
2. 'Only 15 paise reaches the needy': SC quotes Rajiv Gandhi in its Aadhaar verdict | Latest News India - Hindustan Times

connected therewith or incidental thereto. There were shortcomings in this Act but the bigger issue was that of proper implementation.[1]

In the year 2013, Manual Scavengers and their Rehabilitation Act was introduced with an aim to include a wide range of manual scavengers. This Act aims to provide for the prohibition of employment as manual scavengers, rehabilitation of manual scavengers and their families and for matters connected therewith or incidental thereto. This statute has 8 chapters and 39 sections. There is a chapter which includes the identification of insanitary latrines, the identification of manual scavengers in urban and rural areas and their rehabilitation, and the institution of implementing authorities and vigilance committees. This Act also contains miscellaneous provisions on the duties of local authorities and other agencies to use modern technology for cleaning of sewers, etc., It also refers to the jurisdiction of civil courts, power of appropriate government to make rules, power of central government to make model rules, power to exempt, etc.[2]This Act seems to be very revolutionary in nature yet, in practice, it is openly defied. The sewer deaths continue to rise. As many as 110 people died of asphyxia while cleaning sewers and septic tanks in the country in the year 2020.[3]In a response to the question in parliament Union minister, Ramdas Athawale said 57 people died cleaning sewers and septic tanks in 2015, 48 died the next year, 93 in 2017, and 68 in 2018. Uttar Pradesh topped the list of sewer deaths last year at 21, followed by Maharashtra (17), Gujarat (16), and Tamil Nadu (15).[4]

The decision of Hon'ble Supreme Court in the year 2014 made a positive intervention by laying down the provision of payment of rupees 10 lakh in case of sewer death along with other compensations.[5]But it has not yet been able to prevent the deaths of workers, and manual scavenging and sewer deaths are still continuing. In the case of the death of a manual scavenger in the sewers, the devastation wrought on his family leaves little hope left for the children.

1. https://www.indiacode.nic.in/bitstream/123456789/1581/1/199346.pdf
2. https://www.latestlaws.com/bare-acts/central-acts-rules/service-labour-laws/prohibition-employment-manual-scavengers-rehabilitation-act2013/
3. 110 people died cleaning sewers last year, highest since 2015: Athawale - India News (indiatoday.in)
4. No Reports of People Being Convicted for Employing Manual Scavengers: Centre (thewire.in)
5. https://indiankanoon.org/doc/150996920/

Contractualization of Lower Services

The decade of the 90s witnessed counter-revolutionary changes in the economic policies. In the name of liberalization and globalization, there is an increase in privatization of services and contractualization. Yet, the supporters of liberalization and capitalism, give several arguments in support of these policies. A few Dalits such as Chandrabhan Prasad[1] also joined this chore to defend capitalism. However, on the question of exploitation of labour and increased reinforcement of the *status quo* and downward mobility of the lower castes, these people remain silent. Privatization puts a brake on the progress of the working class. During the initial days of its establishment of the government sector, labourers including sanitation workers were recruited permanently. This resulted in fair wages and social security which in turn led to the possibility of better education for their children. This provided an opportunity of occupational mobility for the next generation.

Most of the middle class Dalits today are the progeny of the third generation of government servants. Their journey to their present occupations was built on the foundation of their grandparents working as labourers or peons. Their salaried jobs, social security and comparatively better habitations, sometimes due to the availability of government quarters or otherwise because of their ability to rent houses with better infrastructure, provided an opportunity for their children to perform better in education. As a result, their children found it easy to become clerks, teachers or get into other such white collar jobs and occupations. The middle class jobs of the second generation of Dalits proved to be even more beneficial for their children as they got better education, support, and guidance that resulted in their elevation into officer ranks. This chain of occupational mobility from one generation to another has resulted in the occupation of some top rank jobs to the Dalits. If this process continued for a few more decades or for a century, there was a possibility that none of the Dalits would have remained in the trap of their traditional caste occupations. However, this effective chain of mobility was broken by the contract system and privatization.

At present a contract labourer or sanitation worker under a private contractor gets such a low wage that he is unable to fulfill his basic needs. The parents are unable to spend on the education of their children and therefore they have an uncertain future. Moreover, the decline in quality of education in government schools further plays an important role in

1. His articles defending liberalization and privatization have been appeared in Rashtriya Sahara and the pioneer.

making their lives miserable to such an extent that they have no other option than to become sanitation workers. Once one slips down in the downward occupation, it results in the permanent downfall of his family and generation. The system of contractualization and privatization thus craftily rejuvenated the traditional caste structure, which was once heavily crushed by the Constitution of India. In the era of the contract system, the one who is born in a family of labourers will remain a labourer while those born in elite families will get wide support and facilities to move forward and upward and to make their presence in the global market. The class system as a result becomes an enclosed system. As Ambedkar mentioned in his first seminal research that any enclosed system ultimately becomes caste. Therefore, it is not surprising that this new economic policy is recreating the strictest caste system based on graded inequality. Privatisation and contractualisationare nothing but a new social code of globalized Manu which is turning the lower classes into lower castes, and ultimately turning them into outcastes.

Therefore, unless there is a revolt in the socio-economic and political system there is no hope for the scavenging and other vulnerable communities. To overcome this problem of stagnation, there is a dire need to abolish the contract system. To root out the problem and to break the vicious circle of poverty, exclusion and discrimination, the State must change the policy of recruitment and the contract job system. Without regularization of services, there is neither any hope of safety and security for the workers nor is there any scope left for a better future for their children. Regularization of sanitation work alone could provide job security, better wages and open a channel for occupational mobility of the future generations of the scavenging and other vulnerable communities. Otherwise, they remain in the trap of this vicious circle.

Non-implementation of Labour Laws

It has been observed that in the matter of labour laws, the lower levels of officers are not sincere. In practice, labour laws are not applicable to the sanitation workers. It has been observed that the working hours of a Sweeper are more than other staff members. This is so because they have to clean the office premises before its formal opening. Therefore, the presence of a Sanitation Worker becomes a must before the actual office time. Further, in most instances, the closing of the office also becomes an additional responsibility of the Sweepers.[1] Thus for both these important

1. This is based on primary information collected during field work in Sagar where it a common practise in government offices.

duties and tasks, their presence is required in the office for much longer hours than the other staff. This is a clear defiance of labour laws. The extra and strenuous work affects the Sweeper's family life and it also results in affecting their duty as a parent towards their children. As a result, the children do not get proper support, love, care and guidance from their parents. This naturally affects their performance in school.

Another important event is forcible labour in religious gatherings. On such occasions,sanitation workers are even more exploited and forcible manual scavenging was imposed on them. This fact is discussed in detail in Chapter 3 that on religious occasions the government takes a proactive role by fixing the duties of Sweepers working in the Municipal Corporation, who were posted at the sites of this religious function which is generally located far off from the main cities. As a result, they had to be out of their home for 5-6 days but they were neither compensated with any leaves nor provided any overtime. And in the case of Jain religious retreats, the Sweepers are forced to perform manual scavenging. During the mass gatherings of Hindus, such as *Kumbha Melas* the Sweepers are transferred to the sites, no matter how far is that place from their hometown. Under the contract ship, their salary and other entitlements are dependent on the whims and fancies of the contractors. In hospitals, authorities force the Sweepers to conduct a post-mortem which is technically the duty of Surgeons. In many instances, the labour laws are not applied to the Sanitation workers. The extra and strenuous work affects the family life and thus the parental care is affected.

It is the responsibility of the government to strictly implement labour laws in both organized and unorganized sectors. The rag pickers and the garbage collectors collecting door-to-door or elsewhere should also be brought under the protection of labour law.

The Poor Infrastructure of Schools

We have observed all across that the schools of the scavenging community students are poor in terms of infrastructure whether it is a government school or a private one. In the case of schools catering to poor students, private schools are often worse than government schools. In most cases, the quality of schools in terms of imparting education as well as in terms of infrastructure is worse. The private schools where the poor Dalit children study are in a deplorable condition. Buildings are small, there are no separate classrooms, there is an absence of a playground, there are no library facilities, and toilets are badly maintained. The unusable toilets for girls further add to girls' poor attendance and often result in them dropping out. Teachers are paid a meagre salary by the management; therefore, their quality and commitment are poor. This is the condition of private schools of the poor caste-class students. The marginalized section's preference for private schools is the result of a parent's desire to impart quality education to their children despite their tight economic conditions, without knowing the truth of the efficacy of these schools. As a result, private schools are increasingly gaining the admission of poor children. The poor infrastructure and lack of basic facilities nullify the dreams of their parents in later years when they find their children making no progress in the field of education and end up becomingdropouts. However, this process takes a long time of about 6-12 years. During this long duration, schools can extract money from poor parents' pockets and the result comes at the end when there is no option left for them. There are reasons behind the poor infrastructure and improper maintenance apart from the sheer negligence from the school authorities. In an interview, a principal of a private school inKorba shared:

> The state government is providing enough funds to the government schools. It is an amount that is well utilized. You can see the proper boundary wall, toilets, and sports ground there. The buildings are also well managed but… we are a private school catering to the poor students, we are not able to spend any amount on its maintenance. Our fee is low and we do not get any funds or grants from the government. But we have to pay our staff and run our activities only with the amount that we receive as a fee from our students. In such conditions, how can we repair and renovate our building?[1]

However, as mentioned above, the deplorable condition is not the problem of private schools alone, government schools are equally facing this problem, especially in the states of Madhya Pradesh, Chhattisgarh, Bihar, Rajasthan, Jharkhand, and many other places. There are some common reasons for this but in some cases, there are also specific reasons. For instance, in Sagar, most of the government schools lack basic infrastructural facilities because of a legal factor. Being a cantonment area, reconstruction of the building is strictly prohibited in this city no matter how deplorable school buildings are. The school authorities are not allowed to reconstruct it in any way. Because of such restrictions, the school runs in a limited building. In one of the schools, the classes from 1st to 8th run in one hall. The students of various classes sit together in

1. Discrimination and Exclusion in Education…Madhya Pradesh and Chhattisgarh p. 96.

this hall. The students of each of the classes have to face in one particular direction in the same hall according to their class. There is not even a curtain or any other sort of division to mark the boundary between various classes. In the absence of any partition, it is very difficult for teachers to instruct the students of their class. Also, it is more difficult for the students of a particular class to listen to the instruction of their respective teachers. The scene in this school resembles a village festival. Further, due to the absence of any division of classrooms, there is no question of a separate blackboard. As per the needs, some of the teachers do use the wall to hang the paper blackboard. The teachers share blackboards as per the need. One can easily assume the pitiable situation when on one side Hindi class is going and on the other side, there is mathematics progressing.

In Rajasthan, it is observed that most of the schools have small rooms that are congested, dark with no proper ventilation facilities. Classrooms with tin sheds made students more vulnerable during summers in the case of Rajasthan known for its dry climate. There are no playgrounds in most cases and hardly any space to conduct any cultural event, etc. Most of the school buildings are old and are a threat to the children's safety. Schools, in general, lack basic facilities like toilets, drinking water, and electricity. There is an urgent need to repair the buildings and they need to be properly looked after. Since the schools are located in the slum areas, they are congested and have no place even to conduct classes in the open. In a few cases, there are not even fans in classrooms which is a major concern as during extreme summer, especially in Rajasthan, children get heat strokes and rashes on their bodies. There is an absence of a library in most schools.However, in case if there is one, it is just for a namesake. The books are locked inside the bookshelves. There is no librarian or any authority to issue books to the children. A government school in Gaya, which denied admission to the students of a settlement of a Dom-MusaharTola[1], also described another sad side of the story. This school was covered from all three sides by other buildings.There was one entrance gate of about ten feet in height, and it was fully opaque. This was designed so as to ensure the restriction of rowdies on campus, which is otherwise a common feature in most government schools. But this increased height and opaque structure are also giving a feeling of a jail. There was no free space on the campus.The building was divided into two parts, left and right and the space between is hardly eight feet. This narrow street-like space is the only place that is utilized for morning prayers, games, and other activities. The size of classrooms was so small

1. This matter is discussed elaborately in chapter 4 'The unclean practice in campus.'

that some of the classes were also held in this open space. The higher numerical strength of students is adding more trouble. The limited space is the main reason behind the denial of admission to some children. However, whom to select, and whom to reject certainly depends on the caste and socio-economic profile of children. Of course, the Musahar children are the victims of denial of admission. The teacher present in the school added that the limitation of space is a prominent reason for the denial of admission to some children. 'We have to give first preference to those children whose residence is close to the schools. The children from comparatively far-off locations are sometimes denied admission due to a limited number of seats available.'[1] Unfortunately, even space is the reason for denial of admission and the sufferers are none other than scavenging community students.

In most of the schools, there is a shortage of water and there are no toilets. There are small water tanks used for drinking water. The toilet facility is a major concern in most schools. It was reported in the selected universe of the study that only in a few schools there is a separate staff appointed to clean the school and toilets. In both formal and informal discussions barring a few cases, most of the students claimed that they were asked to clean toilets or school premises. This shows the strictness of state administration against any sort of practice of discrimination in school. Most of the other schools also do not have any gatekeeper facility, therefore, children generally run away from schools by giving excuses of water or toilets. However, in the cities of Jabalpur, Bilaspur and Korba, the school buildings of government schools are found to be better. In this regard, it is the responsibility of the State, to implement the provision of RTE in every school and ensure the proper construction and regular maintenance of these schools.

Lack of Quality Education

The government sector is known for the irresponsible behaviour of employees and government institutes. These institutes are said to be under red-tapism. The worst sufferer of this branding is government schools. For instance, it has been observed in Madhya Pradesh that the enrolment in government schools is on the decline as an increasing number of parents including those of poor sections are preferring private schools for their kids.[2] This is resulting in the merger of girls and boys schools

1. Discrimination and Exclusion in Education…Bihar and Jharkhand p. 81.
2. Madhya Pradesh: EnrollmentIn Classes 1-8 In Government Schools Falls To Almost Half In 2020-21 (ndtv.com)

into one and even the closure of many government schools. However, the trend is different in Bihar. On the one hand, as is the case of other states, there is a flourishing of private schools in Bihar, many of these schools are not recognized by the Education Department of Bihar. Therefore, the students enrolled in such schools are also taking proxy admissions in the government schools (besides being regular in these private schools).[1] This trend is not limited to the middle class alone but it is equally followed by the children of scavenging communities especially in Bodhgaya, where many Buddhist missionary schools impart quality education free of cost. However, most of these missionary schools are not recognized by the government, therefore the scavenging community students studying in these schools also follow the same strategy of registering their names in government schools simultaneously along with their admission in Buddhist missionary schools.[2]

The students studying in government schools shared the non-seriousness of the teaching staff in imparting their duties. The continuous lethargic environment in school leads to students' disinterest in studies and ultimately results in their becoming dropouts. Some narratives of the students tell the reasons for their dropping out. A dropout girl Ruby described the situation of her school in the following words:

> I had exams in our school but we were never told about our results. The school people told everyone collectively that we have passed the exam and have been promoted to another class. Teachers never came on time to our school. Even if they came to school on time, they would never teach. Instead, they used to chat among themselves or used to get busy on their phones. Studies never happened on time at our school. Children used to make noise. If I ever protested against anything wrong then teachers used to scold me and make me sit quietly. No girl in our Ravidas colony has completed her matriculation. All of the girls leave their studies in between. After leaving school I told my father to get me admitted to some other school but he said that what would be the use of resuming school after a gap of one year? He said that I have learned enough to write my name and more study will be of no use. Also, I do not need to do a job. When I told my mother to get me admission to another school, she left me in the lurch by relying on my father's decision. Other caste people discriminate against us by saying that we people

1. Field based information.
2. Ibid.

of Ravidas caste remove the skin of dead animals.[1]

The insincere attitude of teachers is increasing day by day. When we ask about this to the teachers, the common response is 'at one point of time we used to be more serious in our task of teaching. But with the introduction of the RTE and Atrocities Act (PoA), we feel handcuffed. We cannot punish students; neither can we speak to them in a louder tone. Then how come we teach them'. This statement is just an excuse to defend their position.However, in reality, the lack of a proper monitoring system by the Department of Education is the main reason for the lethargy of the teachers. The quality in government schools as well as petty private schools is declining because they are catering to a poor class of students. The teachers' disinterest in teaching is also seen as 'tactical' discrimination. Anyway, for poor and debilitating conditions o f education, theresponsibility lies with the State.

Denial of Reservation on Flimsy Ground

In every civilized society, an individual is free to practice a religion of personal choice. Article 25, of the Constitution, guarantees the freedom of conscience, the freedom to profess, practise, and propagate one's religion to all citizens. But this article comes in conflict with restrictions on religious conversion. The matter becomes grave when a person of Scheduled Caste origin gets converted to Christianity or Islam. In such a case, this person loses the Scheduled Caste identity. This provision was not included in the original Constitution but was amended in 1956. The Constitution Order (Amendment) Act 1956 says:

> No person who professes a religion other than the Hindu or the Sikh religion shall be deemed to be a member of a Scheduled Castes.[2]

This restriction was however challenged by the Buddhist converts who embraced Buddhism under the guidance of Dr Ambedkar. As a result, this act was altered under the Scheduled Castes Order (Amendment) Act, 1990.[3]This opens the entitlements to the Buddhists from among the Scheduled Castes. However, the limitation of this amendment is that it extends this facility to Buddhists alone. The Sikhs are also included in this but the converts to other religions, for instance, Christianity and Islam, are still not included in this amendment.

1. Ibid p. 164.
2. SCHEDULED CASTES AND SCHEDULED TRIBES ORDERS (AMENDMENT) ACT 1956 (commonlii.org)
3. This amendment was done in the constitution at the time of VP Singh, who was known for his pro-active Dalit and OBC agenda.

It is observed that there are a sizable number of scavengers across the nation who follow Christianity. We have particularly found Christian scavengers in Jabalpur, Korba, Bilaspur, Solan, Shimla, Panipat and Faridabad. The Muslim scavengers are equally high in number in many states. Yet both these groups of people are denied SC status on account of their religion. The Muslim scavengers are included only in the OBC category in some cases although their status is much below that of the Pasmanda Muslims. The scavengers irrespective of their religious faith are facing equal challenges in all walks of life. Therefore, it is the responsibility of the government to take their concern seriously. There is no point in denying their entitlement.

We have also come across a number of instances where inter-state migrants tend to lose their SC status in the new state. In such a case, there is a limitation from the Constitution to ensure that the benefits of reservation reach the native scheduled caste. This measure is all right as far as it is in contradiction with the local Dalits however when their presence is not affecting the entitlements of the local Dalits their case is to be taken seriously by the state. In the case of admission in a government school, there is no competition between the local Dalits and the migrant Dalits. It is a fact that in all the government schools the seats are available for admission in the school. This has happened to such a level that there are ample cases where two or more schools got merged into one school and in some instances, the schools were closed down due to the non-availability of the students. In such a situation the government must facilitate the admission of SC and ST students irrespective of their native state and ensure them pre-matric and post-matric scholarships. In such a case the respective state government may find it a financial burden.Therefore, in order to avoid this contradiction, the scholarships of migrant SCs and STs are to be funded by the Ministry of Social Justice and Empowerment, Government of India, to the respective state governments. This step by the government could open the possibility of accessing education. Secondly, the migrant Dalits and tribals shall be included in the EWS quota, which at present is available only to the elite castes. This provision is anyway anti-constitutional[1]but if it is in practice, it shall be open to all irrespective of their castes and creeds. On logical and humane grounds, the migrant scavengers shall be the first category of beneficiaries of such provision. Also, the government has to seek the possibility to have a separate

1. A Supreme Court lawyer MP Raju has extensively shared his ideas questioning the unconstitutionality of this amendment in his talk at Indian Social Institute, New Delhi.

quota for sanitation workers and all those involved in 'unclean' castes irrespective of their caste and tribe.

The data collected from Bihar show that Musahar is the most numerous caste engaged in scavenging occupation. This caste and its various subcastes are at present listed in the SC category in Bihar. But the ethnographic details of this caste and features suggest that this social group is more like a tribe than a caste. The traditional livelihood of this caste was rat hunting and at one time they used to live in jungles. There is very little interaction of Musahars with other Dalit castes and despite being most lowly among the Dalits, the Musahars consider themselves ritually superior to other Dalits and they forbid accepting food and water from the Rajak caste. These peculiarities bring them closer to tribes than to the Dalits. The practice of untouchability against Dalits was common among the Gonds of Madhya Pradesh at one time. They refuse to accept water from Dalit houses. The practise of untouchability by Musahars against Rajaks seems to bring them to the Gonds which are recognized as Scheduled Castes in Madhya Pradesh, Chhattisgarh and many other states. Moreover, among 52 castes listed in the SC list of Bihar, the Musahars get very little representation in government services and other entitlements. Therefore, if the Musahars are reclassified into the ST category, instead of SC, this would be logical on the ethnological ground as well as it proves to be beneficial for Musahars to claim their rights and better representation as there are fewer STs in Bihar.

Exclusionary Syllabus

The syllabus of the schools is not inclusive. We have seen in the recent past that despite the claim of inclusivity in the NCERT syllabus, the worst case of insensitivity has been depicted in the textbooks, wherein a cartoon, Dr. Ambedkar was shown beaten by Nehru with a whip.[1] Strangely, on the one side, RTE is strongly opposing corporal punishment but the authors of this book do not hesitate to include this violent cartoon in the textbook. This is one example of the insensitivity of NCERT. The syllabus overall is not inclusive and the Dalit icons and legends are found missing or have a subsidiary place. It also ignores Dalit literature and issues related to caste, gender, secularism, peace, compassion, marginalization, and discrimination. The overall environment, whether in a private or government school there is no space for Dalit culture, ideology and icons, and such related things. In such a case, students from marginalized communities find it extremely difficult to be in tune

1. https://www.pravakta.com/cartoon-debate-and-controversy/

and empathize with the school system. In such cases, the students from Dalit backgrounds feel alienated and they are not able to develop their attachment with the school.

The syllabus should be more neutral and all-encompassing, not a monologue from a particular majoritarian point of view. More and more biographies and stories of the marginalized communities such as that of Dalit and Adivasi leaders and their struggles and their achievements are to be included in the syllabus.

Teacher-pupil ratio

In most of the surveyed government schools, it was observed that there were very few teachers as compared to students. The teacher-pupil ratio in some cases is just 1:74 and 2:115. This shows utter negligence on the part of the government. Teachers are an integral part of the school and are the backbone of the educational institutions and play a crucial role in the development of students. Teachers have to maintain more than one class and more students at a time. Due to limited space in one classroom, teaching becomes a major burden as most of the time gets lost in maintaining the decorum of the class and teaching becomes a minimal priority. Teachers complain about a lack of support and resources which are major hurdles in imparting quality education. While in the case of private unaided schools surveyed, most of the teachers were under-qualified 12th pass or Graduates and were hired at a very low salary. This way the quality of education is being compromised. Children would only like to stay in school if they get a congenial and friendly environment which would be possible only when teachers have a manageable number of students. The teacher-pupil ratio directly affects the quality of education of children. An overcrowded school with few teachers and limited space cannot provide a pleasant environment for learning.

The Burden of Extra Responsibility to Teachers

There are an increasingnumber of complaints against the teaching staff for their irresponsible and insincere attitudes. One of the common reasons for this is burdening teachers with administrative responsibilities and other tasks that are in no way related to teaching. Most of the state government teachers are given responsibilities of surveys such as for census, adult illiteracy, ration card, etc. They are also involved in making voter cards and polling duties. Apart from these additional responsibilities, whenever there is a shortage of human resources in any government department, the teachers are called to fulfill the need.

These external works that are being imposed upon the teachersaffect their main tasks and responsibility. Apart from it, there is a lot of paperwork and administrative duties such as clerical work related to scholarships, uniforms, school management, budgeting, etc., to such an extent that the principal and many teachers are bound to work even for 10-12 hours a day. Such non-teaching responsibilities result in the absence of teachers from classrooms. The external duties occur on certain occasions while the internal non-teaching duties almost become their daily affairs. The continuous absence of teachers affects the education of students very much and also leads to loss of interest in studies.

There is a dire need to keep teachers away from such tasks and duties. Therefore, to avoid such a situation, there is also a dearth of clerical staff in each school.

Insensitivity of Teachers

Teachers can play an important role in making a humane and egalitarian society. Their words and actions have a direct and staunch imprint on the mind of children. However, we have observed that the teachers in India do just the opposite. They are recreating a casteist world within the classroom situation. In all the government schools, the teachers are predominantly of the upper class and dominant castes. This is more so in urban areas where the wives of bureaucrats and other higher officials took the job of teachers as they find this job comfortable and highly paid but the students in these schools are only from marginalised communities. There is thus a big class-caste gap between teachers and students. This difference creates a hurdle between teachers and students to come on the same level and understand each other. The language spoken by the teachers and the dialects and slang used by the children is different to such an extent that both of them are unable to understand each other. During teaching, if queries emerged due to linguistic differences or because of an inability to understand the concept,it remains unaddressed. The poor students are unable to clear their doubts emerging in the classroom. Moreover, there is no outside support like a private tutor or seniors available to them where they can clear their doubts. They have no option other than to carry the doubts in their minds. This obstructs them to move further in education and results in their loss of interest in studies.[1]

1. For details see my article, 'Exploring Lack of Interest as a Cause of Dropout of the Children of Scavenging Communities, Social Action, October-December Issue: NO.04, Volume: 68 pp. 411-422 New Delhi, 2018.

This is a practical problem that every student of marginal categories faces in their schools. Therefore, to curb this problem, the teachers have to be effectively sensitized on the issue of caste and class. A proper course during the D.Ed. and B.Ed. courses should be prepared for the teachers to develop humanitarian and scientific temperaments in them where Dalit literature and Black literature must be included. The teachers need to be especially taught to be more humane and emphatic towards the students of disadvantaged sections.

Poor Implementation of Government Schemes

The Government of India, as well as the state government, has introduced several welfare schemes concerning the student community of marginal castes. While there are some schemes applicable to all the students irrespective of their castes such as the supply of free textbooks, stationery, and uniforms, scholarships, bicycle to girl students, mid-day meals, RTE, etc. Most of these schemes are followed across the country. However, when the question of the actual implementation of these schemes is concerned, there is always a gap visible between theory and practice. It is commonly observed in all schools that the supply of these benefits takes a long time. The textbooks reach school sometimes even 4-5 months after the beginning of the academic session. Such delay negatively affects a child's performance and their position in the school. Interestingly despite the claim of free supply of stationary in none of the cases, there is any beneficiary of free stationery that was found in the selected field.

The Government of India enacted RTE Act in the year 2009. Later, in subsequent years, it has gone through some modifications. As per provisions of RTE, it is the right of every child to get a free and compulsory education. This Act also ensures proper infrastructure, perfect teacher-student ratio, facilities of library, boundary wall, playground, etc., in the campus. However, none of the government schools was found to fulfill these obligations. The lack of basic facilities directly resulted in the inconvenience of children which ultimately resulted in their dropping out from the schools.

Meagre Amount of Scholarship

The Government of India is implementing the Scheme of Pre-Matric and Post-MatricScholarships to SCs, STs, and OBCs. Moreover, there is also a provision of scholarships for children whose parents are engaged in 'unclean' occupations. This could be a good supportive and motivational factor for the students. However, it failed to be so because the amount is meagre. It is Rs 225 per month for a day scholar and Rs 525 per month for a hosteller for ten months and contingency of Rs 750/- and Rs 1000 per annum respectively for a day scholar and hosteller.

The scholarship for unclean occupation has an even worse fate. The amount of scholarship under this scheme is just Rs110 per month for day scholars and Rs 700 per month for a period of ten months. The beneficiaries of this scholarship include a) Persons who are Manual Scavengers as defined under section 2(I) (g) of Manual Scavengers Act 2013; b) Tanners & Flayers; c) Waste Pickers. This scholarship is so poorly applied that there are very few beneficiaries of this scheme. The state of Bihar is found ignorant of this scheme. During the survey, none of the school authorities were aware of this scholarship. This meagre amount of scholarship instead of giving any support or benefit to students only adds branding as a receiver of the freeship among the general student community and teachers.[1] In the era of inflation, this small amount is just a drop in the ocean.

When the Mid-Day Meal (MDM) scheme was launched by the government, then Prime Minister, Narasimha Rao envisioned that this scheme provides food for which a student will come to school. But he or none of the other governments thought that the hike in scholarships could better retain the students in schools. If both these scholarships are to be raised to the level of Rajiv Gandhi fellowship for higher studies, there is a high possibility that there will be a massive rise in admissions and a big fall in the dropoutsamong the students.

Emphasis on English in Services but Least Care to Spread it to the Masses

English was a foreign language to Indians, which was introduced to them by the Britishers as India was the colony of British rulers. In Chapter 2, we have discussed how the elite castes have taken advantage of their relationship with the Britishers in learning and developing command and mastery over English after their successive generations were exposed to English education and university education. The elite Hindus are generations ahead of the subaltern masses in terms of their access to modern education. Therefore, they were in governing positions in British India. However, after the Independence of the country and even after the enactment of the Constitution, English continued to be a

1. As discussed in chapter 4 of this book.

language of the State despite the fact that the status of the official language (Rajbhasha) was provided to Hindi, along with the other eight languages that were granted the status of the recognized languages.[1]All the official communications especially by the central governments and the bills in Parliament are drafted in English.

English has no doubt remained the language of rulers after Independence. Even the states that are created on a linguistic basis, for instance, Odisha, uses English even in its websites and certificates instead of its regional language Oriya. The access to English education on the other side was limited to elite Indians. We have discussed in Chapter 3 how convents and other private schools are out of reach of the common masses, therefore, they have remained untouched by English education. The children of the scavenging community are the worst victims of this exclusion.

Moreover, the new economic model consistently demands English. The knowledge of English plays an important role in grabbing jobs in the private and government sectors. The competitive exams of UPSC, SSC, banking and the services in elite private companies require fluent knowledge of English. Children from the scavenging community lag in this skill. The schools, whether private or government, do not impart English education, therefore the students, in general, find their education worthless. Some of the students who have dropped out of school say that the education they are receiving does not give them access to any jobs, so what is the use of such education? The lack of senior role models in their schools has led them to think of the worthlessness of school education. Ramesh a dropout of Korba says:

> I left school in 9th standard, now I am about 27 years old. I have no regret for my actions. Some of my friends continued their education. They are now graduated. But what is the use of this degree? They are still jobless. They used to share that in all competitive exams, there is a compulsory English paper which they are unable to pass. They can't even get a teaching job in a good private school, as the students of primary class speak fluent English.How can they accept a teacher who doesn't know English at all? Many of these friends after facing such problems in the market are now taking our traditional work. I started this work at an early age, so my job is at least secured and I can save some money… at least I have my own house… but my "educated" friends have now started coming back to take this job

1. At present altogether 22 languages have been recognized by the state.

> which is not even of permanent nature! They are paid less and there is no job security for them. Who is responsible for this situation?.. What was wrong with me leaving school? This education and school are not for our community. I know that there are a few individuals of my caste who are doctors, lawyers and engineers. I do not want to comment on them as they are not in my touch, but what about the people with whom I am living and sharing my joy and sorrow? If there is not even a single person from my caste who can get any good job after schooling what is the use of such education for us? … Education is fruitful till a student becomes able to learn reading and writing. These two skills are useful to me and my community, but what is the use of spending time and energy in schools otherwise?[1]

The government is directly responsible for sustaining and deepening the class division through the imposition of English. It is, however, the duty of the government to act according to the spirit of the Constitution to establish equality in society. This can be achieved either by stopping the imposition of English in all walks of life or to make English easy and accessible to the common masses.Overall, it is the responsibility of the state to take proactive action to bring a change in the situation. These suggestions are not impractical but are based on the spirit of the Constitution of India, which promises a quality life for its citizens. In the words of Ambedkar:

> We must remove this contradiction at the earliest possible moment or else those who suffer from inequality will blow up the structure of political democracy which this Assembly has so laboriously built up.[2]

1. Discrimination and Exclusion in Education…Madhya Pradesh and Chhattisgarh p. 97-98.
2. BAWS Vol. 13, p. 1216.

Bibliography

Ali, M. (2012, October 20) Suspension of former, present Principals of Mahavir medical college demanded.*The Hindu*. Retrieved from www.thehindu.com/news/cities/Delhi/suspension-of-former-present-principals-of-mahavir-medical-college-demanded/article4015857.ece

Ambedkar, B. R. (1979). *Writings and Speeches (BAWS)* Vol. 13. Mumbai: Education Department, Government of Maharashtra.

Ambedkar, B. R. (1989). *Writings and Speeches (BAWS)* Vol. 1. Mumbai: Education Department, Government of Maharashtra.

Ambedkar, B. R. (1989). *Writings and Speeches (BAWS)* Vol. 2. Mumbai: Education Department, Government of Maharashtra.

Ambedkar, B. R. (1989). *Writings and Speeches (BAWS)* Vol. 5. Mumbai: Education Department, Government of Maharashtra.

Ambedkar, B. R. (1989). *Writings and Speeches (BAWS)* Vol. 7. Mumbai: Education Department, Government of Maharash.

Ambedkar, B. R. (2008). *Writings and Speeches (BAWS)* Vol. 3. Mumbai: Education Department, Government of Maharashtra.

Ambedkar, B. R. (2014). *Writings and Speeches (BAWS)* Vol. 15. New Delhi: Dr Ambedkar Foundation, Ministry of Social Justice and Empowerment.

Apte, D. G. (2015). *Universities in Ancient India*, Faculty of Education and Psychology. New Delhi: Life Span Publishers.

Brighouse, H. and Unterhalter, E. (2010). *Education for Primary Goods or for Capabilities?* In H. Brighouse and I. Robeyns (Eds.), Measuring Justice: Primary Goods and Capabilities, Cambridge: Cambridge University Press, pp. 193-214. Retrieved from doi:10.1017/CBO9780511810916.009

Bronkhorst, J. (2011). *Buddhism in the Shadow of Brahmanism*. Brill. Retrieved from 10.1163/ej.9789004201408.i-294.

Byrne, R. (2006). *The Secret*. New York: Atria Books.

Carothers, C. (2016, November 16) Trains & Toilets: Why India's Railway Stinks — Literally. *Global Citizen*. Retrieved from https://www.globalcitizen.org/en/content/toilets-trains-india/?template=next

Chakraborty, R. (2009). *Women's Education and Empowerment in Colonial Bengal*. In Hans Hägerdal (Ed.). Responding to the West: Essays on Colonial Domination and Asian Agency, Amsterdam University Press. Retrieved from http://www.jstor.org/stable/j.ctt46mt0s.9.

Chakravarty, A. (2018, January 18). Salman Khan and Shilpa Shetty summoned for "bhangi" comment. Retrieved from https://www.newsbytesapp.com/news/entertainment/salman-and-shilpa-in-trouble-again/story

Chandra, B. (1990). *Modern India*, New Delhi: NCERT.

Chaudhary, L. (2012). *Caste, Colonialism and Schooling: Education in British India* (May). Retrieved from SSRN: https://ssrn.com/abstract=2087140

Choudhary, S. and Koh,T. (2019). The Contribution of Christian Missionaries to Educational Development: A Study of Tribals in Jharkhand, *Asian and African Studies*. 28(2): 180-204.

Das, B. (2011). *Main Bhangi Hun.* Delhi: Gautam Book Centre.

Deb, P. (2014, October 2014). British Education Policy in India: The Legacy Still Continues, *Indian Journal of Applied Research*, 4(10): 202-203.

Deb, S., and Walsh, K. (2012). *Impact of physical, psychological, and sexual violence on social adjustment of school children in India.* School Psychology International, 33(4), 391–415. Retrieved from https://doi.org/10.1177/0143034311425225 2012.

DFID (2005) *Girls' Education: Towards Betterment of All.* London: Department for International Development. Retrieved from https://www2.ohchr.org/english/issues/development/docs/girlseducation.pdf

Dube, S. C. (2017). *Indian Village*. New Delhi: Routledge.

Fernandes, D., and Kumar, R. (2014). *Delhi on Margins: A Study of Delhi Metro Contract Workers: A Study Report*, unpublished, New Delhi: Indian Social Institute.

Ghai, R. (2019, February 19). Dalit Activists leaders decry Prime Ministers 'Christ-like' act. *Down To Earth*. Retrieved from https://www.downtoearth.org.in/news/waste/dalit-activists-leaders-decry-prime-minister-s-christ-like-act-63353

Ghatwai, M. (2012, July 10). Mystery, tragedy in MP student suicide. Retrieved from http://archive.indianexpress.com/news/mystery-tragedy-in-mp-student-suicide/972415/1

_________ (2012, July 17). In death as in life,mystifying all who knew him. *Indian Express*. Retrieved from https://indianexpress.com/article/news-archive/latest-news/in-death-as-in-life-mystifying-all-who-knew-him/

Gouh, K. (1952, May 24). The Social Structure of Tanjore Village, *Economic and Political Weekly*, 531-536. Retrieved from https://www.epw.in/system/files/pdf/1952_4/21/the_social_structure_of_a_tanjore_village.pdf

Gupta, S. (2012, March 24). Two dalit girls in Madhya Pradesh stripped in examination hall.*The Times of India*. Retrieved from https://timesofindia.indiatimes.com/india/two-dalit-girls-in-madhya-pradesh-stripped-in-examination-hall/articleshow/12386251.cms

Haralambos, M. and Heald R. M. (2011). *Sociology: Themes and Perspectives,* 3rdEdition, New Delhi: Oxford University Press.

IANS (2017, December 25) Bhangi' Comment Row: Shilpa Shetty Apologises For Hurting https://www.news18.com/news/movies/bhangi-comment-row-shilpa-shetty-apologises-for-hurting-sentiments-1613663.html

ICF (2019, February 26) Mr Prime Minister, Manual Scavenging Work is Neither Spiritual Nor Glorious. *Newsclick*. Retrieved from https://www.newsclick.in/mr-prime-minister-manual-scavenging-work-neither-spiritual-nor-glorious

Jamanadas, K. (2000). *Rajput Period was Dark Age of India* http://www.ambedkar.org/research/Rajput_Period_Was_Dark_Age_Of_India.html

Katulkar, R. and D' Souza P. (2019). *Workers in Sanitation Work: Vulnerabilities of Inter-State Migrants in India,*In Denzil Fernandes and P.O. Martin (Eds.) Labour Migration Post Liberalization Era, Delhi: ISPCK.

Katulkar, R. (2012, May 18). *Cartoonvad aur Vivad.* Retrieved from https://www.pravakta.com/cartoon-debate-and-controversy/

__________ (2018). Exploring Lack of Interest as a Cause of Dropout of the Children of Scavenging Communities,*Social Action*, 68(4): 411-422.

Kausalyaayan, B. A. (2013). *31 Dino Main Aawashyak Pali*, New Delhi: Samyak Prakashan.

Kosambi, D. (2011). *Bhagwan Buddha Jeevan Aur Darshan*, New Delhi: LokbharatiPrakashan.

Kosambi, D. D. (2016). *The Culture and Civilization of Ancient India in Historical Outline*, Bombay: Popular Prakashan.

Kumar, R. (2017). *Discrimination and Exclusion in Education: A Study of Children of the Families Associated with 'Unclean' Occupations of Uttar Pradesh, Rajasthan, Himachal Pradesh and Haryana,A* report submitted to ICSSR, (unpublished), New Delhi: Indian Social Institute.

Kumar, R., and D' Souza, P. (2018). *Discrimination and Exclusion in Education: A Study of Children of the Families Associated with 'Unclean' Occupations of Madhya Pradesh and Chhattisgarh.*(unpublished), New Delhi: Indian Social Institute.

__________ (2019). *Discrimination and Exclusion in Education: A Study of Children of the Families Associated with 'Unclean' Occupations of Bihar and Jharkhand.* (unpublished). New Delhi: Indian Social Institute.

Lankina, T. V. and Getachew, L. (2013). Competitive religious entrepreneurs: Christian missionaries and female education in colonial and post-colonial India. *British Journal of Political Science*, 43(1): 103-131. Retrieved from 9692031.pdf (core.ac.uk).

Macaulay T.B. (1835, February 2) Macaulay's Minute on Education. Retrieved from http://home.iitk.ac.in/~hcverma/Article/Macaulay-Minutes.pdf

Meghwanshi, B. (2020). *Why I cannot be a Hindu: The Story of a Dalit in the RSS*, Translated by Nivedita Menon. New Delhi: Navayana.

Mukul, A. (2012, August 4). Caste, gender biases blight mid-day meal scheme in four states. *The Times of India*. Retrieved from https://timesofindia.indiatimes.com/india/Caste-gender-biases-blight-mid-day-meal-scheme-in-four-states/articleshow/15347784.cms

Nambissan, G. B. (2012, October 13). Private Schools for the Poor: Business as Usual?,*Economic and Political Weekly*, 47(41): 51-58.

Narasu, P. L. (2009). *A Study of Caste*. New Delhi: Samyak Prakashan.

National Commission for Scheduled Castes (2008) Report of the National Commission for Scheduled Castes in to the Incidents of Caste-based Discrimination and Harassment at All India Institute of Medical Sciences. New Delhi: NCSC, Government of India. Retrieved from https://ncsc.nic.in/files/mgz0001.pdf

National Herald (2019, July 27) Schoolgirls in Haryana allege daily harassment, ask High Court to provide protection. *National Herald*. Retrieved from www.nationalheraldindia.com/gender/schoolgirls-in-haryana-allege-daily-harassment-ask-high-court-to-provide-protection

Neel Kranti Media (2012, November 17) I Want to Motivate Our Students to Join Universities: Narinder Jakhu, *Round Table India*, Retrieved from https://www.roundtableindia.co.in/i-want-to-motivate-our-students-to-join-universities-narinder-jakhu/

Nehru, J. L. (2010). *The Discovery of India*. New Delhi: Penguin Books.

Nigam, D. D. (2022, October 10). We Do not sit at their Doorpost: Sanitation Castes and the Untouchability within. *Newsclick*. Retrieved from https://www.newsclick.in/we-sit-doorpost-sanitation-castes-untouchability-within

__________(2023). Our Society: My Observation. *Academia*. Retrieved from https://www.academia.edu/104779592/Our_Society_My_Observation

Nyaradi, A., Li, J., Hickling, S. C., Foster, J and Oddy, W. (2013). The role of nutrition in children's neurocognitive development, from pregnancy through childhood. *Frontiers in Human Neuroscience.7*(97): 1-16. Retrieved from 10.3389/fnhum.2013.00097.

Pant, A. (2019, May 29) Three Mumbai Doctors, Accused of Driving Junior to Kill Herself, Arrested. *NDTV*. Retrieved from https://www.ndtv.com/india-news/mumbai-doctor-bhakti-mehre-who-allegedly-targeted-her-junior-dr-payal-tadvi-with-casteist-remarks-le-2044288

Patel, S. (2007). Tribal Girl Education: Prospects and Problems, *Women's Link,13*(1):32-33.

Prado E. L. and Dewey K. G. (2014). Nutrition and Brain Development in Early Life, *Nutrition Reviews*, 72(4): 267-284. doi: 10.1111/nure.12102. Epub 2014 Mar 28. PMID: 24684384.

Prashad, V. (2000). *Untouchable Freedom: A Social History of a Dalit Community.* New Delhi: Oxford University Press.

Press Trust of India (2021, December 20) Madhya Pradesh: EnrollmentIn Classes 1-8 In Government Schools Falls To Almost Half In 2020-21. Retrieved from https://www.ndtv.com/education/madhya-pradesh-enrollment-in-classes-1-8-in-government-schools-falls-almost-half-in-2020-21-2661990

_____________ (2022, August 17) Dalit boy death: Father took child to 6 hospitals over 23 days, but failed to save him.*The Economic Times*. Retrieved fromhttps://economictimes.indiatimes.com/news/india/dalit-boy-death-father-took-child-to-6-hospitals-over-23-days-but-failed-to-save-him/articleshow/93620841.cms

Rai, S. (2017, October 24). Beaten up for polluting garbage bin, dalit dies. *The Times of India*. Retrieved from https://timesofindia.indiatimes.com/city/meerut/beaten-up-for-polluting-garbage-bin-dalit-dies/articleshow/61191230.cms

Ramachandran, R. (2012, March 6). Suicide exposes ills of system in AIIMS: Thorat Committee had suggested remedial coaching for SC/ST students. *The Hindu*. Retrieved from www.thehindu.com/news/national/suicide-exposes-ills-of-system-in-aiims/article2964427.ece

Ramaiah, A. (2015, October 24). Health Status of Dalits in India,*Economic and Political Weekly, 50*(43): 70-74.

Reddy, A. (2018, June 30). How caste is marring mid-day meals. *Down To Earth*. Retrieved from https://www.downtoearth.org.in/news/governance/how-caste-is-marring-mid-day-meals-60898

Rezavi, S. A. N. (2018, July 18). Revisiting Aurangzeb. *Frontline*. Retrieved from https://frontline.thehindu.com/the-nation/article24441441.ece

Round Table India (2012, June 20) Memorial Addressed to the Education Commission. Extract from Selected Writings of Jotirao Phule, Education Commission, Bombay, Vol II, Calcutta, 1884, pp 140-145. *Round Table India*. Retrieved from https://www.roundtableindia.co.in/memorial-addressed-to-the-education-commission/

Sankrityayan, R. (2009). *Vinaya Pitaka*. Taipei: The Corporate Body of the Buddha Educational Foundation.

Selvaraj, A. (2017). *Discrimination and Exclusion in Education: A Study of Children of the Families Associated with 'Unclean' Occupations of Karnataka, Tamil Nadu, Telangana and Andhra Pradesh*, (unpublished), New Delhi: Indian Social Institute.

Sharma, R. S. (1990). *Ancient India* Delhi: NCERT.

Srinivas, M. N. (1980). *The Remembered Village,* California: University of California Press.

Thaliath, J. (1961). Notes on the Scavenger Caste of Northern Madhya Pradesh, India. *Anthropos*. 56(5/6): 789-817. Retrieved from http://www.jstor.org/stable/40455595

The Wire (2019, July 10) No Reports of People Being Convicted for Employing Manual Scavengers: Centre. *The Wire*. Retrieved from https://thewire.in/rights/manual-scavenging-ramdas-athawale-parliament-questions

Times of India (2021, May 10) Taarak Mehta's Munmun Dutta issues an apology for her 'bhangi' comment in recent video. *The Times of India*. (E Times, Mumbai Edition), Retrieved from https://timesofindia.indiatimes.com/tv/news/hindi/

taarak-mehtas-munmun-dutta-issues-an-apology-for-her-bhangi-comment-in-recent-video/articleshow/82521866.cms

TNN (2019, December 11) Dalit Students Made to Sit Separately During Mid Day Meal in Mandi School. *The Times of India*. Retrieved from https://timesofindia.indiatimes.com/city/shimla/dalit-students-made-to-sit-separately-during-mid-day-meal-in-mandi-school/articleshow/72465065.cms

Tulasiram. (2016). *Murdahiya.* New Delhi: Rajkamal Prakashan.

Umarji, V. (2021, June 11). India's gross enrolment in higher education rose marginally in 2019-20, *Business Standard.* Retrieved from https://www.business-standard.com/article/education/india-s-gross-enrolment-in-higher-education-rose-marginally-in-2019-20-121061001249_1.html

Vaidya, P.L. (1952). *On the Use of Prakrit Dialects in Sanskrit Dramas*. Annals of the Bhandarkar Oriental Research Institute. 33(1/4): 15-25. Retrieved from https://www.jstor.org/stable/i40083588

Valmiki, O. (2018). *Joothan,* Translated by Arun Prabha Mukherjee.New York: Colombia University Press.

Varma, S. and Fernandes, S. (2016, February 5). 70 Generations Ago Caste Stopped People Intermixing. The Times of India.Retrieved from https://timesofindia.indiatimes.com/india/70-generations-ago-caste-stopped-people-inter-mixing/articleshow/50859632.cms

Video Volunteers (n.d.) Caste Discrimination keeps Dalit Children from Schools. *Video Volunteers*. Retrieved from https://www.videovolunteers.org/caste-discrimination-keeps-dalit-children-from-schools/

Wadhwa, W. (2019, January 15). Equity in Learning?,In*Annual Status of Education Report (Rural) 2018 (Provisional)*. New Delhi: ASER Centre. Pp 17-19. Retrieved from https://img.asercentre.org/docs/ASER%202018/Release%20Material/aserreport2018.pdf

Wagh, S. (2016). Ancient Buddhist Universities in India. Mumbai: Department of History, University of Mumbai. Retrieved fromhttps://mu.ac.in/wp-content/uploads/2014/05/2016-Ancient-Buddhist-University-in-India-compressed.pdf

Wani, H. A. (2012). Madrasah Education in India: A Need for Reformation. *Atikan, 2*(2): 235-252. Retrieved from https://www.researchgate.net/publication/312146408_Madrasah_Education_in_India_A_Need_for_Reformation

Wordpress (2011, July 6) The Death of Merit: Manish Kumar (IIT Roorkee) [A Documentary]. *Wordpress* Retrieved from https://thedeathofmeritinindia.wordpress.com/2011/07/06/the-death-of-merit-manish-kumar-iit-roorkee/

Xavier, J. (2018). *Excluded and Victimized City Makers: Economic, Social and Cultural Rights of Dalits among Dalits*. Madurai: Shanlax Publications.

Zelliot, E. (2005). *Ambedkar's Conversion*, Delhi: Critical Quest.